THE EARTH STORY IN GENESIS

The Earth Bible, 2

THE
EARTH STORY
IN GENESIS

edited by
Norman C. Habel &
Shirley Wurst

THE PILGRIM PRESS

Copyright © 2000 Sheffield Academic Press

Published by
Sheffield Academic Press Ltd
Mansion House
19 Kingfield Road
Sheffield S11 9AS
England

ISBN 1-84127-085-7

Published in the USA and Canada (only) by
The Pilgrim Press
700 Prospect Avenue East
Cleveland, Ohio 44115-1100
USA

USA and Canada only
ISBN 0-8298-1407-8

Typeset by Sheffield Academic Press
and
Printed on acid-free paper in Great Britain
by Bell & Bain Ltd, Glasgow

British Library Cataloguing-in-Publication Data

A catalogue record for this book is available
from the British Library

Library of Congress Cataloging-in-Publication Data

A catalog record for this book is available
from the Library of Congress

Contents

Foreword

Desmond Tutu

Planet Earth is in crisis. More and more life systems are being threatened. Scientists estimate that at least half, and perhaps as much as 80 per cent, of the world's animal and plant species, are found in the rainforests. The rainforests are the lungs of the planet producing much of the oxygen that humans and other oxygen-dependent creatures need to survive. The rainforests, alas, are still being destroyed at an alarming rate.

Resolving the ecological crisis of our planet, however, is no longer a problem we can leave to the scientists. Just as we are all part of the problem, we are also part of the solution. We all need to come to terms with the forces that have created this crisis and the resources within our traditions that can motivate us to resolve the crisis. One of those traditions is our biblical heritage.

It is significant, therefore, that the Earth Bible Project has chosen to take the Earth crisis seriously and to re-read our biblical heritage in the light of this crisis. The Earth Bible Team has listened closely to ecologists and developed a set of principles to re-read the biblical text from an ecojustice perspective. The concern of Earth Bible writers is not to defend the biblical text blindly, but to identify those passages that may have contributed to the crisis and to uncover those traditions that have valued Earth but been suppressed.

I commend the Earth Bible Team for including representative writers from around the globe, including the Southern hemisphere. I commend the team for confronting the biblical tradition honestly and openly in dialogue with ecologists. And, in particular, I commend the writers for daring to read the biblical text afresh from the perspective of Earth. Feminists have forced us to confront the patriarchal orientation of much of the biblical text. Earth Bible writers are now confronting us with the anthropocentric nature of much of the biblical text. We now ask: does the text devalue Earth by making the self-interest of humans its dominant concern?

I recommend you read the Earth Bible series with a critical but empathetic eye. As a critical reader you will want to assess whether writers make their case for their interpretation of the text in terms of the principles employed. As an empathetic reader, however, you will need to identify with Earth and the suffering Earth community as you read the text.

I hope that the promise of 'peace on Earth' will be advanced by this laudable project as scholars probe our heritage to understand and assist in resolving the crisis of our planet.

Editorial Preface

Norman Habel and Shirley Wurst

Volume 2 in the Earth Bible series follows the same principles outlined in Volume 1 and given on page 20 of this volume. We read the text in the light of these principles as we seek to develop an ecojustice hermeneutic appropriate for the ecological crisis that faces our planet. These principles, formulated in dialogue with ecologists, assist us in reading the text from the perspective of Earth.

All writers in this volume read the text in the light of one or more of these principles and explore whether a given principle is affirmed or negated. There is still a tendency among ecotheologians and ecoexegetes, willy-nilly, to find a way to retrieve a positive message about Earth in the text. They are reluctant to recognize that biblical books—written after all by humans—are likely to be anthropocentric and need to interpreted as such.

Again, the writers in this volume come from several countries of Earth. We are privileged to have the voice of an Indigenous Australian, Wally Fejo, included. As a person who knows the voice of Earth in his country, he brings a radically new understanding of the flood. Many of the narratives of Genesis, like the Babel story or the Cain text, can be read in a completely new way when viewed from the perspective of Earth. Ecofeminist approaches, reflected in the articles by Newsom, Wurst and Fontaine, generate further new insights into the Genesis texts. A diversity of approaches, consistent with an ecojustice orientation, is reflected in the spectrum of articles selected for inclusion in this volume. In this volume we also include the first in a series of dialogues between the Earth Bible Team and key people representing issues that emerge as we read the Bible from the perspective of Earth.

The same collaborative process was employed in the reviewing, vetting and formulation of articles by the Earth Bible Team. Some writers did not agree with our editorial suggestions and their wishes were honoured. One area where there is still some difference of opinion is in relation to the use of the term 'Earth'. The team believes that 'Earth' capitalized without the definite article is the option most consistent with our principles. However, where writers have chosen—and sometimes strongly supported—'earth' or 'the Earth', we have honoured their choice.

The core members of the team continue to be Vicky Balabanski, Charles Biggs, Norman Habel, Duncan Reid, Michael Trainor, Marie Turner and Shirley Wurst. Shirley continues to be the team editor and has developed a consistent format for articles in this volume.

We again express our gratitude to those who have supported the project in various ways, whether with funds, in kind or in person. The project is now located in the Centre for Theology, Science and Culture, associated with the Adelaide College of Divinity and Flinders University of South Australia. The body whose financial support has underwritten the project to date is the Charles Strong Memorial Trust. This trust is named after Charles Strong, the founder of the Australian Church which operated from 1885 to 1955. The trust promotes the sympathetic study of all religions and fosters dialogue between religion and other disciplines. This project is the result of a dialogue between religion, especially Christianity, and ecology. Other supporters of this project include Flinders University, Adelaide College of Divinity and the Columban Mission.

We wish to thank those scholars who have promoted this project as international consultants in various countries. These include Heather Eaton (Canada), Gerald West (South Africa), Ellen van Wolde (Netherlands), Keith Carley (New Zealand), Diane Jacobson (USA) and Gene Tucker (USA). We appreciate that some writers, such as Laura Hobgood-Oster, have become strong advocates of the project. We would appreciate the support of representatives from other countries and communities willing to act as sponsors for the project.

We have enjoyed working with the staff of Sheffield Academic Press in the publication of the Earth Bible series: we mention especially David Clines and Philip Davies (the publishers), Jean Allen, Judith Willson and Lorraine Bottomley among others. Their professionalism and commitment to this new venture has been very welcome.

We especially thank Desmond Tutu for a forceful and constructive foreword to this series and Charles Birch for a stimulating preface.

Preface

Charles Birch

We do not go to the book of Genesis to find science. It has none. But we do find there something science does not tell us—the value of the creation. Science puts an instrumental value on nature and so does the book of Genesis. But Genesis also emphasizes another value of nature we miss today—the intrinsic value of all the entities of creation. Intrinsic value, a key principle in the Earth Bible project, is the value of an entity in itself, for itself and for God. The Genesis way of saying this is that the creation is very good. And that was the case well before humans arrived on the scene. We are not the only pebbles on the cosmic beach. Before us came lots and lots of creatures who had value in themselves, for themselves and for God. The creatures in the desert in the heart of Australia or Africa, where no human lives, have value and always have had value. This is a message we do not generally hear these days. We tend to place value on humans and what they use for their well-being. This is why theologian John Cobb, in what he calls the Earthist challenge, says somewhat startlingly:

> Earth is a far more inclusive and suitable object of devotion than Christianity, a nation, or economic growth... Jesus points us to the God who is the God of all creatures. For practical purposes this directs us to the Earth with *all* its inhabitants, especially the human ones, as the locus of our Christian service.

What gives intrinsic value to creatures who share the Earth with us? The only answer that makes any sense to me is that feeling gives intrinsic value. We recognize the capacity of sentience or feeling in ourselves. It is our feelings that give value to our lives. It is our feelings that God also feels. But not only our feelings. Not a sparrow falls to the ground but that God knows of it. This is not saying that God is a counter of dead sparrows. It is saying that even the loss of a single sparrow is a loss to God. God feels that loss. Nor is it only sparrows that feel the world around them. We know that all mammals, all birds, probably all frogs and all snakes, feel; science adds, perhaps honey bees as well.

But a thoroughgoing perspective of this sort leads John Cobb and others, including myself, to find this subjective element in all of nature down through molecules, atoms, electrons and quarks. The world is a feeling world and not just a machine world. Ours is a world of subjects and not just objects, as the principle of voice specified in the Earth Bible project affirms. Genesis foreshadows this vision, as do many of the psalms and understandings of nature in the thought of Jesus. The belief that human beings and all other creatures have value for themselves and that they are valued by God becomes the ground for ethical attitudes towards nature.

The Genesis account of creation implies an ordering of intrinsic value: animals above plants and humans above other animals. Otherwise the authors would hardly have considered it morally acceptable for animals to eat plants and humans to eat plants and animals. At the same time the recognition of the intrinsic value of all animals clearly implies the expression of compassion and justice to them all. This is brought out in the extraordinary account recorded in Numbers 22 about a prophet by the name of Balaam who saddles his donkey and drives off on a dubious mission. Suddenly the animal stops short and turns off the road into the field. Balaam strikes the donkey, but it refuses to go on and scrapes Balaam's foot against a wall. When he strikes it again the donkey lies down underneath him. But then the donkey speaks to Balaam: 'What have I done to you, that you have struck me these three times?' Balaam replies: 'Because you have made a fool of me I wish I had a sword in my hand! I would kill you right now!' To this outburst the donkey retorts, 'Am I not your donkey, which you have ridden all your life to this day? Have I been in the habit of treating you this way?' Balaam ashamedly replies, 'No'. According to the story, the donkey stopped because he saw an angel standing on the road with a drawn sword. Not until Balaam replied to the donkey were his eyes opened so that he too could see the angel. Balaam is scolded by the angel, who tells him that if the donkey had not turned back Balaam would have been killed, since his errand was displeasing in God's eyes. A critical element of the story is that the donkey is presumed to have experiences not unlike those of his master. He says to Balaam in effect: 'You have hurt me; how would you like this done to you?'

The recognition of intrinsic value in a donkey, in all donkeys and in all other creatures, has not been a dominant attitude in Western Christianity. There are various reasons for this. One is the doctrine of *Imago Dei*, humans made in the *image of God*, which is traced back to Gen. 1.26. This text has been interpreted to mean that humans, and humans alone, are created in the image of God. The biblical story does indeed single out humans beings as those for whom God is peculiarly concerned. The habit of reflecting only this interpretation has often led to an arrogant attitude that is not commended in the Bible. A more balanced reading of the story is required. The particular significance of humans within the textual context of Genesis has been largely lost in Western Christian thought—though not in Eastern Christian thought.

The Genesis context focuses on the goodness of the whole creation. It is not the authors of Genesis who have promoted this exclusive thesis but their interpreters. The story of Noah and the flood emphasizes the preservation of species. 'Keep them alive with you' is the injunction to Noah (Gen. 6.19). The covenant that God establishes with Noah includes 'every living creatures that is with you, the birds, the cattle and the beasts of the Earth with you' (Gen. 9.10). A rainbow in the sky is the symbol of that covenant.

The Judaeo-Christian Scriptures have been used to warrant three human attitudes to other creatures besides ourselves. They can be summarized in the three words: compassion, exploitation, stewardship. *Compassion* says we are fellow companions of other creatures, all of whom rejoice in the beneficence of God and where all the Earth 'sings a new song'. Saint Francis of Assisi is famous for having lived out this attitude. A second view in Western thinking, which is also the dominant view, is the assumption of our absolute rule over nature—*exploitation*. It assumes that all things are created for human use and for no other purpose. 'Having dominion over' creation is the source of the environmental crisis we face. This view regards the great forests of the world as worth more dead than alive. The industrialization of the world, together with population growth, has caused the death of much of nature and the disappearance of many of the resources of the Earth. A third view, *stewardship*, sees humans as trustees responsible for the care of their fellow creatures. Adam is placed as a gardener in Eden 'to dress and keep it'. But the garden is kept because it is the source of food and other resources that Adam needs. This notion of trusteeship is the dominant ethic of the conservation movement. We look after nature because nature looks after us.

Stewardship is well and good but it does not go far enough. Leading forest ecologist John Terborg wrote a book in 1999 entitled *Requiem for Nature* in which he expresses grave concern about the inadequacies of the environmental movement and the programmes of the United Nations to save the Earth. Terborg's strong message is that we should conserve nature in all its biodiversity for its own sake and not for any utilitarian value, and that arguments for conservation must be spiritual and aesthetic. This stance would mean a return to recognizing the intrinsic value of all creatures. So far only one country in the world—Aotearoa New Zealand—has incorporated the phrase 'intrinsic value' in its conservation legislation. This degree of ethical enlightenment was to a considerable extent a result of the influence of so-called deep ecologists who call for an organic relationship between humans and nature that recognizes we are what we are by virtue of our internal relationships with nature. Western thought focuses on external relationships. A relationship is external when it does not affect the nature of the things involved. If you slap my face, that may affect my view of you, but it does not affect my nature. If, however, you show me great friendship, I may be internally affected. Then my relationship to you is internal, not external.

Christians are called to act with respect and reverence towards these 'least of our brothers and sisters'. This is both an act of mercy and justice. Romans 8 speaks of the whole of creation groaning in labour pains. The passage goes on to say that the liberation of nature is directly linked to the emergence of 'God's new family', which is experiencing 'the fruits of the Spirit'. This passage links the redemption of nature with the redemption of human beings. It does not say 'save people and they will save the world'. Rather, it implies that redeemed people have an obligation to save the world. These ancient texts speak eloquently to our time and circumstance. Nature is groaning. We have not heard these groans. Let us hear them now as nature's cry to us for mercy and justice.

ABBREVIATIONS

AB	Anchor Bible
ABD	David Noel Freedman (ed.), *The Anchor Bible Dictionary* (New York: Doubleday, 1992)
ABR	*Australian Biblical Review*
AbrN	*Abr-Nahrain*
ANET	James B. Pritchard (ed.), *Ancient Near Eastern Texts Relating to the Old Testament* (Princeton: Princeton University Press, 1950)
BA	*Biblical Archaeologist*
BibSem	Biblical Seminar
BJRL	*Bulletin of the John Rylands University Library of Manchester*
BR	*Bible Review*
BZAW	Beihefte zur *ZAW*
CBQ	*Catholic Biblical Quarterly*
ConBOT	Coniectanea biblica, Old Testament
FOTL	The Forms of the Old Testament Literature
HBT	*Horizons in Biblical Theology*
HSM	Harvard Semitic Monographs
IBS	*Irish Biblical Studies*
ICC	International Critical Commentary
IDB	George Arthur Buttrick (ed.), *The Interpreter's Dictionary of the Bible* (4 vols.; Nashville: Abingdon Press, 1962)
Int	*Interpretation*
JBL	*Journal of Biblical Literature*
JES	*Journal of Ecumenical Studies*
JSOT	*Journal for the Study of the Old Testament*
JSOTSup	*Journal for the Study of the Old Testament*, Supplement Series
JTS	*Journal of Theological Studies*
JTSA	*Journal of Theology for Southern Africa*
NICOT	New International Commentary on the Old Testament
OBO	Orbis biblicus et orientalis
Or	*Orientalia*
OTL	Old Testament Library
RTL	*Revue théologique de Louvain*
SBL	Society of Biblical Literature
SBLDS	SBL Dissertation Series

SBT	Studies in Biblical Theology
SJT	*Scottish Journal of Theology*
TD	*Theology Digest*
TDOT	G.J. Botterweck and H. Ringgren (eds.), *Theological Dictionary of the Old Testament*
TT	*Teologisk Tidsskrift*
TTod	*Theology Today*
TynBul	*Tyndale Bulletin*
VT	*Vetus Testamentum*
VTSup	*Vetus Testamentum*, Supplements
WBC	Word Biblical Commentary
WW	*Word and World*
WWSup	*Word and World*, Supplementary Series
ZAW	*Zeitschrift für die alttestamentliche Wissenschaft*

List of Contributors

Charles Birch is Emeritus Professor of Biology at Sydney University. His internationally recognized works include *On Purpose, Regaining Compassion: For Humanity and Nature* and a work jointly written with John Cobb, *The Liberation of Life: From the Cell to the Community*. He continues to research and write on the interrelationship of biology and ecology.

Suzanne Boorer is a lecturer in Old Testament Studies at Murdoch University, Western Australia, and the author of 'The Promise of the Land as Oath: A Key to the Formation of the Pentateuch' in *BZAW* 205 (1992) and 'The Dark Side of God? A Dialogue with Jung's Interpretation of Job' in *Pacifica* 10 (1997).

Mark Brett is Professor of Old Testament at Whitley College, Melbourne and author of *Biblical Criticism in Crisis* and *Ethnicity and the Bible*. His current research is in the book of Genesis.

Wali Fejo is an Elder of the Larrakia Nation and the first Indigenous Principal of Nungalinya College. His areas of research include pastoral theology, Indigenous spirituality and Aboriginal reconciliation.

Carole Fontaine is Professor of Hebrew Scriptures at Andover Newton Theological School. Among her major works are listed *Traditional Sayings in the Old Testament: A Contextual Study* and *A Feminist Companion to Reading the Bible: Approaches, Methods, Strategies*, written jointly with Athalya Brenner. Her current research relates to genre and gender studies in wisdom literature, folk medicine and Song of Songs.

Anne Gardner is Senior Lecturer in the History Department of Latrobe University, Melbourne. She has written a range of journal articles on the Maccabean period and feminist exegesis. Her current work is on the book of Daniel.

Norman Habel, the Chief Editor of the Earth Bible Project, is Professorial Fellow at Flinders University of South Australia and Adelaide

College of Divinity. His major works include a commentary on Job in the Old Testament Library, *The Land is Mine* and *Reconciliation: Searching for Australia's Soul*. His current research extends to ecoliturgy and ecojustice writings for the wider community.

Laura Hobgood-Oster holds the Elizabeth Root Paden Chair in Religion at Southwestern University. Her major publications include *Crossroad Choices: Biblical Wisdom Literature in the 21st Century* and *The Sabbath Journal of Judith Lomax*, which she edited. Her current research includes ecofeminism, animals in Christian tradition and environmental practices of congregations in North America. She is on the editorial board of *The Encyclopedia of Religion and Ecology*.

Eugene C. McAfee is lecturer in the Study of Religion and Allston Burr Senior Tutor of Lowell House, Harvard College. His publications include 'Ecology and Biblical Studies', in *Theology for Earth Community* edited by Dieter Hessel and *The Place Belongs to God: Twenty-five Years of the Preaching Ministry of Peter Gomes in the Memorial Church, Harvard University*. His current areas of research are ecology and biblical studies, and ancient and modern mythmaking.

Carol Newsom is Professor of Old Testament/Hebrew Bible at Candler School of Theology, Emory University. Her publications include a commentary on Job in the *New Interpreter's Bible* and a critical commentary on *Songs of the Sabbath Sacrifice* in *Qumran 4: VI; Poetical and Liturgical Texts, Part 1*. Her current area of research is in the book of Job and Apocalyptic Literature.

John Olley is concurrently Senior Lecturer in Old Testament at Murdoch University and Principal of The Baptist Theological College of Western Australia. His writings include 'Righteousness' in *The Septuagint of Isaiah* and numerous articles in missiological journals. His current research is on the text and theology of Isaiah and Ezekiel.

Desmond Tutu is former Archbishop of Cape Town, South Africa, and currently Archbishop Emeritus of the same city. Two of his major publications include *The Rainbow People of God* and *No Future Without Forgiveness*

Ellen van Wolde is Professor of Exegesis, Old Testament and Hebrew, in the Faculty of Theology, Tilburg University, The Netherlands. Her major publications include *Words Become Worlds: Semantic Studies in*

Genesis 1–11 and 'Who Guides Whom? Embeddedness and Perspective in Biblical Hebrew and in 1 Kings 3:16-28' in *JBL* 114 (1995), 623-42. Her current research is in the Jacob Cycle in Genesis, text-linguistics and Job.

Howard N. Wallace is a Professor of Old Testament at The Uniting Church Theological Hall, Melbourne. One of his major publications is *The Eden Narrative;* a recent article typical of his work is 'What Chronicles has to say about Psalms', in *The Chronicler as Author.* His current research includes the Psalms in Christian ministry and developing an inductive introduction to the Hebrew Bible.

Gunther Wittenberg is Emeritus Professor of Old Testament in the School of Theology, University of Natal, Pietermaritzburg, South Africa. His major publications include *I have Heard the Cry of My People: A Study Guide to Exodus 1-15* and *Prophecy and Protest: A Contextual Introduction to Israelite Prophecy.* Both these volumes are in the ISB Bible in Context series.

Shirley Wurst is an editor for the Earth Bible Project and Equity and Diversity Officer for the Equity and Diversity Unit and Tutor at University of South Australia. Her recent doctoral thesis, entitled *Dancing in the Minefield: Feminist Counterreadings of the Women in Proverbs 1–9,* reflects her current research in feminist theory, hermeneutics, epistemology and social justice.

Six Ecojustice Principles

1. *The Principle of Intrinsic Worth*
The universe, Earth and all its components have intrinsic worth/value.

2. *The Principle of Interconnectedness*
Earth is a community of interconnected living things that are mutually dependent on each other for life and survival.

3. *The Principle of Voice*
Earth is a subject capable of raising its voice in celebration and against injustice.

4. *The Principle of Purpose*
The universe, Earth and all its components, are part of a dynamic cosmic design within which each piece has a place in the overall goal of that design.

5. *The Principle of Mutual Custodianship*
Earth is a balanced and diverse domain where responsible custodians can function as partners, rather than rulers, to sustain a balanced and diverse Earth community.

6. *The Principle of Resistance*
Earth and its components not only suffer from injustices at the hands of humans, but actively resist them in the struggle for justice.

The principles listed here are basic to the approach of writers in the Earth Bible Project seeking to read the biblical text from the perspective of Earth. For an elaboration of these principles see The Earth Bible, 1: *Readings from the Perspective of Earth*, Chapter 2, 'Guiding Ecojustice Principles'.

Conversations with Gene Tucker and Other Writers

The Earth Bible Team

Preamble

This opening chapter in Volume 2 of the first Earth Bible series is designed to focus on specific issues raised by writers and readers of Earth Bible Project materials and to explore these issues through dialogue and conversation with the Earth Bible Team. Some of these issues are methodological and others relate to the ecojustice dimensions of the Earth Bible project. In the course of these conversations we will refer to articles in the first two volumes in this series which illustrate our point.

As the starting point for our first conversation we have chosen key issues raised by Gene Tucker in his response to the ecojustice principles guiding the project. Tucker's response was delivered at the annual Society of Biblical Literature conference in Orlando in November 1998 and reflects his continued commitment to ecological issues (Tucker 1997).

Quotations from Tucker's speech may be supplemented by statements from others who have responded to the approach and principles of the Earth Bible Project at various times. In this way we hope to encourage the development of an ongoing dialogue between participants in the project and scholars at large, and that subsequently biblical scholars will contribute to public conversations about ecojustice as an issue of public concern and part of an ongoing educational strategy to change the way we view Earth.

The conversations in this chapter are a continuation of the conversations among scholars involved in the project, students in related courses and ecologists. While individuals in the Earth Bible Team may have differences of opinion about certain readings of the text, we are united in supporting the approach and principles of the project. The following conversation represents our joint response to issues being raised by a number of writers at this stage in the project.

The Use of Guiding Principles

Tucker: *The very idea of principles to guide a project of biblical interpretation raises questions these days that would not have come up 20 or 30 years ago. Most of us were taught to avoid imposing our preconceptions on the text, or even deciding in advance what we wanted to discover. Preferred has been an inductive rather than a deductive approach: just read the text and see what comes out.*

But we were kidding ourselves. Principles of interpretation are both essential and inevitable. Until recently, our unacknowledged principles for the most part were Western, male and historical. In the guild, theological and moral goals were suspect.

One cannot enter new terrain without both a map and some idea of destination or goal. Many different kinds of maps may be useful, depending upon what we want to find. Even geography includes physical geography, political geography, economic geography and geology. Just what are we looking for as we head out into a strange—or even a supposedly familiar—country? And the destination may of necessity change as we learn more about the land.

Some of the most hazardous principles—like those that have guided so much of scholarship for the past century—are the ones which are unacknowledged and/or unexamined. It isn't possible to know everything that shapes our journey or drives our exploration, for many of our principles are so close that we cannot see them. All the more reason to set out as much as we can and check it out in public. Principles, including principles of interpretation, can and must open up new problems and possibilities of the terrain.

Team: In this statement Gene Tucker, like others, warns us of the danger and necessity of using guiding principles to interpret the biblical text. Tucker rightly notes that members of the guild, until relatively recently, employed unstated principles of interpretation that were basically Western, male and historical. Recent critical approaches, including reader-response studies, have forced us to acknowledge that each interpreter has a set of governing assumptions about what questions to pose when reading the text—whether these questions are consciously articulated or not.

The ecojustice principles developed for the Earth Bible project do not preclude the interpreter analysing the text in terms of its literary, historical and/or cultural dimensions. On the contrary, these strategies are encouraged both as a first stage in the reading of a text and as a continuing interactive process of engagement with the ecojustice principles. The ecojustice principles for this project are not to be applied arbitrarily to discover willy-nilly whatever ecological idea the reader is hoping to find—a tendency that seems to be present in some works on ecotheology. When used in conjunction with traditionally accepted modes of analysis, the ecojustice principles will guide us in asking new questions of the text, confronting new dilemmas and raising new potential readings. With fresh questions being posed from a new, consciously espoused, perspective, we are in a position to discover new concepts, insights and dimensions embedded in the text that may not have been seen before.

The writers in the first two volumes have used a wide range of critical approaches as their points of departure. Some, like Sue Boorer and John Olley, have assumed the basic findings of source hypothesis scholars. Mark Brett employs a deconstructive approach. Laura Hobgood-Oster adopts a more thematic approach as she explores the significance of wells in Genesis. Carole Fontaine explores the Canaanite cultural background as a crucial initial step in her reading of the text.

As writers in this series, in addition to our basic critical approach, we come to the text with challenging questions posed by the Earth Bible project's ecojustice principles. Although writers may disagree with the precise wording of a given principle, these principles set the agenda for readings in this series, and lead us to see the text with new eyes—hopefully the eyes of Earth.

The Contribution of Feminist Models

Tucker: *A good example of such enlightenment of the text from principles of interpretation is the contribution of a wide range of feminist readings of the Bible. We—that is, the prevailing male scholarly tradition—had not recognized the angle of vision of texts toward women and gender issues. When the legal codes of the Hebrew Bible use almost exclusively masculine language, are they being 'inclusive' of women or not? By asking such simple questions as 'Where are the women in this narrative?', or 'What value or authority is attributed to women?', new vistas have opened up.*

Consequently, I would prefer 'principles' to be stated in the interrogative rather than the indicative or any other mood, that is, as questions rather than statements or instructions. So each of the Earth Bible principles is followed by a series of questions. To pose questions of the text does not mean that one abandons perspective or a structure of values, because particular questions lead in certain directions and not in others.

Team: Gene Tucker points to the model of feminist approaches to the Bible as enlightening examples. His comments provide us with an opportunity to answer the concerns of some writers who have questioned the openness of the project by pointing to what they see as a heavy dependency on feminist methodologies.

From the outset, we acknowledge that the hermeneutic of suspicion and retrieval appropriated by feminist methodology has also been adopted in the Earth Bible project, while recognizing that the primary object of the suspicion and retrieval strategies in our project is quite discrete. We also acknowledge that the Western dualisms, so sharply delineated by feminist scholars in recent years, are also challenged by our ecojustice approach. Identifying these dualisms and pursuing this hermeneutic are not, however, the sole preserve of feminist interpreters.

The advent of the feminist approach represents a turning point in biblical interpretation. Feminist hermeneutics have opened our eyes to biases and strategies in reading the text that have radically changed the possibilities of biblical interpretation. Without that change, an ecojustice reading of the text would probably not have been possible. The Earth Bible Team acknowledges that debt as a given.

Ecofeminist approaches—one logical development of bringing feminist and ecojustice approaches together—are represented in the first volume of this series. While our approach seeks to focus on justice for Earth, justice for women is a closely related—and some would say necessarily related—dimension of the interpretative process, as Heather Eaton (2000: 54-71) and Elaine Wainwright (2000: 162-73) have both demonstrated in Volume 1.

Some writers have adopted specific techniques developed by feminist interpreters. Shirley Wurst has employed feminist retrieval strategies to discover the voice and agency of Earth behind the text. Elaine Wainwright describes her ecofeminist approach as a struggle towards potential transformation for each member of the Earth community.

Sources of the Ecojustice Principles

Tucker: *It is important to acknowledge that principles of interpretation do not derive from the subject of inquiry into the biblical text, but they are accountable to it. To return to the metaphor of the map: we must be willing to adjust and correct our map as we learn more about the territory. If we expect to discover anything new, we have to let the terrain guide us as we rewrite our maps.*

Therefore, any principles need to be flexible and responsive to what is in or comes out of the texts; that is, they should facilitate a dialogue. With regard to the Earth Bible principles, it is obvious that there was no environmental science in antiquity. But there are attempts to understand the earth and all

*that dwells within, including some classifications of natural features and liv-
ing things.*

*And, while nature and culture are among my favourite categories, neither
one is biblical. Asking questions in terms of those categories does reveal some
of the relationships between human beings and the world. It also shows that
'nature' does not fit the biblical tradition, which uses the language of 'creation'.*

Team: Gene Tucker's comments raise the question of the source of the
ecojustice principles employed in this project and their relationship to
what he calls 'the map' of the Bible. This question can be answered in
two ways—pragmatically in terms of the specific processes used in
the project, and theoretically in terms of our assumptions about Earth
as creation.

The process of identifying these principles involved consultations
and dialogue with ecologists—in person and through their literature.
The principles were debated, explored in courses and their viability as
guides to interpretation evaluated by a body of scholars. They reflect,
therefore, the formulation of a school of thought represented by the
members of the Earth Bible Team and widely accepted by ecologists.

A second way of investigating the source of these principles is to
explore our assumptions about Earth as creation where we discern
these principles in operation. We do not view Earth as a massive
machine as philosophers like Descartes, Newton and their successors
suggested. Earth is a living creation that functions according to myriad interrelated systems. By close observation, personal experience
and sympathetic listening, human beings can discern the laws and
principles that govern this creation called Earth. In this we affirm the
quests of scientists from ancient to modern times.

This process of observation, experience and listening is illustrated
admirably by those who belonged to the wisdom traditions of the
ancient world, including the biblical world. It is fundamental to wisdom practice that the wise sought to discern the laws, design and
order of the cosmos. That search to understand the principles that
govern the cosmos, from the ways of the ant (Prov. 6.6-9) to the ways
of the constellations (Job 38.31-33), is integral to the wisdom tradition.

Significantly, in Job 28, this search for wisdom in creation is also
God's search. When God surveys all the phenomena of Earth and
sky—from the weight of the wind to the laws of lightning—God discerns the principles of wisdom in the cosmos (28.23-27). Our search
for the governing principles of ecology and ecojustice is likewise
derived from empathetic scholarly observations of the natural

world—the world of creation—and our experience of that world. We believe that we are following the way of wisdom when we affirm the ecojustice principles identified by scientists and observe the Earth closely ourselves. Yet, as Tucker says, our principles need to be flexible: they need to be altered as our knowledge of ecology and Earth changes. We also need to be flexible in our reading strategies as the insights within the text move us.

The Principle of Intrinsic Worth

Tucker: *Some of the Earth Bible principles seem more fundamental than others. I am tempted to argue that the first two and the fifth would be sufficient. The first, the principle of intrinsic worth, is a moral claim. I know of no better guide to further reflection on this principle than Holmes Rolston's* Environmental Ethics *(1988). The subtitle of his text is 'Duties to and Values in the Natural World', and his work is a profound and poetic exploration of values inherent in the earth and all its components. And then with regard to the moral authority of human beings he emphasizes duties or responsibilities and not rights, consistent with principle five, the principle of custodianship.*

Team: The significance of the first principle is evident from the number of writers in the first two volumes who explore this principle from a variety of perspectives. Paul Trebilco (2000: 204-20) argues that 1 Tim. 4.1-4 clearly asserts the intrinsic worth and goodness of the Earth against opponents who view the created order as evil or tainted. This text, however, goes a step further and declares that creation has also been 'sanctified' by God's word; by this act another dimension of value has been added. Howard Wallace, in this current volume, discerns the principle of worth reflected in the original act of God sanctifying the seventh day as the culmination of creation.

In his analysis of Genesis 1, Norman Habel highlights that God not only orders the existing components into a cosmos governed by laws of time and space, but also examines what has been ordered/created. God, the wise one, is explicitly said to 'observe/see' what is made. And God's evaluation of these observed phenomena is 'very good'. According to this text, it is not God's pronouncement that makes creation good; it is already good. God discerns its intrinsic worth in what God 'sees'.

The Principles of Interdependence and Custodianship

Tucker: *The second principle, that all 'living things…are mutually dependent on each other for life and survival', may be indebted to traditional religious beliefs, but it summarizes what earth, biological and ecological science has taught us. Anyone who observes the world closely knows this to be true. Moreover, the only principles that make sense are those which see human beings as part of the natural order.*

The exemplary questions following the principle, however, suggest that 'hierarchical' is inconsistent with 'community', 'interconnected' and 'mutually dependent'. But in this community of living and even non-living constituents, certain citizens at times inevitably rule over others. The most obvious of these hierarchical relationships is the food chain. All species seek to survive and to reproduce themselves, and do so at the expense of other life. All life, at least all sentient life, lives on life. And lest we as homo sapiens *believe we stand at the top of the food chain except when a larger mammal meets us on the trail—even some of the smallest forms of life, such as viruses, can easily exercise dominion over us. For that matter, so can rock and wind and water.*

Furthermore, all living things shape their environments, or seek to. To be sure, ours is the most powerful species, in the sense of exerting direct influence over that environment.

That brings us to the principle of custodianship. This directly addresses the role and responsibility of human beings as partners with the earth, but not without tension. There is a fine line here, between custodian and ruler, and between custodian and partner or citizen. I find it difficult to avoid linking responsibility with power and authority.

Team: As Gene Tucker has observed, these two principles—interconnectedness and custodianship—are closely related. In recent times we have come to appreciate the reality that each species and each component of Earth are connected in a complex web of interdependent ecosystems. Kinship with the members of these systems has always been integral to our identity as human beings on Earth. We in the contemporary Western world are rediscovering this reality again now. Within these systems some elements will have greater physical strength; others have more sophisticated techniques for survival, and still others have more developed instincts for territorial control. In the food chain, life is indeed dependent upon life to survive.

Do these realities, however, necessarily constitute a hierarchy of domination among life forms and a corresponding hierarchy of rights?

We would answer, no! Is the human species necessarily intended to dominate the entire Earth? Again we would answer, no! Unfortunately, it seems, human beings have the capacity at this point in time to unleash physical, biological and chemical forces that could annihilate life on the planet as we know it—or even destroy the planet itself.

This ominous thought raises the issue of the specific role of humans in Earth's ecosystems. Earth is host to myriad life forms, many of which are hosts to smaller life forms and so on. Normally these various life forms do not destroy their hosts. There is a mutual dependency between host and guest—a mutual custodianship. Similarly, humans ought to be custodians of their host, Earth. We have chosen the term 'custodian' not only because it fits the model of ecological science, but because it is also used to portray the way in which many Indigenous peoples describe their relationship with other species as kin and Earth as mother.

Custodianship obviously involves responsibility, but it also involves respect for the bonds of life between humans and other creatures as well as the enduring connection humans have with Earth as the reservoir of life. The idea that the Earth is also a custodian who takes care of its own is developed in William Urbrock's analysis of the Tobit story (2000: 125-37) in Volume 1.

Wittenberg, in his article on Genesis 4 in Volume 2, explores one biblical tradition about how this connection between humans and Earth is viewed as broken already in the primordial era. A fundamental separation from Earth and its life-giving *adamah* (surface soil) is expressed in a way that points to a primal violation of the principle of interconnectedness. The Cain community is alienated from Earth as home and kin.

Carol Newsom returns to the preceding narrative of Genesis 2–3 to demonstrate that the 'original sin' can be understood as a 'fall into anthropocentrism'. Human beings have violated their interconnectedness with the rest of creation from the beginning.

A number of writers explore the way in which biblical texts deal with the connection or disconnection between heaven/sky and Earth. Ed Conrad's article in Volume 1 demonstrates that translating the term *malak* as 'angel' brings to the text a hierarchical dualism, a separation between heaven and Earth (2000: 86-95). Conrad argues, however, that in the Old Testament there is an interrelatedness between sky and Earth as the abode of the human and the divine where YHWH's messengers reside. Similarly Duncan Reid (2000: 232-45), in his analysis of Revelation 21, discerns how the fluid boundaries between heaven and Earth finally disappear in the new creation.

Vicky Balabanski (2000: 151-61) argues that the Lord's Prayer destabilizes the distinction between heaven and Earth by calling upon God to do away with the distinction. Specific petitions also assert a mutual connectedness and mutual dependency between members of the Earth community for life and survival.

The Principles of Voice and Resistance

Tucker: *The principles that give me most pause are principles three and six: that the earth is capable of 'voicing its cries against injustice' and 'actively resists' human injustice. Is this language poetic or literal? Taken literally, it appears to personify the earth in human terms, and thus moves contrary to the other principles. This could be the most anthropocentric perspective of all. To be sure, there are biblical texts that speak poetically of the earth's voice.*

On the other hand, the principle of voice could be turned around and taken as a summons to respect, that is, to look again (re-spect), or listen again to the earth and all its wonderful features. In 'Teaching a Stone to Talk', Annie Dillard said, 'Nature's silence is its one remark, and every flake of world is a chip off that old mute and immutable block' (1982: 69). But her essay invites you to pay attention.

Is there a design and a will within the earth to actively resist human injustice? This is not unlike certain—for the most part theologically formulated— interpretations of disasters such as earthquake, flood and drought. The best I can muster here is the recognition that actions have consequences, as set out in Hos. 4.1-3: failure of faith leads to disorder within human society that leads to the suffering of the land and the disappearance of its creatures. If we foul our nest, we will live in a foul nest. Houses built on fault lines or in the paths of hurricanes likely will fall, and their owners might think the earth is angry.

Team: The principle of voice has evoked considerable discussion. As we argued in the second chapter of Volume 1, we need to move beyond assuming that the voice of Earth will be a human voice. Such an assumption would indeed be anthropocentric. The ways in which Earth and the numerous members of Earth community communicate will reflect their own distinctive natures. Understanding the various ways in which humans may hear these voices, however, is a continuing search. Ecojustice requires a new way of listening to Earth and giving voice to what we hear.

Terence Fretheim (2000: 96-110) analyses how the prophet Jeremiah heard the cries of Earth ringing in his ears because of the desecration caused by God's people. In Volume 2 we have deliberately included an Indigenous reading to illustrate that for some peoples, hearing the voice of Earth—including animals, trees, birds and rocks—is quite natural. The difficulty many of us face is our intellectual conditioning as Western scholars. We have extended the dualism between culture and nature to include intelligent and dumb, verbal and mute.

One of the goals of this project is to begin identifying with Earth and viewing ourselves as kin of the wider Earth community. For Wally Fejo, an Indigenous Australian, that is already a reality. He reads the Bible with Earth as his mother and the Earth community as his relatives. As a result, his insights into the flood story are quite striking. He hears what many of us have never heard: he hears Earth speaking. He hears, for example, God within Earth suffering with Earth beneath the flood waters.

Iustitione Salevao (2000: 221-31), from within his Samoan world-view, knows the Earth as a living entity that communicates with its people. For him to read in Heb. 6.7-8 that so-called unproductive land is to be burned is to devalue and destroy what his people knows to be good—the land as the source of life and the centre of their universe. Earth, and Indigenous peoples, cry out against this message in Hebrews.

It has been difficult for male scholars to enter the world of feminist thought and interpretation. It took time for male readers to grasp how feminist readers could find the suppressed voice of women in the text. Similarly, it will take time for most Western readers to hear the suppressed voice of Earth in the text. Indigenous readers like Wally Fejo may need to lead us in this process. Perhaps women, as Shirley Wurst does in her chapter in this volume, will first discern the suffering of Earth as mother.

Principle of Purpose

Tucker: *The principle of purpose, principle four, opens the door to explicit theological reflection. That is important but dangerous ground. Is that 'dynamic cosmic design', in which we all participate, within or beyond the earth and all its components? Certainly the biblical texts affirm or assume that the world is good because it is God's creation and God's design, but it is not God. In short, the Hebrew Bible is essentially theocentric rather than anthropocentric.*

The related problem, the rejection of this world in favour of a heavenly one beyond history—clearly present in important biblical traditions—is the root of many ecological evils. The most vivid statement of this perspective was a cartoon of James Watt, *the evangelical Christian who served as Ronald Reagan's Interior Secretary. He is shown holding a sign that says, 'Jesus is coming soon. Cut down all the trees.'*

Team: Writers in the first volume did not focus extensively on this principle. In connection with two eschatological texts, however, this principle plays a significant role. Brendan Byrne (2000: 193-203), in his discussion of Rom. 8.18-22, highlights an inherent principle of purpose relating to Earth. The material universe is evolving into the age of salvation rather than dying or being destroyed. The groaning of creation represents birth pangs not death cries.

Similarly, Duncan Reid (2000: 232-45), in analysing Rev. 22.1-22, recognizes that God's purpose for Earth in the end times is not replacement but renewal; not the annihilation of 'raw material', but the transformation of creation; not a return to origins/Eden, but the removal of the ecological death introduced by humans. Renewed Earth is a transformed domain where no 'ladder to heaven' is necessary.

Ecojustice and Social Justice

Tucker: *The Earth Bible project means to focus on understanding (and comprehending the biblical understanding) of the earth and all its components. But the very use of the terms 'ecojustice' and 'justice' in the heading serves as a reminder of the context within which we raise concern with the earth. That context includes nature and natural science, politics and economics. It is not possible to address ecological concerns without opening questions of social justice.*

Tensions are unavoidable, for principles and interests conflict with one another. Examples of this are all around us. In this country (America), concern for the environment frequently is perceived to be—and often actually is—in conflict with economic interests, both legitimate and illegitimate: owls or jobs, economic development or protection of the environment, real estate or open space, and on and on. It is easy to blame human greed, technology and overpopulation. But as we consider the earth, we must struggle with the relationship between ecological responsibility and social justice.

Team: Here Gene Tucker touches on an issue with which the Earth Bible Team struggled at some length: should we formulate a set of ecojustice principles without also including a specific principle that recognizes social justice as a necessary component of the process? The Earth Charter mentioned in the first chapter of Volume 1 seeks to emphasize a necessary connection between respect for Earth and respect for the dignity of human life. The social, economic, political, spiritual and environmental factors are integrated within the structure of the charter.

Members of the Earth Bible Team have been heavily involved in social justice issues and recognize that ecological responsibility cannot be divorced from social justice. We have not made explicit reference to social justice within our principles, in order to limit the scope of the project, and to focus attention on the ecological dimension of the problem, and most clearly to differentiate our approach from feminist, liberationist and other approaches that explore social justice from alternative perspectives.

Writers who wish to explore the social justice ramifications of an ecojustice principle in a given text are welcome to do so. David Jobling and Nathan Loewen (2000: 72-85) demonstrate this link in the prophet Amos. The principles of interconnectedness and custodianship also embrace relationships between human members of the Earth community and the impact of these relationships on the environment.

Additional Principles?

Tucker: *Perhaps we need an additional principle, not for exegesis but for what comes next: all normative claims should be based on our best current scientific, environmental and ecological knowledge. And I suggest—and would require if I could—some intense and sustained experience of the earth before one is allowed to comment on it. One needs now and then to stand on real earth with nothing but the sky overhead. Strolling in the woods, or fishing, or hiking, or viewing the stars at night may be recreation, but it is also essential work toward understanding the world. To view the world mainly through those rectangular pieces of glass might lead one to think of it as an abstraction, just a picture.*

Team: Quite a number of writers have suggested additional principles to complement the six outlined for the Earth Bible project. The principle suggested above by Gene Tucker is already an assumption of this project as outlined earlier in our discussion of the sources of our six principles. As our ecological knowledge increases these principles may need to be modified, even if that is not evident to us at the moment.

Diane Jacobson, in her response to the six principles at the 1998 SBL Conference in Orlando, USA, suggested two additional theological principles: the principles of incarnation and promise. The first assumes that the creation, while not identical with the Creator, provides a range of 'earthen vessels' through which God is manifest. The second is suggested as a guide to distinguish between eschatology, which promises a future for Earth, and some apocalyptic traditions, which imply the destruction of Earth.

These two suggestions are valuable for theological reflection upon the findings of an ecojustice reading. In our dialogue with the ecological world of science we have opted to articulate our principles in non-theological language and ground them in recognized ecological scientific discourse. This does not mean that writers in the project will ignore the fact that the biblical text reflects diverse theologies about the cosmos as God's creation; Earth Bible writers will examine these theologies in the light of these principles.

Geophany: The Earth Story in Genesis 1

Norman Habel

Introduction

The creation story in Genesis 1 (1.1–2.4a) has long been proclaimed by scholars to be a structured literary unit, characterized by poetic symmetry, majestic order and consistent terminology. This narrative is viewed as an introductory masterpiece of the so-called Priestly writer who provided the overall structure for the narratives of Genesis (cf. Westermann 1964; Anderson 1994: 42-55). As a structural unit, the content of the passage is generally understood to outline the creation and ordering of the various parts of the cosmos, with the creation of humans as the climax and the day of rest as a celebrative closure. Genesis 1 is read as a literary unit dealing with the origin of the world, focusing especially on the origin of human beings.

In this article, I read Genesis 1 as a story with a setting, narrative progression and closure. Some seek to identify the underlying characteristics of a liturgy, a confession, a theological proclamation or a primordial history—partly to avoid the fundamentalist alternative of viewing the text as a literal account of how the world was actually created. The present form of the text, however, remains a narrative, a story with a sequence of events and a series of subjects or characters. In my opinion, Genesis 1 as a literary work is, first of all, a story about Earth comprising a series of brief sequential episodes.

In focusing on Earth as a central character or subject of the story my approach differs significantly from those who discern Earth, land or landscape as themes in the narrative of Genesis 1–11 (e.g. Johnson 1995; McKeown 1997). By reading Genesis 1 as a 'story' I am also seeking to shed the baggage of our Western concepts of creation. As Michael Welker has so clearly demonstrated, readings of the text have been influenced by Western theological assumptions about *creatura* (1991-92). I read the text as an origin story in which Earth and *Elohim* are both characters with major roles to play. In so doing I also explore whether the intrinsic value of Earth (principle 1) is espoused as an integral part of the story.

When I began reading this story with a concern for Earth, including justice for Earth, I operated with an assumption that the Genesis 1 narrative was a coherent literary unity, and with a suspicion that the entire text would be governed by an anthropocentric orientation. I discovered, however, that neither of my assumptions were valid, but that

- the primary subject of the primordial setting and subsequent days of creation was not the entire cosmos, nor humanity, but *erets*, Earth;
- if the story of the creation of humans in Gen. 1.26-30 is removed from the text, the resulting narrative is a consistent story about Earth that affirms the intrinsic value of Earth;
- when Genesis 1 is read as a story of Earth, the account of God creating humans does not represent a climax to the narrative, but a sharp conflict of plot and perspective within the narrative.

It is my contention, after reading the text with ecojustice eyes, that Genesis 1 is about the origin, appearance and activating of Earth—albeit within the context of a framework about creating Earth and sky. At the heart of the story is a 'geophany', a manifestation or revelation of Earth. The various acts of creation prepare for, depend upon or relate to this manifestation of Earth. The secondary story of human entry onto Earth scene (Gen. 1.26-30) poses a conflict of orientation within the Earth story that remains unresolved. In Genesis 1 'geophany' and 'anthropophany' stand in ecological tension.

I shall first explore the geophany of Genesis 1 as a unified Earth story and subsequently examine how the story of human appearance in Gen. 1.26-30 disrupts both the plot and the perspective of this Earth story.

Erets *Hidden*

The Hebrew Scriptures begin with a story of Earth (*erets*). There are many biblical stories about the Earth, even about the origins of the Earth; the Earth story at the beginning of Genesis is a dramatic account that celebrates the wonder and worth of Earth as a geophany. In the primordial setting of that story, however, the *erets* remains hidden, awaiting its revelation.

The precise intent of the opening verse of the chapter has long been under dispute. The three major options for reading this verse are neatly summarized by Barr (1998: 55-65).

- *Option 1*: it describes an initial act of creation, previous to the creation of light in Gen. 1.3, which is the first event of the seven-day scheme of the chapter.
- *Option 2*: it is actually a temporal expression, something like 'in the beginning of God's creating heaven and Earth', and thus attached to the description of the chaotic state in Gen. 1.2.
- *Option 3*: it is a summary of the total work of creation, placed at the beginning, and followed by a detailed account that goes back over the same process of creation in seven days.

Barr clearly demonstrates that option 1 is excluded by the internal logic of the text. Following option 2, we would render the text, 'When God began creating the sky and Earth, Earth was...', thereby expressing these words as an opening formula typical of several ancient Near Eastern creation myths. Option 3 reads the opening verse as a summary statement of all the creative activities that follow in Genesis 1: 'In the beginning God created the sky and Earth.' Verse 1 then forms an *inclusio* with 2.4a at the end of the literary unit (cf. van Wolde 1998: 23).

Whether we follow option 2 or option 3, Earth (*erets*) is present from the beginning of the creating process. Genesis 1.2 explicitly begins with *erets*, the primordial Earth. This opening focus, I would argue, is not on Earth as 'pre-existent' in some philosophical or scientific sense, but rather on the Earth as 'present but hidden from view'. Earth is present as the primary subject of the story, the main character of the plot. Throughout the story, the listener anticipates the future appearance and transformation of this mysterious hidden entity called Earth. The summary caption 'sky and Earth' provides the framework for the story, but *erets* is the dominant subject of the story.

The image projected in Gen. 1.2 is one of total darkness. It is a picture of a mysterious primordial realm where nothing is visible. There is no negative verdict on the darkness, no designation of the darkness as evil, sinister or forbidding. The darkness is simply a condition that hides the presence of several components in the primordial domain. Without light the primordial state—and any subsequent states of reality—remain hidden and unseen. Within this darkness, three central components or characters of the subsequent story are specifically identified: *Elohim*, the waters and Earth.

Elohim is present as a breath or spirit (*ruach*) moving across the waters within the darkness, not outside of it or beyond it (cf. Wyatt 1993: 543-54). The *ruach* is hidden deep within the primordial domain, waiting in the darkness, with Earth. In the Earth story of Genesis 1 there is no reason to assume this divine presence departs from the primordial or any subsequent domain. The psalmist speaks of the same *ruach* creating life on the face of the ground (Ps. 104.30). This story of creation embraces the presence of God as an integral part of the cosmos, perpetually moving within the cosmos.

The *ruach* of *Elohim* is described as *merachepet* ('hovering'). The translation of this rare term varies, depending partly on whether the interpreter assumes the verse refers to chaos. If the *ruach Elohim* is read as a 'mighty wind' or 'mighty storm' (von Rad 1961: 47), the descriptive verb is rendered something like 'swept' (NRSV) or 'raged'. The use of this verb (*rchp*) in Deut. 32.11 speaks of an eagle 'hovering' over its young and spreading its wings—not in some fierce act of disturbance, but apparently to lift them up in the nurturing act of teaching them to fly.

The presence of *Elohim* is described in terms of this mysterious movement deep in the darkness. Perhaps, as Luise Schottroff suggests, this movement suggests a 'giant mother bird' (1993: 24-25). In the next verse (1.3) the moving *Elohim* becomes the speaking *Elohim*. There is no reason, therefore, within the logic of the story, to read *Elohim* as meaning 'mighty', or *ruach* as a chaos wind. *Elohim* is one of the key characters of the story from the beginning.

The second component of the primordial state is 'the waters'. These seem to be described in two ways: simply as 'waters', or as 'the deep' (*tehom*). A detailed linguistic analysis of *tehom* in Hebrew and related Near Eastern languages by Tsumura, demonstrates that

> [t]here is no evidence that the term *tehom* in Gen. 1.2 is a depersonification of an original Canaanite deity as Day assumes. The Hebrew term *tehom* is simply a reflection of the common Semitic term *tiham* 'ocean' and there is no relation between the Genesis account and the so-called *Chaoskampf* mythology (1989: 65).

Tehom, usually translated as 'the deep', apparently refers to the primordial oceans—they have still to be ordered into known seas and water sources. These waters remain hidden in the darkness together with the hovering breath or spirit of God. No negative verdict is pronounced on these waters—there is no indication that they are threatening powers or turbulent forces of chaos. They are part of the benign dormant primordial order that awaits transformation. Especially significant, however, is that the waters cover *erets*, Earth. Earth, therefore, is hidden—by both the darkness and the waters.

Erets *Uninhabited*

The third and pivotal character in the primordial setting is the *erets,* Earth. Earth is the dominant subject in the setting of the story; the condition of the Earth is a primary focus. Earth is in darkness, located beneath the primordial waters. It is described as *tohu wabohu.*

Debate over the meaning of *tohu wabohu* has raged long and hard over the years. Given the analysis above, it seems reasonable to assume that this designation does not represent a negative verdict on the condition of Earth, but is simply a description of the state of Earth prior to its appearance and transformation. After working through the linguistic evidence provided by Tsumura (1989: 16-43), I believe that one of the clearest texts to illustrate the import of *tohu* is Isa. 45.18 which reads:

> God did not create it *tohu,*
> God formed it to be inhabited.

Within the specific creation context of this verse, the explicit parallel of *tohu* is 'uninhabited'. *Tohu* and its extended form *tohu wabohu* seem to refer to a prior condition of Earth: it is without life, vegetation or habitation. Primordial Earth is bare, still to be inhabited or made productive. This condition parallels that of the Earth in Gen. 2.5: here the ground has no water or human beings to make it productive. Tsumura concludes:

> both the biblical context and extra-biblical parallels suggest that the phrase *tohu wabohu* in Gen. 1.2 has nothing to do with 'chaos' and sim-ply means 'emptiness' and refers to the earth which is an empty place, i.e. 'an unproductive and uninhabited place' (1989: 43).

Many of the scholars who have commented on this passage in recent years have discerned in Gen. 1.2 an allusion to 'chaos', fre-quently understood in terms of turbulent threatening waters that must be overcome by the Creator to produce the cosmos, the order of the world as ancient Israelites perceived it (e.g. Brueggemann 1982: 29). This chaos connection is often made by linking *tehom* with the Babylonian chaos deity Tiamat who, in the Babylonian myth *Enuma Elish*, was conquered by Marduk so he could establish order. Others view the *ruach* of *Elohim* as a raging wind rather than the breath or spirit of God. The story of Genesis 1, from this perspective, in-volves God's creative deeds, designed to overcome the forces of chaos and create a cosmos. For some, the Genesis 1 account was written to improve on the Genesis 2 account by employing the model of Marduk's victory over Tiamat:

> The Priestly Writer found in this divine sovereign scene the model he needed for transforming the unsatisfactory Yahwistic portrait of a naive and inexperienced creator [*sic*] into that of an omnipotent and omniscient Creator. This was accomplished by prefacing the Yahwist's with a prior scene (Gen. 1.1–2.3) which tells how the Creator tamed the Abyss and then brought into existence everything that is according to a well-conceived orderly scheme (Batto 1992: 34-35).

I have no doubt that a *Chaoskampf* tradition of some kind probably lies behind a number of biblical texts such as Ps. 74.12-14 and Sir. 51.9-10. My analysis of Gen. 1.2 suggests, however, that the Genesis portrayal of the primordial state has no necessary connection with the chaos tradition (see also Fretheim 1994: 356). Rather, it is a completely consistent story about Earth's manifestation. The Earth story makes complete sense without recourse to assuming a 'state of chaos' prior to the acts of creation in Genesis 1. My findings are consistent with those of van Wolde:

> This is the primeval situation: no 'nothing', nor a chaos that needs sorting out, but a situation of 'before' or 'not yet' in view of what is coming. Even God is not yet the Creator, but an indefinable spirit of God moving on the face of the waters. These are the main characters of the story to come (1998: 25).

One may speculate, given a growing ecojustice awareness, why scholars found it so appealing to discern the conquest of chaos motif in Genesis 1. The answer may be found in the relentless drive of many biblical scholars to find the setting of biblical texts in the wider ancient Near Eastern world of myth, history and cosmology. Another possibility lies in making connections between other biblical texts where this motif has been incorporated but radically transformed.

I suspect, however, that the reason may also lie in the fact that male scholars, like myself, were 'conditioned by our times'. The conquest of a threatening chaos—associated with female forces like Tiamat—by the rational 'word' of a powerful male deity appealed to our gendered view of the world. God's control over chaos could then be seen as precedent for the control of Earth assigned to *adam* in the latter half of Genesis 1. I also suspect that the dualistic contrast between chaos and order appealed to Western androcentric patterns of thought relating to conquest and 'power over'—especially as one element is overcome, conquered by might.

The portrait of the primordial state in Gen. 1.2 can be summarized as follows:

- Earth is bare and uninhabited, but not turbulent and chaotic;
- Earth is hidden beneath the primordial darkness and primordial waters;
- the breath/spirit of *Elohim* hovers over the waters; Earth lies beneath the waters;
- the presence of God is hidden within the darkness of the primordial;
- beneath the waters, the darkness, and in the presence of God, Earth silently 'awaits' manifestation;
- the setting is devoid of apparent conflict or dualism.

Erets *Staging*

The process of creation is introduced in 1.3 with the words of a voice, 'And *Elohim* said…' The primordial setting of the story introduced the presence of *Elohim* in the form of a breath or spirit. In 1.3 the breath of *Elohim* becomes the voice or word of *Elohim*. As in Ps. 33.6, the word and the breath are alternative images to express the presence of God as a creating power; they are two modes of God as Creator. *Elohim* hidden as a breath in the darkness is now revealed as a word that splits the silence and begins to transform the primordial.

Much has been made of the action of *Elohim* first creating light in the primordial darkness. From the perspective of Earth as a subject hidden in the darkness, light is essential for Earth—or any other reality of the known world—to be revealed and made visible. Without lighting there is no manifestation, no appearance, no visible Earth, no geophany. Without lighting, Earth and its goodness remain forever hidden.

Light is, first of all, therefore a functional prerequisite for the manifestation of Earth. Within the parameters of the Earth story, there is no duality between light and darkness, no equation of light with life and darkness with death. Light and darkness are complementary realities, expressions of the natural order, separated as domains of time and function. Accordingly, light is called 'day' and darkness is called 'night'. The darkness is transformed from an eternal condition of the primordial domain into a functional division of the present reality. The darkness is not evil or threatening; it is not a residue from a threatening chaos. It is part of the 'everything' that is declared 'good' by *Elohim* (Gen. 1.30).

The second prerequisite for Earth to be made manifest is that the waters covering and hiding Earth's presence need to be structured into a new reality. This structuring takes place in two stages, the first on day two and the second on day three.

On day two, *Elohim* constructs a dome or canopy (*raqia*) which is explicitly named *shemayim*. It is clear from the immediate context that this term refers to the sky as part of the visible order of things, and not to some distant celestial place called 'heaven' where, according to some biblical traditions, God is said to dwell in distant splendour. The references to *shemayim*—in the opening summary statement of Gen. 1.1 and the corresponding closure in 2.4a—within the language of the narrative logically also refer to a visible 'sky', and not to an invisible celestial heaven. Genesis 1, according to Gen. 1.1, is therefore a story about the creation of sky and Earth. The central subject of the story, Earth, is introduced in 1.2.

The initial function of the sky is to enable part of the primordial ocean to be relocated above, presumably as a source of rain. The sky also functions as a canopy to provide the open space within which Earth can appear. Elsewhere the formula 'the one who stretches out the heavens/skies' seems to refer to the pitching of the skies as a cosmic tent where YHWH is revealed to those on Earth (Habel 1972). In Genesis 1 the heavens are stretched out as a canopy beneath which the Earth, not God, is to be revealed.

The absence of a divine response to the sky as good in 1.8 may be due to the fact that the work of ordering the primordial waters happens in two stages. When both stages are complete in 1.10, the appropriate verdict is pronounced. The setting for Earth's appearance has the director's approval; the lighting and the staging for Earth's appearance centre stage are in place.

Erets *Revealed*

On the third day *erets* is revealed, the hidden is made visible, the mysterious is uncovered. On the third day *erets* rises from the waters, an epiphany from below—a geophany.

I use revelatory language in the preceding paragraph quite deliberately. According to the text:

> And God said, 'Let the waters under the sky be gathered in one area, and let the dry domain appear.' And it was so. And God called the dry domain *erets*. And the waters God gathered together God called seas. And God saw that it was good (Gen. 1.9-10).

The verb *ra'ah* is rendered 'appear', though it could well have been translated 'be revealed'. The niphal form used here is used elsewhere when God or an angel of God is revealed or 'appears'. In Gen. 18.1, 'YHWH appeared to Abraham' (cf. 12.7; 35.1). In Gen. 1.9 the language of God's theophanic appearance to humans is associated with the appearance of *erets*.

This gives *erets* a unique character, distinct from all other components of creation. *Erets* alone is revealed from below, a hidden mystery made manifest, a sacred domain in the cosmos.

When the waters are pulled back into their own domain, the form of *erets* is described as the *yabashah*, the 'dry domain'. This dry domain that has emerged from the watery deep is specifically called *erets* ('land or Earth'). It refers to land/Earth as that domain, at present bare, which is potentially habitable. Just as when the light was separated from the darkness, *Elohim*—the character behind the breath and the voice—responds. *Elohim* not only speaks but also 'sees' in a distinctive way, responding personally to what has now appeared, 'is seen'. When '*Elohim* sees' Earth is good, the storyteller implies a subtle word play on Earth 'being seen/appearing'.

God does not pronounce light and Earth 'good', thereby imprinting them with integrity from a position of authority. Rather, they 'are good', and God experiences them as good; *Elohim* 'sees' they are good. The integrity of *erets* is a given, discovered by God in the creation process. The 'good' which God experiences in the *erets* is probably not 'good' in some dualistic or moral sense. 'Good' is God's response to what is seen, experienced in the moment of creation.

A similar idiom is used to describe the response of Moses' mother when he is born. When she first bonds with the child 'she sees he is good' (Exod. 2.1). God beholds Earth emerge from the waters below and 'sees it is good'. God is delighted with what appears! God bonds with Earth. The intrinsic value of Earth is something God discovers and something humans have yet to appreciate fully. The principle of intrinsic worth is evident, therefore, not only in the nature of Earth as a primordial 'revelation' but also in God's response to that revelation as 'delightful'!

Appealing as it may be, there is no evidence within the text to suggest that *erets* is an oppressed character within the chaos waters who needs to be liberated (Deane-Drummond 1996: 17). The act of God separating the waters of the Reed Sea to expose the 'dry land' may have been a stage in the liberation of Israel, but the appearance of the dry land on the third day of the Earth story is not a rescue operation. It is a revelation of a hidden reality. In Genesis 1, *Elohim* the Creator is not necessarily a prototype of YHWH the liberator in Exodus. The Earth story stands as an origin story in its own right, whatever its ancient Near Eastern roots may have been.

Erets *Activated*

Elohim now speaks to 'newborn' Earth and summons it to come alive, replete with all the vegetation typical of land. 'And *erets* put forth...' a range of plants complete with seeds to enable regeneration. The immediate source of this plant life is not strictly the command of God, but *erets*, Earth. When God activates *erets*, the potential life forces within Earth emerge as fauna and flora of all kinds. The revealed *erets* is the dormant source of living creatures.

On the fifth day the waters are activated and bring forth creatures; these creatures have no prior existence as chaos forces as in other ancient traditions. The sky too is filled with birds that explicitly fly 'above *erets*', the narrative centre of all creation (Gen. 1.20). All these creatures are given the divine blessing necessary to procreate and to 'multiply in Earth'. The Earth story depicts *erets* as both the source of life and the home of all living creatures. The creation process continues; life is stimulated by the divine word, emerges from the *erets*, and persists through the blessing of pro-creation.

On the sixth day *erets* is again activated and animal life emerges, including domestic animals, creeping creatures and wild animals that are specifically identified as 'living things of *erets*'. Creatures of the wild belong to *erets*. Earth is the source, home and haven of living creatures. Earth is a co-creator with *Elohim* (Fretheim 1992: 14). As a life source, *erets* supplies both body and spirit, the animated being. There is no duality here—this is not a picture of the material or body deriving from Earth, and the spirit or life-breath deriving from God.

The response of Earth to the voice of *Elohim* points to the ecojustice principle of voice. Not only is Earth a character in the story—there is also an interaction between God and Earth that leads to life emerging from Earth. Life from Earth is the living value of the Earth.

There are a number of indigenous creation myths—sometimes called emergence myths—that describe all life, including animal and human life, as emerging from the land or sea and returning there at death. It is typical of Aboriginal Australian origin stories that animals and humans emerge from the ground as part of a sacred cycle of life and death. A person's identity is determined not only by virtue of their origin from the land as mother, but also in terms of specific places on the land where that person shares a common spirit with animals and ancestors. Earth is a spiritual source of life. At this point I acknowledge my debt to indigenous Australians, including the Rainbow Spirit Elders, for my appreciation of the deep significance of Earth/land in the Bible, including Genesis 1 (Rainbow Spirit Elders 1997).

Erets *Illuminated*

The purpose of the sun and moon created on the fourth day is to regulate the light created on the first day. They are specifically called 'lights' or 'lamps', and emit and regulate the light from the sky. The specific purpose stated for regulating the light is to 'give light upon Earth', a purpose which is stated twice (Gen. 1.15, 17). The sun regulates light during the day, and the moon regulates the night. By regulating day and night, the 'lights in the sky' also regulate time—'signs, season, days and years' (1.14).

Some scholars would argue that the word 'sun' is avoided as a polemic against an ancient deity who bears that name. It is just as valid—in terms of this narrative as an artistic Earth story—to suggest that the emphasis lies on the function of these bodies as light-givers for Earth, rather than on deliberately negating any specific ancient Near Eastern rival mythology. On the fourth day, the great lights illuminate *erets* and thereby regulate the pattern of light over time.

This regulation of the light is described at one point as 'rule over the day and over the night'. The verb rendered 'rule' is *mashal*, a term used for both 'ruling over' (Gen. 45.26) and 'being responsible for' (Gen. 24.2). Just as Abraham's servant was 'in charge of/responsible for' Abraham's household, the sun and moon are responsible for/rulers over day and night. The function of this 'ruling' is not to dominate, but to regulate light for *erets*. Their role as custodians above is in the service of *erets*, 'to give light to Earth'.

Erets *Complete*

The Earth story concludes with the narrator announcing that the sky, Earth and their inhabitants were completed after six days. The once latent Earth is now fully revealed, whole, complete. The focus of the narrative in the final scene moves to *Elohim*. This character, who once hovered endlessly as a mysterious breath or spirit in the primordial darkness, orders Earth in a six-day burst of activity and then rests. The narrative progression is one of movement from anticipation, through execution, to satisfaction and rest.

It is striking that the activity of God in revealing, activating and illuminating Earth is called 'work', a word for everyday labour that occurs three times in this scene (Wenham 1987: 35). The focus is not on transcendent edicts that enter the earthly domain like verbal shafts from heaven. *Erets* is the 'earthy' work of *Elohim* within the cosmos, a work in which *Elohim* takes genuine satisfaction. Rest naturally follows this kind of work: effort yields to peace and satisfaction.

The *erets* work and rest of *Elohim* is the pattern for all life on Earth. The day of rest is sanctified so that all creation joins in this same pattern. All is in order, complete and at peace with *Elohim*. This day of rest is designated a sabbath day. No connection is made with the moon or celestial order. Rather, it is linked especially with *Elohim*'s cessation of work on Earth (Wenham 1987: 35).

Erets *Subdued*

The Earth story analysed thus far presents a beautifully unified narrative, with Earth as the primary character. The story commences with uninhabited Earth hidden beneath primordial waters and darkness. *Elohim* is also present in the darkness as a mysterious moving breath or spirit.

On the first two days, *Elohim* introduces light into the darkness and a canopy into the waters. These provide the lighting and staging for the revelation of Earth on the third day, when Earth emerges from the deep and is revealed as a dry domain above the waters and beneath the sky. This event is a geophany, an epiphany of *erets*, the chief character in this Earth story.

Once Earth is manifest, the life forces within Earth are activated by a word of *Elohim*. The Earth, supported by the waters and the sky, brings forth flora and fauna as living realities. Earth is a subject, a character who participates with *Elohim* in the creation process. *Elohim* places two lights in the sky to regulate time, and to illuminate Earth. Finally *Elohim* rests, celebrating the 'work' of creation on the seventh day.

This story emphasizes the intrinsic value of Earth as the centre of the cosmos and the source of life. All components of the cosmos are related to Earth as an integrated interconnected whole, free from hierarchies of power in relation to Earth (principle 2). It is precisely *erets* that *Elohim* experiences as 'good'. Earth at creation is pristine, evoking God's pleasure and celebration.

With the appearance of human beings onto the scene, however, power relations shift radically. The orientation of the human story

(Gen. 1.26-30) stands in direct conflict with the orientation of the Earth story in the preceding verses. The radical conflict between the two can be summarized as follows.

Elohim is introduced as saying, 'Let us make humans'. The 'us' seems to refer to beings in a celestial realm that is not part of the cosmos as constructed thus far in the story (von Rad 1961: 57). *Elohim* apparently moves from being a breath and voice within the cosmos to being the head of a heavenly council beyond the cosmos of the Earth story.

1. Human beings, unlike all other living things, do not emanate from Earth as the logic of the story would seem to dictate, but are created by fiat of *Elohim* in council. This special mode of creation already differentiates human beings from all other forms of life. The technical term *bara* 'create', while used to introduce and conclude the creation story (Gen. 1.1; 2.4a) is not used of the basic acts of creation except for humans and, oddly enough, the sea monsters (Gen. 1.21). Humans are 'created'; other realities emerge or are constructed through different processes.

2. Human beings are further differentiated from other living creatures by being made in 'our image'—apparently the image of the celestial beings (Gen. 1.26) or of *Elohim* (Gen. 1.27). Humans are elevated to the side of God/celestial beings over against Earth.

3. The function of the special form and status of humans as 'images of *Elohim*' is to give them dominion over all other living things 'upon *erets*'. The focus moves from *erets* as the source of living creatures to *adam*, a new creature with power over all the life that has emanated from *erets*. Both *erets* and the life that has been born of Earth are devalued by being made subservient to humans.

4. The fertility blessing given to all life assumes a new dimension when extended to humans. Not only are humans to be fruitful, multiply and fill Earth; they are also authorized to 'subdue' Earth. *Erets* is further devalued by being portrayed as a force that humans are expected to 'subdue'. The verb *kabash* ('to subdue') not only confirms the status of humans as having power over Earth; it also points to harsh control. Elsewhere the term involves forceful subjugation, including enslavement (Jer. 34.11; Neh. 5.5), the crushing of hostile nations (2 Sam. 8.11) and the rape of a woman (Est. 7.8). The

specific expression 'subduing the *erets*' recalls the 'subduing/
conquest of the land (*erets*)' of Canaan. Moses, Joshua and
David were all involved in 'subduing' the land by conquest
and subjugation of Israel's enemies (Num. 32.22; Josh. 18.1; 1
Chron. 22.18). Subduing the land meant crushing opposing
forces. There is nothing gentle about the verb *kabash*. To
suggest that this verb means something like 'receive a divine
gift' or 'tend' ignores, it seems to me, the basic usage of the
term. Nor is there any indication in the text that this 'subdu
ing' is temporary or limited in any way as D.T. Williams sug
gests (1993).

5. The orientation of the human story (Gen. 1.26-28) is overtly
   hierarchical: humans are authorized to rule other creatures
   and to subdue Earth. The preceding Earth story of the uni
   fied cosmos is interrupted by the human story which reduces
   Earth to a force or thing that must be subjugated. The two
   stories are in conflict; humans are set over Earth and against
   Earth.

Erets *Redeemed?*

It is not the intention of this analysis to survey the many ways that
scholars, including ecotheologians, have sought to redeem the text of
this human story by interpreting the expressions 'image of God',
'rule' and 'subdue' in environmentally friendly ways (cf. Halkes 1989:
132; McAfee 1996: 33-36). My concern here is to highlight that the
human story (Gen. 1.26-30) violates the spirit of the Earth-oriented
story that precedes it (Gen. 1.1-25). The assumed dominance of the
human story over the Earth story is illustrated by the reading of
scholars like Brueggemann who writes:

> With careful regard to the rest of creation in verses 3-25, the special
> clustering of the word 'create' in verse 27, suggests that the text wishes
> to *focus on the creation of humankind*. The liturgy celebrates the creation of
> humankind (1982: 31; italics in original).

This anthropocentric interpretation of Genesis 1 necessarily leads to
the relegation of Earth story to a secondary status. The human story is
seen to override the Earth story; the story of humans subduing Earth
has suppressed the story of a pristine Earth of intrinsic worth. Within
the narrative of the Earth story, no reason is given as to why a pristine
Earth, having just been revealed as a source of life and fertility,
should need to be 'subdued'. No weakness or wildness is identified

that needs to be controlled. On the contrary, *Elohim* finds Earth a reality to be celebrated as good.

Nor is there is any hint here that the narrator is specifically living in the harsh environment of Palestine, and views the land as an alien force that must be harnessed by arduous labour to produce food or to maintain order. The story is, first of all, about the primal era—before humanity has spoiled the pristine Earth, or any act of God or humanity has made Earth recalcitrant.

Given that the human story has an assumed primacy among interpreters, can the Earth story be redeemed? Or must *erets* remain forever under 'human subjugation' from the beginning? In terms of justice for Earth, the text of Genesis 1 moves from honouring Earth by describing its revelation as a geophany, to negating Earth as a force to be overcome by humanity.

It is high time, it seems to me, that we return to honouring Earth, recognizing the intrinsic value of Earth, and restoring the Earth story to its rightful place as a genuine counterpart to the human story with which it interacts in subsequent narratives of Genesis. The challenge before us is to face the problem and potential of this text squarely and reinstate the Earth story so that justice for Earth is initiated by our readings. In our reading of the Scriptures, we have negated the Earth story by giving the human story complete primacy.

If we restore the Earth story to its proper place of honour in Genesis 1, how will we read the rest of Genesis? How does the Earth story, from the perspective of justice for Earth, unfold? Have interpreters, assuming the primacy of the human story, also suppressed the Earth story, and the voice of Earth, in subsequent narratives of Genesis? How would *erets* tell the Earth story? How can we retrieve the Earth story and in so doing contribute to the contemporary task of redeeming Earth in the context of our current ecological crisis?

These questions will be explored in various ways in the essays that make up the remainder of this volume.

Rest for the Earth? Another Look at Genesis 2.1-3

Howard N. Wallace

Introduction

'Thus the sky and the earth were finished, and all that was within them.'[1] Thus begins the account of the seventh day of creation (Gen. 2.1-3). This day is special in the order of creation in Gen. 1.1–2.3 by virtue of both the content and shape of its account. It stands alone, the odd day at the end of the sequence, the day without a mate as the rabbis have called it (*Gen. R.* 11.8.1-2) (Neusner (1991: 87-88)). It is part of the creation account of Genesis 1, and yet it is not.

My aim in this paper is to ask what part the earth has to play in this seventh day and/or what the seventh day has to offer the earth? Of course the earth is only mentioned once in our passage (Gen. 2.1). That might suggest that the earth has little role or place in the text. However, I believe that would be a distortion of the text. I will endeavour to show that in fact the earth receives considerable attention by virtue of being part of the whole of creation. In the first section of the paper I will look at the text of Gen. 2.1-3 itself, both in isolation and in connection with Genesis 1. This investigation will be from the point of view of the modern reader of the text. It will involve the retrieval of an emphasis on the earth as a significant part of a whole. In the second section of the essay I will look briefly at some ways Gen. 2.1-3 has been interpreted within Scripture and without, again with an eye to the consequences for the earth. I will argue that little attention has been given to the place of the earth as an important part of the whole of creation. In terms of the ecojustice principles that guide the Earth Bible project, this essay is concerned principally with the

---

1.   The Hebrew word *shamayim* (שמים) is often translated 'heaven(s)' (e.g. in the NRSV). This could give the sense of referring to a 'spiritual' realm or heavenly sphere which is the dwelling place of God only. It is clear from the parallel treatment of *shamayim* and *erets* (ארץ) in Gen. 1.1–2.3 that the material creation is encompassed by both terms. *Shamayim* should thus be translated 'sky' or something similar which gives the sense of part of the material universe.

first two, namely the principles of intrinsic worth and interconnectedness.

Genesis 2.1-3 in the Context of the Creation Account (Genesis 1.1–2.3)

I have already indicated Gen. 2.1-3 stands out in a number of ways at the end of the creation account. It breaks with the set formula established for the other six days[2] that binds those days together and gives a sense of the orderliness of creation. In contrast the account of the seventh day consists of three parallel lines (Gen. 2.2-3a), each with seven words and with the repetition of basic phrases. Each of the first six days had been counted off by a single ordinal at the end of the account. The naming of the seventh day occurs three times within the body of the account. This day has no evening or morning. The absence of verbs of action or indicators of time, as well as the repetition, changes the rhythm of the reading of the text and focuses attention on this day.

In spite of the differences between Gen. 2.1-3 and Genesis 1, it is still clear that Gen. 2.1-3 is to be read as part of that account. The seven-day structure, the *inclusio* around the words *bara Elohim* (ברא אלהים, 'God created' in Gen. 1.1 and 2.3b, and the similar vocabulary, especially in relation to Gen. 2.1, all go to bind together Gen. 1.1–2.3.[3] The seventh day is thus part of the creation story, yet it is distinct within it. In terms of the day structure, the seventh day is placed both within the temporal sequence of days one to six and yet beyond it. The seventh day is both part of the 'history' of creation, and yet not part of it.

In contrast to accounts of the other days, Gen. 2.1-3 does not begin with God as subject. The accounts of the other six days all begin with the statement 'God said'. Nouns other than 'God' govern verbs only as they stand under that introduction. The seventh day begins in Gen. 2.1 with 'the sky and the earth...and all that was within them' as the subject of the passive verb form *waykullu* (ויכלו) 'they were finished'. Thus prominence on the seventh day is initially given to 'the sky and the earth...and all that was within them'. Only after this, in Gen. 2.2a, is God introduced as the subject. The use in Gen. 2.2a of the active piel form of the same verbal root as in Gen. 2.1 (*killah*, כלה, 'he finished') maintains a link between these verses and roots the completion of the

2.   The formula runs: God said: 'Let there be... God made... It was so... God called... God saw that it was good...there was evening and morning, day...' See Gen. 1.3-31.

3.   For more detail see Wallace (1988). Note also Anderson (1977: 151) who argues that the story is a 'meticulously wrought composition'.

sky and the earth and all within them in God's action. It is only after this that God becomes the subject in the text and, in fact, remains so for the rest of the account of the seventh day.

On the seventh day God's activity changes. God does not do any work. On the other days God undertook the tasks of making, creating and naming. Now God's work is complete and God blesses and sanctifies the seventh day.[4] It has been argued that the terms 'bless' and 'sanctify' are basically synonymous in this text, but it can also be the case that each term brings its own nuance to the text.[5]

A number of points should be noted when seeking to understand the sense of 'bless' and 'sanctify' in Gen. 2.3. First, the parallelism between the verbs in Gen. 2.2-3, and the fact that the verbs 'bless' and 'sanctify' are surrounded by notices that God rested on the seventh day, point to a close connection between the completion of God's work and God's blessing or sanctifying the seventh day. The latter actions have to be seen in light of the former state. Secondly, it is the seventh day, a period of time, which is blessed and sanctified. In Gen. 1.22 and 28 God blessed the creatures and humans in terms of procreation. In each case the blessing fell on a certain part of creation and expressed God's desire for the increase of those creatures. Thus the blessing in Gen. 2.3 is not the same as those earlier in the story. Thirdly, sanctification of places, times or people in the human sphere has the effect of setting them apart so that they might aid communion between the divine and the human. In Gen. 2.3 only God is involved.

Bearing these points in mind, a limited use of analogy from other contexts within which the terms 'bless' and 'sanctify' are used might help in the case of Gen. 2.3. Elsewhere in the Hebrew Bible days can be blessed or not blessed (e.g. Jer. 20.14).[6] The blessing designates the day, in Gen. 2.3 the seventh day, as a successful or favourable time. The Sabbath, as well as other holy days, is also regularly said to be sanctified (e.g. Exod. 16.23; 20.8). On the analogy of certain days being sanctified for humans one could say that the seventh day is a time set apart for special observance by God. Speaking about sanctification is appropriate as the day shares with all other sacred things the quality

---

4.   On the meaning of the root *shbt* (שבת) in Gen. 2.2b see Cassuto (1961: 63). G, *Sam.* and *Syr.* (abbreviations for various existing ancient versions of the text of the Hebrew Bible) all emend Gen. 2.2a to read 'on the sixth day' to make it clear that God does no work on the seventh day. Cf. also *Jub.* 2.16. See Westermann (1984: 168-70) for a discussion of the understanding of *killah* (כלה) in Gen. 2.2a. Andreasen (1972: 63 n. 2) provides a summary of opinions.

5.   On the case for synonymity see Dressler (1982: 29).

6.   This is the case also in Phoenician. See Scharbert 1975: 282.

of being part of the world (in time), and yet sharing in a reality that transcends it. God's blessing and sanctifying of the seventh day mark this day out as significant and different to the other days. The same point is made by noting that on this day, in contrast to the preceding six, God rested because God's creation was complete.

Of primary concern in the account of the seventh day is the notion of the completion of creation. This completion has already been marked in Gen. 1.31. In the evaluation formula in that verse, 'all which [God] made' is seen as 'very good'. G. von Rad correctly sees the sense of 'very good' in Gen. 1.31 as 'completely perfect', referring to harmony, not beauty.[7] Thus a sense of completion is already present at the end of the sixth day and it has to do more with interrelatedness than with just a task being at an end.

While Gen. 1.31 functions as a concluding verse for the acts of creation in Gen. 1.3-30, it also anticipates the focus of the seventh day. The notion of completion is taken up in Gen. 2.1-3 by the repetition of the verb *klh* (כלה, 'to be complete'), and by the phrase 'all that was within them' and the clause 'all his work which he/God had done/created'. The last two echo 'all which [God] made' in Gen. 1.31 as well as the sevenfold occurrence of *kol* (כל) 'all, everything' in Gen. 1.29-31. It is this completion which is celebrated at the start of the seventh day.

The interrelatedness of the whole creation is further indicated in the remark in 2.1 that 'the sky and the earth...and all that was within them' were complete. This combination not only draws together all aspects of the six previous days in the words 'all that was within them',[8] but also brings together the sky and the earth as joint subjects for the first time in the creation account. The two nouns sky and earth have not appeared together since Gen. 1.1 where they formed the object of God's creating. In the body of the account 'sky' (*shamayim*, שמים) and 'earth' (*erets*, ארץ) appear separately. Creation proceeds by means of division or separation on four of the six days, with some days focusing on the sky and others on the earth. In Gen. 2.1, however, the completeness and interrelatedness of the whole of creation is again stressed and celebrated.[9] Moreover, this completeness is not a quality of creation itself. The link between Gen. 2.1 and 2.2a around

---

7.   Von Rad (1972a: 61), cf. Westermann (1984: 166) and Cassuto (1961: 59).

8.   The word *tsaba* (צבא) 'host, multitude' is often associated with the sky but rarely with the earth. In this context it clearly covers all the individual creations within the more general frame of the creation of the sky and earth in Gen. 1.3-30. Cf. Isa. 34.2 where *tsaba* (צבא) is used as a synonym for 'nations'.

9.   See also Lincoln (1982: 348).

the common verb *klh* (כלה), but with a change of subject to God, suggests that completion has its origin in God.

In stressing this sense of completeness it is implicit that no one act or part of creation brings the greatest accolade from God. This is true of humans as much as anything else. In Gen. 2.1 humans are subsumed within 'all that was within' the sky and earth. In Gen. 1.28 they were given dominion over other creatures and over the earth. But in Gen. 2.1 they are not afforded a special place. Moreover, all creation is held under the sovereignty of God as I will argue. Thus Gen. 2.1-3 stands as a check against any interpretation of the role of humans in Gen. 1.28 that ignores the harmony and wholeness of all the work God has done in creation.

Genesis 2.1-3 is not the only passage in the creation story that sits outside the structure of the six days of creation. Genesis 1.2, as a prelude to the acts of creation, also fits this case. In that verse earth is described as being *tohu wabohu* (תהו ובהו), possibly a chaotic, desolate or empty state, with 'darkness upon the face of the deep'. The seventh day in Gen. 2.1-3 stands as the antithesis of the situation described in 1.2. Whereas the earth was chaotic or desolate in Gen. 1.2, it is part of the complete, harmonious creation in 2.1. In Gen. 1.2 the *ruach Elohim* (רוח אלהים)[10] hovered over the waters in what could be a faint echo of a battle motif, and God had not yet begun to create, while in Gen. 2.2-3 God rests and blesses the day creation is complete. Thus while Gen. 2.1-3 brings the creation story to a close with the *inclusio* already noted, it also stands in opposition to what existed before the acts of creation. Michael Fishbane makes a similar observation:

> Between the stillness of the prologue and the calm of the epilogue there is a world of difference. The first silence precedes time, the second sanctifies it. The torpid waste of the primal beginning has been transformed (1998: 9).

The meaning of God's rest in Gen. 2.1-3 can only be understood in light of the whole creation story. I have argued at length elsewhere that in the shaping of the creation account in Gen. 1.1–2.3, a traditional motif, namely that of the 'rest of the gods', which in Akkadian and Ugaritic creation myths closely follows the motif of the creation of humankind, has been elevated to the important concluding position (Wallace 1988: 241-47). In the process the motif of rest has been changed. In the Akkadian texts the rest of the gods is achieved at the

---

10. Variously translated as 'wind from God' or 'spirit of God' or 'mighty wind'.

expense of humankind who are created in order to relieve the gods of manual labour. In Genesis God does not take rest at the expense of humans. Rather the fact that the later institution of the human Sabbath in Exod. 20.8-11 and 31.17 is based on Gen. 2.1-3 suggests that humans are meant to share in God's rest.

The elevation of the motif of the 'rest of the gods' in Gen. 1.1–2.3 has been achieved at the expense of another motif, namely that of the proclamation of the sovereignty of the creator god in association with temple building. This latter motif is the point of conclusion of creation in some non-biblical myths. If the final form of Gen. 1.1–2.3 is to be dated to the exilic or early postexilic period then the explanation for the replacement could be that the symbolism of the ruined first Jerusalem temple powerfully denied any sense of the sovereignty of Judah's God. By elevating the motif of the 'rest of the gods' and by subtly relating it to the Sabbath tradition, the writers of Gen. 1.1–2.3 gave the people a new way to recognize the sovereignty of their God without employing symbolism that spoke strongly against that sovereignty.[11] If this argument is convincing then the fact that God does no work, as well as the order of Gen. 2.1-3, proclaims the sovereignty of God who has controlled the desolation and darkness of Gen. 1.2 through his word and action. That sovereignty is explicit in God not doing any further work at the completion of the whole of creation, or, to put it another way, it is explicit in the statement that God has brought into being and maintains the interrelatedness and harmony of the whole.

To summarize the points on Gen. 2.1-3 so far. By means of the shaping of the account of the seventh day, with both its connections to the other days and its distinct features, attention is drawn to this day. It is part of the sequence of days of creation and yet, at the same time, it stands apart from the sequence. It signals a new type of period when the completion of creation leads into an ongoing period of blessing by God. The seventh day is one in which the sovereignty of Judah's God over chaos or desolation is proclaimed and as such it introduces the note of redemption to the story. That not only has implications for moral or religious reforms, as stressed in some passages in the Hebrew Bible on the Sabbath, but it has implications for ecological reforms as well. In particular, it calls for redemption from any misappropriation of the notice in Gen. 1.26, 28 that humans are given dominion over the earth and other creatures.

The earth does not figure prominently in the text of Gen. 2.1-3 if we

11. Cf. Levenson 1988: 100-11.

simply regard the frequency of references as indicative of importance. On the other hand, the emphasis on the interrelatedness of the whole creation will not let any part of creation fall from view (van Wolde 1998: 28). The text, in bringing 'the sky and the earth…and all that was within them' together, plays out the intention of God in creation itself and brings all parts of God's creation into relationship. God completes the work of creation as all parts find their completion in relationship with each other.

The Earth in the Interpretation of Genesis 2.1-3

We have noted above that Gen. 2.1-3 stresses that the completion of creation involves the interrelatedness of the created order under the sovereignty of God. The earth, the sky and all that they hold within them are of importance to God and God's rest is only exercised at the completion of the whole.

While the text readily lends itself to this exegetical conclusion, only rarely has much been made of this understanding. The general lack of interest in the place of the earth in this text can be traced right back to the biblical interpreters themselves. Of course, we cannot assume that the interpretation I have outlined reflects the intention or outlook of the writers. In fact, it would probably even be unreasonable to assume that the writers of the passage, in their own social, economic and agricultural contexts, would have given much consideration to the place of the earth in the creation story.

There is a small number of Hebrew Bible texts that are based on an interpretation of Gen. 2.1-3. For the most part the interest in Gen. 2.1-3 in these texts focuses on the issue of human Sabbath observance. This is true in Exod. 20.8-11, the passage on the Sabbath from the Ten Commandments, and Exod. 31.17 where, in relation to the construction of the tabernacle, the Sabbath is seen as a sign of the perpetual covenant. There is no overt thought for a Sabbath for the land or earth in either passage. That is also true of many other texts concerning the Sabbath that do not refer to Gen. 2.1-3, for example Exod. 35.2-3; Lev. 19.3, 30; 23.3; 26.2; Isa. 58.13-14. In these texts the Sabbath is largely discussed in terms of human observance. The closest one comes to a discussion of the Sabbath in relation to parts of creation other than the human is in Exod. 20.10 and Exod. 23.12 where it is commanded that one's livestock or ox and donkey will do no work on the Sabbath.

The idea of the land or earth observing a Sabbath is raised in Lev. 25.1-22 which speaks of a fallow year in every seven and the year of Jubilee every fifty years. These periods of rest for the land are referred to as Sabbaths (cf. also Lev. 26.34-35 and 2 Chron. 36.21) but nowhere in these passages is Gen. 2.1-3 clearly indicated as the basis for the law. In Exod. 34.21 the Sabbath is stressed as a time of rest even in periods of ploughing and harvest. The passage could lend itself to the idea that the land might rest, but the point of the text is more likely to be a matter of human discipline and trust in God even in the busiest of times.[12]

Genesis 2.1-3 is certainly structured in such a way that it alludes to the institution of the Sabbath day.[13] However, it is not an aetiology for Sabbath observance and the noun 'sabbath' (*shabat*, שבת) does not occur in the passage. The aetiology for Sabbath observance comes in Exod. 31.12-17. Genesis 2.1-3 is about creation and God's Sabbath. Of course, it is not unreasonable given the allusions to the institution of Sabbath observance in Gen. 2.1-3, especially in the many expressions characteristic of Sabbath regulations, that Gen. 2.1-3 should be incorporated into discussion of Sabbath observance. Where things seem to get distorted is in the emphasis given to human Sabbath observance rather than to seeing Sabbath in connection with the whole of creation. To the degree that any consideration is given to an understanding of the relation of Sabbath to the whole of creation, it is usually within the context of human observance and rest. The roots of any modern ecological problems to which an emphasis on Gen. 1.28 and human domination of creation has contributed, would thus seem to be embedded in the biblical text itself and its own internal means of interpretation.

Preoccupation with humankind as the subject of Sabbath is also found in modern commentaries and discussion on Genesis. Inasmuch as commentators see Gen. 2.1-3 connected with Sabbath observance, it is again mostly anthropocentric in orientation.[14] On the basis of what I have argued above this would seem, at the least, to ignore the full implications of the text, or at most involve a misappropriation of the text. The human Sabbath, as discussed in Exod. 31.12-17, is meant to be a reflection of the divine Sabbath. As such it ought to involve more of a 'refreshment' of a sense of humility in humankind than rest and recuperation for further domination and exploitation. An anthropocentric interpretation of Gen. 2.1-3 in relation to Sabbath obser-

12. See Hiebert 1996c: 129.
13. For a fuller discussion, see Wallace (1988: 242-43); cf. also the view of Meier (1991: 8-9), who relates the creation story to seven-day cycles of purification rites.
14. See Kahn 1990: 125-26; Westermann 1984: 169, 171; Scharbert 1975: 295. Cf. also the passages on Gen. 2.1-3 in *Gen. R.* 11, cited in Neusner (1991: 78-89).

vance can also overemphasize the human place in redemption. The unity of creation expressed in Gen. 2.1 suggests a close connection between creation and redemption. An anthropocentric interpretation of Gen. 2.1-3 in relation to Sabbath observance only fosters the division between creation and redemption promoted by an earlier generation of biblical scholars and theologians.[15]

There have been some recent comments and arguments that have tried to correct a narrow reading or misappropriation of Gen. 2.1-3. While some arguments by G. von Rad have seemed to contribute towards the situation outlined above, other statements by him suggest another direction. In regard to the seventh day he says in his *Old Testament Theology* that 'what is spoken of is much more than just something affecting only God himself: even here it possesses a hidden relationship to the world and man [*sic*], which will, though of course only later, become completely clear'(von Rad 1965: I, 148). He goes on to speak principally about humankind and Israel in particular, but he at least acknowledges that the Sabbath rest which is 'a good gift of salvation' is open to 'the world' beyond humankind.

A more substantial consideration of the place of the whole created order in the acts of creation by God is to be found in J. Moltmann's work *God in Creation*. He strongly stresses all aspects of the creation in his discussion. In relation to Gen. 2.1-3 he says, 'When people celebrate the sabbath they perceive the world as God's creation, for in the sabbath quiet it is God's creation that they are permitting the world to be' (Moltmann 1985: 6). This world embraces the human soul and body, individuals and groups, humans and animals, living things and all inanimate objects of the sky and earth (1985: 277). The blessing of the Sabbath is universal. Even those creatures over which humans have dominion are to share the Sabbath. In that he says: 'The celebration of the sabbath leads to an intensified capacity for perceiving the loveliness of everything' (1985: 286). Moltmann goes on to recognize that the Sabbath lies both within time and in what he calls 'messianic time' (1985: 286).

However, while I believe Moltmann has a good feel for the interpretation of Gen. 2.1-3, in places his arguments are based on interpretations of the passage that are not always exegetically rigorous. In particular, while trying to understand the metaphor of God's 'rest' on the seventh day, Moltmann states: 'The God who rests in face of his creation does not dominate the world on this day: he "feels" the

---

15. See esp. von Rad (1966: 131-43) for an argument regarding the separation of creation and redemption in the Old Testament.

world; he allows himself to be affected, to be touched by each of his creatures' (1985: 279). In this I do not think Moltmann fully grasps the motif of rest. I have argued that it has to do with the proclamation of the sovereignty of God. Moreover, that sovereignty is asserted through the overcoming of chaos or desolation by word and action. It is not that God does not dominate creation on the seventh day, somehow letting it be free to be itself. Rather, I would say that God's dominion over creation as the one who has declared creation to be 'very good' and who holds it by his word over against chaos or desolation is seen most clearly on that day. Moltmann also states: 'The sabbath quiet is diametrically opposite to all the notions and cultic imitations of struggles between the gods out of which the world emerges' (1985: 284). But I think this is only partly true. Certainly the act of creation is not one of struggle in this particular text in the Hebrew Bible.[16] Rather creation is by unopposed word and action. On the other hand, the rest at the end still carries a faint echo of the old battle myths of creation, as possibly does the scene in Gen. 1.2.

Finally I will comment on some implications of my reading of Gen. 2.1-3 for our contemporary situation and no less in its ecological aspects than in others. Genesis 2.1-3 calls us to affirm the sovereignty and effectiveness of the work of God in the world, on the seventh day as much as on the other six. The seventh day is a recognition that the creation is held together by God and that God is the one on whom it is totally dependent. The dependency is not just applicable for the first six days. Genesis 2.1-3 seems to me to be a call to recognize that. It is a call to see ourselves, as human beings, from another perspective in the context of the whole of creation, or to put it in words similar to Moltmann's, to permit the world, including ourselves, to be God's creation.

My reading of Gen. 2.1-3 also calls for a recognition that there are forces in the world that act against the movement towards God's rest. Moltmann's view of the seventh day connects it both to time and 'messianic time'. Genesis 2.1-3, as well as having a timeless sense, still keeps the seventh day connected to the temporal sequence. To recognize that the rest of God is a statement about the sovereignty of God over against the forces of chaos or desolation is to recognize that striving for the wholeness of creation involves an ongoing struggle against chaos. This struggle is both one 'in time' and beyond time. Inasmuch as it is the former, we are involved in it. However, it is only

16. See Levenson (1988) on this.

in the latter that victory is assured, and then by virtue of the sovereignty of God.

Moltmann concludes his discussion with a practical step in the direction he has been moving. He suggests that, as is already the case in some congregations, Saturday night could be a time of devotion that leads into a Sabbath stillness on Sunday. The latter can then become an 'authentic Christian feast of the resurrection'. This day is also to be an 'ecological day of rest' (Levenson 1988: 296).

Moltmann's suggestion is both faithful to the Christian tradition and a challenge to contemporary faith. However, we live in an increasingly complex and technologically sophisticated world. With increasing pressures of work expectations, family life and leisure activities, greater flexibility is needed in 'Sabbath observance'. By that I do not just mean the Christian tradition has to accommodate itself to the 'ways of the world'. It is no longer simply a question of a quiet Sunday or even Saturday evening plus Sunday. Individual Christians and their denominations need to be more creative in their thought on and understanding of Sabbath in the Christian context. On an individual basis stress on Sabbath is important, and not just in terms of rest. In a culture that emphasizes human domination over creation, and individual control over time and space, there is a prophetic task for Christians. It is to proclaim that humans are part of creation. As such they are partly responsible for their environment in its broadest sense, but are also the recipients of gifts, words and expectations from outside themselves. As I remarked above Sabbath rest needs to be a 'refreshment' of a sense of humility in each of us in the light of our place in the whole creation and before God. Christians and their denominations must give further thought to what Sabbath is about and to ways to proclaim the value of the whole creation, especially the earth, apart from humans. On the corporate level this is important also. Issues to do with the environment are often portrayed in the media in terms of conflict, especially between the environment and employment. Such portrayals are not true in many cases and need rebuttal in words and actions.

In these situations faithful people must continue to be prophetic in the best biblical sense of that word. To overcome the ecological crisis fuelled in part by an anthropocentric misappropriation of Gen. 1.1-31, we need to rekindle our imaginations in relation to the biblical heritage in Gen. 2.1-3.

Common Ground: An Ecological Reading of Genesis 2–3

Carol A. Newsom

Nobody owns the Bible. Though from time to time various religious traditions have attempted to restrict who might read and interpret it, the Bible always manages to evade its chaperones and sneak out for a tryst with unauthorized interpreters. In recent years some of the most creative and provocative ecological readings of the Bible have been produced outside of the traditional theological circles of interpretation. In this essay I want to present, engage and adapt some of these readings in an effort to bring them before a new set of readers.

Several years ago, *Ishmael*, a novel with an unusual premise was published by Daniel Quinn. In this book, an idealistic, but rather disillusioned young man sees an ad in the personal column of his newspaper. The ad reads, 'Teacher seeks pupil. Must have an earnest desire to save the world. Apply in person' (Quinn 1992: 4). Against his better judgment he goes and is more than a little surprised when the 'teacher' turns out to be an enormous gorilla, the Ishmael of the title. Ishmael, it turns out, is a remarkable being, who discovered a capacity to communicate with human beings and for many years had been befriended by a Jewish man whose family had perished in the Holocaust. Now, after his benefactor's death, Ishmael lives on a stipend and has embarked on a new phase of his life, seeking a human being who can understand what he knows.

Ishmael announces to the young man that his subject is 'captivity'— not his own, but human captivity. He became interested in this subject through conversations with his Jewish benefactor. How had it been possible that not only Jews were held captive by Hitler but that millions, too, had been held captive, that is, captivated, by Hitler? It was not by force, not by terror, not by the charisma of a demagogue. Hitler had captivated the nation, Ishmael says, by giving it a story, '[a] story in which, under the leadership of Adolph Hitler, the Aryan race would burst its bonds, wreak vengeance on its oppressors, purify mankind of its defilements, and assume its rightful place as the master of all races'. Although many Germans 'recognized this story as rank mythology... [t]hey were nevertheless held captive by it simply because the vast majority around them thought it sounded wonderful and were willing to give their lives to make it a reality' (Quinn 1992: 34-35).

The gorilla's purpose is not to analyze Nazism, however, but to bring his young pupil to see that modern Western culture is in general in an analogous situation, captive to a story with fatal consequences. The young man has trouble recognizing and then articulating the story, the myth of our culture that Ishmael warns is so dangerous. This is scarcely surprising, since the story is so woven into our assumptions that we seldom tell it explicitly. Eventually, the young man does manage to speak it: '*the world was made for man, and man was made to rule it*' (Quinn 1992: 72; italics in original), 'the world is a human life-support system, a machine designed to produce and sustain human life' (Quinn 1992: 69). For the most part, this 'story', this fundamental myth of our culture, is taken as self-evident and true. But perhaps more alarmingly, Ishmael points out, even those who would not be comfortable with articulating it in such terms, even those who are dismayed by it, act in accordance with it. And yet, the disastrous consequences of this story for the whole Earth, including its human inhabitants, become increasingly apparent.

To be a Jew or a Christian listening to Ishmael can be a rather uncomfortable experience. To what extent has the Bible been a contributor to the destructive culture myth that Ishmael exposes? Over 30 years ago historian Lynn White Jr wrote a tremendously influential article in which he argued that the biblical heritage, especially as it had been interpreted in Christian theology, was at the root of the ecological crisis (White 1967). The notion that only human beings were created in the image of God and the belief that human beings had been given dominion over nature and even commanded to subdue it had led, White argued, to an attitude toward the natural world that set the stage for its exploitation and degradation. The number of articles written to refute White's argument would themselves fill a substantial book. Among thoughtful writers on the environment few would still endorse White's sweeping condemnation of the biblical heritage. But the popular image of Christianity as a religion indifferent if not hostile to ecological values remains widespread. Even among ecologically sensitive Christians and Jews discomfort still lingers. Doesn't the Bible privilege human beings as unique and special to God? Isn't it finally a human-oriented, even an anthropocentric, religious perspective, a religion whose genius is for history, not nature? Is the biblical story, even if not quite as culpable as White charged,

nevertheless one of the foundations of that cultural myth that the
world was made for us, and we are to rule over it?

Certainly, the Bible has often been *heard* in that way, but the actual
story it tells of how-things-came-to-be-the-way-they-are and the models it gives for living out the biblical story are much more nuanced
and thoughtful about the place of human beings in the world. The
Bible presents powerful resources for confronting the inadequacies of
the cultural myth of absolute human privilege and for transforming
our understanding of our relation to land and water, to plants and
animals. Indeed, that wise gorilla Ishmael is himself quite taken with
the fundamental importance of the Bible, and in particular the Yahwistic creation account in Genesis 2–3, in recovering an alternative
story to live by.

Paradise Described (Genesis 2.4b-17)

It may seem odd that Ishmael, the gorilla of deep ecology, would turn
to this story, since the narrative seems to begin with a thoroughly
human-oriented, anthropocentric focus. Compared with the Priestly
account in Genesis 1, in which the creation of each element of the
cosmos is described in loving detail, independent of its relation to
humans, the Yahwist moves right to human beings (Gen. 2.4b-7) and
apparently sees them as the central focus for the rest of creation. The
human being is the first thing whose creation is described, and everything else, both the garden and the animals, appears to be created in
response to human need. One might just pass this off as the naive
style of traditional storytelling, in contrast with the more sophisticated Priestly account, which is so rich with parallels to early Greek
scientific cosmology (Cornford 1952: 200). But more is at issue than
that. A recent interpretation of Genesis 2–3, which will be discussed
below, has argued persuasively that the story is about the origin of
anthropocentrism itself. Indeed, that is the 'original sin' of which the
story speaks. Thus one might suggest that the telling of the tale also
exhibits the marks of that fall into anthropocentrism. The narrator, the
one who tells the story, has a consciousness formed by anthropocentrism, that obsessive preoccupation with human beings and their
interests. And so it is natural that he would tell the story as one with
human beings at its center.[1] Poignantly, however, the story he tells is
one that reaches back to the time *before* the human consciousness was

---

1. I use the pronoun 'he' for the Yahwist, for the story is also marked by
androcentrism, male-centeredness.

formed as it is today, before we became so focused on our own selves as the measure of all value and interest. Indeed, he will present this development not as a triumph but as a deeply ambiguous event.

Consequently, even though ecologically minded readers might initially be put off by a creation story that seems obsessed with human beings, it would be misleading to think the story is unhelpful or hostile to ecological reflection. Because it presents the emergence of anthropocentrism as such an ambiguous development, it also looks back with some wistfulness to a primordial human solidarity with the natural world. Moreover, that sensitivity to the non-human world is also part of the texture of the tale.

As many have noted, there is a graphic sense of 'earthiness' that permeates the Yahwist's story. Notice, for instance, the extent to which the narrator perceives the centrality of water—how he speaks of rain, of mist or springs, of rivers and how they define the world (Gen. 2.5-6, 10-14). Or note the way in which soil serves as the basis of human and animal life (Gen. 2.7, 19). Most readers are also aware of the way in which the Yahwist puns on the name for humankind (in Hebrew, *adam*) and the name of Earth (in Hebrew, *adamah*), indicating that we share common ground with the Earth because we are *common ground*. For the Yahwist, as will be discussed below, there is no more telling indication of the intrinsic relatedness of things than the similarity of words. So to call the creature *adam* is to recognize its solidarity with Earth.

Throughout the story there is evidence of how closely observed the physical world is. Genesis 2-3 was written by someone for whom creation was not an abstraction. The very beginning of the story observes that there was a time before the shrubs and grasses grew because then the climate was different (i.e. it was a time before God caused rain to fall)—but also because there was a time before there were human beings to work the soil, a perception that the human presence, as well as climate, affects the environment. What the Yahwist offers to tell us is in effect a story about a time before agriculture existed. And significantly, the end of the story will explain how agriculture (tilling the soil) came to be. That focus is very different from the Priestly writer, who simply takes agriculture for granted.[2]

The narrative gets underway with God causing water to come upon the Earth and then making a human creature out of the mud and

---

2.   The distinction between seed-bearing plants and trees as food for humans and 'green plants' for animals (Gen. 1.29-30) seems to presume the distinction between foods that require cultivation and those available for grazing.

planting a garden in Eden in which the creature could live, a garden
full of wonderful trees, including two specifically mentioned, the tree
of life and the tree of the knowledge of good and bad (Gen. 2.8-9). The
story continues in a rather leisurely fashion, quite different from the
economical and direct account of Genesis 1. Here, the narrator takes
some time simply to describe the location of this forest garden (Gen.
2.10-14). Though that description is not needed for the plot of the
story, it serves to disclose the character of the storyteller, letting us
know what he thinks worth telling. In his description the reader can
continue to see both the elements of sensitivity to the physical world
and a strongly marked anthropocentric consciousness. The narrator
identifies the location of this primeval forest by reference to the rivers
that have their sources there—the Pishon, the Gihon, the Tigris and
the Euphrates. It is not the narrator's folk geography to which I wish
to draw attention but his perception that rivers define land. Instinc-
tively, he thinks in terms of the features of the natural world. But
there is also a note of anthropocentric valuation. The land of Havilah
is singled out for being the land where especially good gold is found,
and also bdellium and onyx. The storyteller's own values and character are complex. He is one who is attentive to the natural world, but
he is also capable of seeing the most important thing about a land
simply in terms of the mineral resources and forest products, a way of
valuing Earth that has in recent centuries caused enormous ecological
degradation.

Following this observation the narrator turns back to the story
proper and describes the relation between the Earth creature and the
forest garden. The text says that the Earth creature, *adam*, was put
there 'to work it and to keep it' (Gen. 2.15). Exactly what this means is
seldom discussed in the commentaries on Genesis. What is *adam*'s
relationship to the land and the environment in which he has been
placed? The narrator describes the place where the human creature is
placed as a *gan*, a Hebrew word usually translated as 'garden'. But
that translation is somewhat misleading, since the English word
'garden' conjures up an image of rows of neatly organized vegetables,
clear of weeds, fenced to keep out the rabbits and browsing deer. But
that is not what is described here. As the narrator has been careful to
say at the beginning, this story takes place before the tilling of the soil,
before agriculture. *Gan* Eden is not a garden in that sense, but a forest,
a place of trees and fruits. The kind of 'working and keeping' that is
suitable to a forest is rather different from that needed to grow vegetables in rows. Indeed, the Hebrew word for 'work' (*abad*), as Phyllis
Trible notes, can also mean to 'serve' (Trible 1978: 85). The image that

Genesis has of the original human relationship to the environment is
one that involves interaction but of a very modest sort. The forest of
Eden is imagined as what we would call a permaculture, where
human attention is part of the ecosystem, but of a nature rather like
'light pruning and raking' (Callicott 1991: 125). And this, the author
suggests, is the image of paradise. This is no fantastic never-never
land but actually the way our ancient ancestors did live, and the way
a few peoples of Earth still live.

Despite its uncanny evocation of that ancient way of life, Genesis
2–3 is not an attempt to do anthropology but a mythic story of human
origins. Consequently, it is less concerned to specify the way *adam*
rakes and prunes the trees than to underscore that there is one tree
that is off limits—not the tree of life, interestingly enough, but the tree
of the knowledge of good and bad. To eat from that tree, however,
does mean death. Like the accomplished storyteller that he is, the narrator does not explain *why* that one tree should be off limits, or even
exactly what it is. But in traditional stories like this one, the reader
knows that a prohibition such as this will eventually be broken. Pan-
dora *will* look in that box; somebody *will* eat that fruit (Niditch 1998:
17).

Humans, Animals and the Question of Companionship (Genesis 2.18-25)

For the moment, however, the story wanders off, apparently in
another direction. It suddenly occurs to God that the creature in the
garden may be lonely (Gen. 2.18), and so God makes the animals.
Here, again, the ecologically conscious reader might initially be irri-
tated at the perspective. It apparently does not occur to the storyteller
that animals might have been created for their own sakes, or for God's
sake, as Genesis 1 seems to suggest. But before one becomes too dis-
missive, it is worth attending to precisely how the creation of the
animals is described and what it seems to say about the relation of
animals and people in God's creation. God, after all, is the one who
believes that there could be that close bond of companionship
between *adam* and the animals. Why does God think that? Because
like the human creature the animals, too, are created from Earth. 'And
Yahweh God formed from the *adamah* every living creature of the
field and every bird of the heavens and brought them to *adam* to see
what he would call them' (Gen. 2.19a). Just as *adam* and Earth share
common ground, so do *adam* and the animals. Some readers have
observed that nothing is said about God breathing the breath of life
into the animals, but the story does not make *adam*'s failure to find a

special companion among the animals turn on that fact. From the perspective of the story the animals are in no sense lesser or lower beings.

More troubling to many readers is the fact that God allows *adam* to name the animals, since they reason that 'the power to name is the power to control'. But whatever the applicability of that saying to other contexts, that is not what occurs in this story. One must be attentive to how this author understands language, and for the Yahwist language is not about power but about identity. That is clear from the Yahwist's use of wordplays. *Adam* is related to Earth (*adamah*) because his name is. So when God brings the animals to *adam* 'to see what he would call them', it is a question of recognition not power.

To be sure *adam* does not find a special companion among these other creatures of Earth, but the story passes no judgment on that fact. God seems to decide that the special kind of companionship that will assuage loneliness in this creature can come only from a very intimate kind of identity and difference, the identity and difference of gender: at once the same in common humanity but different in sexual identity. What was one requires separation, because the space of separation is necessary for companionship; but the two must 'correspond to one another' (Gen. 2.20) so as to be able to come together as 'one flesh' (Gen. 2.24) *Adam*, too, realizes this when he cries out in recognition that his companion is bone of his bone, flesh of his flesh (Gen. 2.23). In keeping with the Yahwist's understanding of language, this close play of identity and difference is marked in the play on words. The new being is called 'woman' (*ishah*) because she was taken from 'man' (*ish*).

In many respects this is a quite wondrous vision of the world as common ground. Both humans and animals are united with the Earth and with each other in their derivation. Women and men correspond to each other as separate parts of one original being. The people tend and keep the trees of the garden, and the trees in turn provide beauty and fruit that is good to eat. If the Priestly writer were telling the story, one would expect the Sabbath blessing to follow. Everything is complete and harmonious. But although the Yahwist's story of the harmony of creation as God intended it is important, for the Yahwist it is not the whole story. Using his characteristic narrative subtlety, the Yahwist first hints at the coming plot complication before actually describing it.

Cleverness, Nakedness and the Birth of Self-Consciousness (Genesis 3.1-7)

The storyteller foreshadows the plot twist in yet another pun. In the last line of the second chapter, as the concluding stroke to the picture of harmonious existence, the Yahwist mentions that 'the two of them, the man and the woman, were naked (*arumim*) and were not ashamed' (Gen. 2.25). In the first verse of the third chapter, the narrator opens the next episode with this observation: 'Now the snake was the cleverest (*arum*) of all the animals that Yahweh God had made' (Gen. 3.1a). Cleverness and nakedness, *arum* and *arumim*—something is up, but the reader does not yet know what.

In keeping with the Yahwist's vision of the original common ground of creation, language seems not to have been a human prerogative. At least nobody in the story seems to think there is anything odd about a talking snake. It is one of those little details that fills out the picture of an originally different relationship between human beings and animals from that which now prevails. Although it remains difficult to read this story apart from the later interpretations familiar from Milton, Augustine and Paul, there is nothing truly evil about the snake. It is simply 'clever', a kind of trickster figure familiar from folk tales all over the world, the sort of figure that uses its wits to stir things up.

The dialogue between the snake and the woman is so familiar that it is difficult to hear it in all its oddity. Disingenuously, the snake asks the woman if God said that the humans could not eat from any of the trees. She replies, with some elaboration, that they can eat from any of the trees, except the one in the middle of the garden, which they cannot eat or even touch, lest they die (Gen. 3.1b-3), to which the snake replies, correctly, 'You won't actually die. God knows that on the day you eat from it, your eyes will be opened and you will be like gods, knowing what is good and what is bad' (Gen. 3.5).

Despite the traditional translation 'knowing good and evil', commentators regularly observe that such a translation is too narrow, too restricted to the moral dimension. The Hebrew words mean good and bad in the broadest sense. Thus, what the tree confers is the ability to discriminate, to make distinctions, to evaluate, to prefer, to choose. But why should this be the subject of the one and only prohibition in the garden? It hardly seems like a divine quality, and the story has not yet made clear what is at stake.

Narratively, what happens next (Gen. 3.6-7) is that the woman takes another look at the tree and sees that it appears good to eat and pleasing to the eye (like all the other trees) but also desirable for making one wise. Then she takes some of the fruit and gives some to her husband, and when they eat their eyes are indeed opened—and what do they see? That they are naked! The third pun shows up again: *adam* and *adamah*; *ish* and *ishah*. Now through the suggestion of the clever (*arum*) snake, they too are clever. But what has it gotten them? The knowledge that they are naked (*arumim*).

Most readers are accustomed to thinking of this new knowledge as somehow signalling awakened sexuality, and there are some overtones of that. The fig-leaf coverings that the humans make for themselves are specifically loincloths for covering the genitals. But sex itself hardly seems to be the main point. Sexual difference was apparently what *adam* was talking about when he first saw the woman God had made from his own flesh and called her *ishah*. Nor can one readily find an exegetical basis for assuming that the woman and the man were 'chaste' in Eden. All that the text says is that they were naked and did not really notice—until now.

But what might this have to do with ecology? There has to be something else about nakedness at issue here that includes but goes beyond the matter of sexuality. What is significant about the term 'naked' is the contexts in which the word makes sense and the contexts in which it does not? One cannot use the term meaningfully about animals. One simply cannot say that a cow or a lion or a trout is naked. 'Nakedness' as a concept can only be applied to human beings. It is a term that radically distinguishes people from animals. Animals make many things. They make shelters; a few make tools, and it has even been argued that one species of ape makes weapons—but no animal makes clothes. Or, as the Yahwist might put it, an animal is naked but not ashamed. Yet the first thing that the man and woman do when their 'eyes were opened and they realized that they were naked' is to make clothes. Now, in retrospect, it becomes even clearer why God had originally brought the animals and birds to *adam* as possible companions. At that time the great gulf that divides human beings from the rest of the animals had not yet opened up like a chasm between us. But now, since the eyes of the man and the woman were opened, the common ground that had united human beings with the other creatures is broken.

Still it may not be clear what this eye-opening knowledge is that suddenly separates us from the rest of created beings. The most persuasive interpretation of this part of the Genesis story has been made by philosopher and ecologist Baird Callicott (1991: 123). He goes back to the moment of the 'open eyes' and the perception of nakedness for his clue. What the man and the woman see is *themselves*. They become *self*-aware, *self*-conscious; and this self-awareness is the prerequisite for the experience of shame. That quality of self-awareness is also what distinguishes us from the other animals.

More perplexing is the question of why the story insists that this self-consciousness is something God did not intend for people to have originally. The snake insinuated that God was selfish and jealous. But Callicott suggests another reason, one that helps explain why this issue is fraught with such ominous potentiality:

> For once aware of themselves, [the man and woman] may treat themselves as an axiological point of reference. Indeed, the text suggests by its very silence on any alternative to Yahweh's banishment, or any compromise, and by the finality of that banishment, that once aware of themselves they *will* inevitably treat themselves as an intrinsically valuable hub to which other creatures and the creation as a whole may be referred for appraisal. Self-consciousness is a necessary condition for self-centeredness, self-interestedness (Callicott 1991: 123-24).

And thus, though not culpable in itself, human self-awareness is fraught with peril.

What Callicott describes is the birth of anthropocentrism, which is, if not the root of all sin, at least of all ecological sin. Who now decides what is good and what is bad? What is the point of reference? Is wheat good? Then what of tares? Are sheep good? Then what of wolves? In God's creation there is no ranking between one creature and another. Each is made from Earth and each is a potential companion for the other. But now human beings have disrupted that original creation and taken for themselves the power to distinguish what is desirable and what is not. And the basis for that discrimination is human value.

Consequences (Genesis 3.8-24)

God's anger at this destruction of an original harmony of common ground is direct and forceful, yet it can be difficult to judge whether to talk about the fates of the snake, the woman and the man in terms of punishments meted out by God or of consequences stemming directly from their actions. Something about each of the punishments expresses the disruption of the harmony of creation that their actions have caused. The snake, too clever for its own good, is cursed. It will be worse off than the other animals, with no legs and in a perpetual state of enmity with human beings. As the only animal character in the story, however, its fate also gestures toward the more general loss of trusting community between animals and humans in the world outside the garden.

The woman's and the man's punishments are even more closely tied to the alienation from nature represented by their choice to be 'like gods'. The woman's punishment involves a social dimension, the loss of a fully mutual and symmetrical relationship with her husband. But it is her other punishment that is of particular interest to an ecologically focused reading of Genesis 2–3. The woman is told that her pain in childbearing will be multiplied. Although stated as a punishment, it might also be seen as the tangible manifestation of the alienation from the animal world that the woman has already chosen. Of all the creatures in the world only human females have such regularly dangerous and painful birthgiving. And the reason is because of the overly developed brains and consequently large heads of human infants. The storyteller of Genesis 3 is correct. That which distinguishes us from the animals, the self-awareness that our highly developed brains makes possible, is directly related to the pain and danger encountered in giving birth. Because we have in a sense chosen to be human, we no longer have the ease of birth that God gives to the animals.

The man's punishment is equally related to the nature of the transgression. The birth of self-awareness and the consequent birth of anthropocentrism are linked by Genesis 2–3 to the birth of agriculture. First, the nature of their food is changed. Where in Eden they ate fruit from the trees, outside Eden they will eat 'the grass of the field', that is, grains, from grassy plants like barley and wheat. It is not incidental that this type of food is obtained only by 'the sweat of the face', for grain requires intensive cultivation (Callicott 1991: 125). Now an alienation exists between *adam* and *adamah*. God says that the ground is cursed 'on account of you' (Gen. 3.17), or as one might translate, 'because of you'. A type of enmity ensues, in which Earth brings forth thorns and thistles, and only the painful and sweaty work of field labor can produce bread. This relation does not arise from some stinginess of Earth, but as the result of its abuse, for as Callicott observes, 'thorns and thistles attend disturbed, eroded, and exhausted soil' (1991: 139 n. 83). With agriculture there begins the paradoxical history of human destruction of the Earth's fertility in the very search for productive land.

The parting 'gift' that God gives to the humans is, fittingly, clothes, the symbol of everything that divides us from animal existence (Oden 1987: 102-103). More tellingly, where the clothes the woman and the man had made for themselves were of leaves, God gives them clothes made of skins. Where formerly we had talked with the animals, henceforth we wear them.[3]

But what about the issue of death? The snake appears to have been right in that the woman and man do not in fact die on the day that they eat from the forbidden tree, although God's expulsion of the humans from the garden is designed to prevent them now from eating from the tree of life and so living forever. Death is somehow tied up in this fateful choice. In Daniel Quinn's book, as Ishmael the gorilla reflects on this part of the story, he draws a sobering conclusion. Ishmael has already characterized the story of Genesis 2–3 as a story of the agricultural revolution. Now in his dialogue with his human pupil, he reflects that this choice was indeed a fatal one:

> 'The disaster occurred when, ten thousand years ago, the people of your culture said, "We are wise as the gods and can rule the world as well as they". When they took *into their own hands* the power of life and death over the world, their doom was assured.'
>
> 'Yes. Because they are not in fact as wise as gods.'
>
> 'The gods ruled the world for billions of years, and it was doing just fine. After just a few thousand years of human rule, the world is at the point of death.'
>
> 'True. But [our culture] will never give it up.'
>
> Ishmael shrugged. 'Then they'll die. As predicted. The authors of this story knew what they were talking about' (Quinn 1992: 166; Quinn's italics).

The expulsion from Eden aptly symbolizes humankind's historic shift from one ecological place to another, from what in anthropological terms we would call a hunter-gatherer state to an agricultural one. And from the Yahwist's perspective this was a deeply ambivalent event. As the succeeding stories make evident, the richness of human culture emerges from the capacity human beings have to discriminate and to choose for themselves. But that same characteristic is also at the heart of the greedy and arrogant violence that characterizes the human societies that emerge from this new economy. Cain, the agrarian, murders Abel, the pastoralist. The first murderer founds the first city (Gen. 4). And the rest, as they say, is history.

What is one to do with a story like Genesis 2–3? It can certainly

---

3.   That there are still a few indigenous peoples who do not regularly wear clothes and whose relation to animals has a distinctively personal quality only serves to underscore the perceptiveness of the story in analyzing the fall of most of humanity.

serve as an explanation, as a theodicy for our broken relationship with the natural world. But is it a story that can also guide us as we seek to find the wisdom to cease our violence against creation and restore harmony? Or is it a tragic story only? It does tell of God's original intention for human beings: that we were created for harmony with the rest of creation; to tend and keep the forest garden; to be related to the Earth, as our name signifies; to see in the other animals potential companions even if not that closest corresponding other. This is a story of loss, but even in its telling it keeps alive the memory of God's original intention. And what God intends can never completely be destroyed; what God intends will eventually find consummation (Isa. 11.6-9; Ezek. 47.1-12). But the story also makes clear that there is no simple going back. The way to Eden is blocked (Gen. 3.24).

The account in Genesis 2–3, with its rather grim account of the human fall into anthropocentrism, should not, however, be cause for despair in regard to humankind's capacity to transform its practices. The story of the emergence of self-awareness and self-consciousness, the recognition that one can make choices, is also the story of the birth of moral agency. Though the narrative reminds us of the ease with which one may choose selfishly, such bad choices are not inevitable. The very self-consciousness that makes self-regarding actions possible also provides the critical capacities for transcending narrow self-interest. With eyes thus opened, it is indeed possible to 'choose life' (Deut. 30.19), not only for oneself but for all the world. Perhaps if we listened to more gorillas, we would make better choices.

Earthing the Human in Genesis 1–3

Mark G. Brett

Framing the Question of Agency

'Can the subaltern speak?' Gayatri Chakravorti Spivak asked in her classic essay on postcolonial theory (1988). How do those who have been systemically marginalized find a voice? Her answer to this question was largely negative: the politics of representation always seem to get in the way. The subaltern voice is usually mediated and interpreted, since the vernacular of that voice is unintelligible to a wider audience. The 'organic intellectual' lends a charitable hand, and immediately the threat of assimilationist distortion arises. In Australia, for example, it could be said that our interest in Aboriginal spirituality has grown in inverse proportion to the erosion of Western cultural resources. But what interests us is not so much the secret–sacred songs of an irreducibly particular tribal tradition, sung for the earth and for the ancestors; it would take too long to learn the dialect of the song-lines (assuming that we could ever earn the right to learn the songs from their custodians). What interests us is the general idea of connectedness to the earth, and the Aboriginal voice is thereby reduced to a cipher.

Such postcolonial problematics belong equally to the quest for an ecological hermeneutic. In what sense does 'the earth' have a voice? Here again, there seems to be no escape from the politics of representation. Who speaks on behalf of the earth? Our interest in environmental matters seems to grow in inverse proportion to the decline of physical resources which are crucial to human survival. What interests us, however, is not so much the particularities of an ecosystem, since it would take too long to learn those intricacies. What interests us is the general idea of environmental interconnectedness. This sort of eco-ideology clearly has strategic value, but one wonders (on analogy with postcolonial hermeneutics) whether the earth is thereby reduced, all too often, to a cipher.

Is it possible to speak of the earth having an authentic 'voice'? Perhaps this formulation of the question still harbours assumptions which are residually anthropocentric, or 'logocentric'. Nevertheless, we need to find ways of appreciating the earth's agency as part of the web of life. Can we broaden the concept of agency in a way which allows us to imagine forms of community that take us beyond the narrower constructions of *human* community?

As a partial answer to this question, the following reinterpretation of Genesis 1–3 seeks to identify the agency and needs of the earth as they are constructed in these classical creation narratives. The practice of biblical interpretation is not itself a listening to the earth, but perhaps in some indirect way this kind of interpretation might stimulate those who inhabit the biblical tradition to appreciate afresh the larger networks of interdependent life which we share. Having engaged with the competing voices represented in the creation stories of Genesis 1–3, we shall then step back and ponder the hermeneutical issues arising.

The First Creation Narrative

In the beginning, *Elohim* created the heavens and the earth.
And the earth, it was welter and waste,[1]
and darkness was on the face of the deep,
and the spirit of *Elohim* hovered on the face of the waters (Gen. 1.1-2).

When the world began, there was earth and water, undifferentiated and lifeless. The Hebrew grammar is ambiguous on the question of ultimate origins. The first verse could be taken to mean that *Elohim* existed before the heavens and the earth. The first creative act, on this reading, brings the heavens and the earth into existence, but the earth is still in a lifeless state—partly uninhabited land and partly dark waters. On the other hand, if the first verse is a prefatory summary of the entire narrative, then the earth and waters are coeternal with *Elohim*. The divine creative action would then begin properly at Gen. 1.3 with the creation of light.

The text of Gen. 1.1-2 simply does not provide enough evidence to arbitrate between the two options. Apart from the opacity of the grammar, the narrative does not set out to answer the doctrinal question of whether this is *creatio ex nihilo* ('creation from nothing') or not (cf. Westermann 1984a: 174). Nevertheless, Gen. 2.4a assumes that the heavens and the earth were brought forth by God: 'These are the gen-

---

1.   I have translated the rhyming phrase *tohu wabohu* as 'welter and waste', following Robert Alter's elegant rendering (1996: 3). There is no need to see here a threatening chaos, but simply an empty wasteland (Tsumura 1989: 43).

erations of the heavens and the earth when they were created.' The term 'generations' (*toledot*) is used throughout Genesis in reference both to genealogies and narratives, but the verb from which it is derived (*yalad*) normally means 'to bear a child'. This parental motif is hinted at in Gen. 1.2 where the spirit of *Elohim* is 'hovering' with creative and caring potential, perhaps like an eagle hovering over its young.[2]

'*Elohim*' is a generic term for divinity, and thus it has no particular connection to Israel. Unlike many creation stories from the ancient world, there is no focus on the author's own people or temple. Nor is there an account of the creation of the gods themselves, a common feature of the mythological literature of the time. For example, the Babylonian *Enuma Elish* begins by describing the birth of the gods from their progenitors, Apsu and Tiamat.[3] We find a great deal of colourful detail about the gods even before Marduk, the god of Babylon, slays Tiamat—the goddess of salt water—in a violent battle, dismembering her body to make the heavens and the earth. By comparison, Genesis 1 is extraordinarily peaceful in its representation of creation and extraordinarily reserved about the nature of divinity. The cohortative verbal form in Gen. 1.26 indicates some form of divine sociality but no hint of disagreement: 'Let us make humankind in our image, as our similitude' (cf. 3.22; 11.7). The Hebrew Bible elsewhere contains several references to a divine council,[4] and these texts are also elusive. There are a few references to violent creation motifs (e.g. Pss. 74.13-14; 89.7-11; Isa. 51.9), but Genesis 1 is markedly free of such violence (Janzen 1994; Levenson 1988). The mood of the story is more of an eirenic inclusivism.[5] In the primordial creativity of *Elohim*, the identity of Israel and of Israel's God are not matters of contest. We might infer then that wherever conflict arises, this will be a matter of divine regret.

However, some sociologically minded commentators have suggested that the divine discourses in Genesis 1 initiate some binary distinctions in the created order, and these discourses foreshadow the possibility of a hierarchy among the creatures of the earth. *Elohim* inaugurates a series of divisions between light and darkness (Gen.

---

2.   Deut. 32.10-11 uses the same verb (*rhp*) of an eagle hovering over its young, comparing the image to Yahweh who found the children of Israel in a wasteland (*tohu*), and cared for them.

3.   The exiles in Babylon would have known this myth, even if some version of it had not made its way to Israel in earlier periods.

4.   See, e.g., 1 Kgs 22.19-22; Isa. 6.8; Jer. 23.22; Job 1.6-12; Ps. 82.

5.   Cf. Habel, 'Geophany', in this volume.

1.4), day and night (Gen. 1.14, 18), and a separation of water above the heavenly vault from the water below it (Gen. 1.7). In each of these cases, the Hebrew word *hibdil* appears (meaning 'to divide' or 'distinguish'), and it is often argued that this is distinctively Priestly vocabulary. For example, the Priestly dietary laws construct a binary distinction between 'clean' and 'unclean' animals, and the Israelite audience of Leviticus is exhorted to 'distinguish (*hibdil*) between the unclean and the clean, between living creatures that may be eaten and those that may not be eaten' (Lev. 11.47; cf. 20.25-26). The discourse of cosmic ordering is thus potentially linked to the discourse of holiness, and on this view, a hierarchy in the species is implied, even if it is not explicitly stated (cf. Kapelrud 1974).[6]

But it seems to me that the evidence points in another direction: the use of *hibdil* refers not to the order of living creatures but exclusively to the cosmic ordering. The language of holiness is largely absent from Genesis, and this sets the book apart from the rest of the Pentateuch (Moberly 1992: 99-103). If Genesis 1 comes from Priestly circles, as most scholars think, then it is all the more remarkable that the distinction between 'clean' and 'unclean' animals is missing from the first creation narrative. The language of holiness is attached only to the Sabbath rest, as we shall see.

The plants and animals are created 'according to their kinds' (Gen. 1.11, 12, 21, 24, 25), without any overt indication of hierarchy, but a distinction certainly arises with the creation of the species which is made in the image of *Elohim*:

> And *Elohim* said, 'Let us make humankind in our image, according to our similitude,
> and let them rule over the fish of the sea and the birds of the heavens, over the livestock, over all the earth, and over all the creatures that move on the earth' (Gen. 1.26).

> So *Elohim* created the human in his image,
> in the image of *Elohim* he created him,
> male and female he created them (Gen. 1.27).

> And *Elohim* blessed them and said to them,
> 'Be fruitful and increase in number, fill the earth and subdue it,
> rule over the fish of the sea and the birds of the heavens
> and over every living creature that moves on the earth' (Gen. 1.28).

But even here, where a basic distinction among the species is asserted, there is an element of continuity between humankind and other crea-

6.   For a discussion of the methodological issues relating to the study of communicative intentions which are indirectly expressed, see Brett (1991).

tures. The first divine speech which contains an imperative is addressed to the creatures of the sea and the birds of the air: 'Be fruitful and increase in number' (Gen. 1.22). That is, the blessing for procreation has already been shared with these creatures, and it is not the exclusive preserve of humankind. Moreover, the earth has also been addressed in the divine discourses: 'Let the earth grow vegetation' (Gen. 1.11), and 'Let the earth bring forth living creatures according to their kinds' (Gen. 1.24). Even if *Elohim* is the focus of creative agency, the earth is a full participant in the process; the earth is an agent, a co-creator, not just the object of divine manipulation. The distinctiveness of the human is thereby undermined, and humankind has to share the divine vocation of co-creation with the earth and with other creatures.[7]

There is, however, no escaping the overt hierarchy asserted by the text: human beings are called on to rule the earth and to subdue it. The use of the verb *radah* ('to rule'), in Gen. 1.26 and 28 probably alludes to royal ideology, and the language of the 'image of God' was commonly associated with pharaohs and kings in the literature of ancient Egypt and Mesopotamia (Bird 1997: 134-38; Lohfink 1994: 1-17). In the immediate context, the only way this image is defined is through the idea of monarchic rule (being male and female is hardly distinctive of humankind as a species). The phrase 'image of *Elohim*' occurs nowhere else in the Hebrew Bible. Indeed, this language is so unusual that we need to look more closely at the intertextual subtleties associated with Gen. 1.27-28.

When humanity as a whole is exhorted to rule over the other living creatures, this is best read as a polemical undermining of a role which is otherwise associated primarily with kings. The characteristic association of the phrase 'image of God' with Mesopotamian kings and Egyptian pharaohs has long been observed, but the implications of this comparison have often been under-analysed. If the health of the created order does not depend upon kings, then the democratizing tendency of Gen. 1.27-28 can be seen as anti-monarchic. Indeed, there is an anti-monarchic tone to Genesis, which begins in Genesis 1 but extends into the second creation story and beyond. The polemical intent is subtle, but the evidence for it accumulates as the narrative unfolds.

Within Israelite royal tradition, one frequently finds a connection

---

7.   This linking of the species is reinforced by the first covenant in Genesis (9.8-17) where the divine promise encompasses all creatures, not just the human ones.

between the ideal king and the fertility of the land, and in this respect the rule of the created order is specifically linked to the monarchy within the Hebrew Bible itself and not just in Egyptian and Meso-potamian literature. Psalm 72, for example, interweaves the expectation that the ideal king is one who defends the weak and afflicted (Ps. 72.2, 4, 12-14) with the claim that this rule is characterized by prosperity and fertility (Ps. 72.3, 6-7, 16-17). In Psalm 72, we even find the impossibly utopian expectation that the Israelite king 'will rule from sea to sea, and from the River to the ends of the earth' (Ps. 72.8), echoing the human vocation in Genesis 1.

One could argue, therefore, that these aspects of Israelite royal ide-ology have also been democratized in Genesis 1, and it is interesting to notice both the continuities and discontinuities which the compari-son invites: in Gen. 1.28, it is humanity as a whole who is to rule 'over all the earth', but there is no expectation that this rule will entail the subjugation of distant enemies and nations, as Ps. 72.9-11 suggests. In Genesis 1, the vision of human expansion over all the earth does not envisage social conflict. This eirenic tone also applies in some respects to the relationship between humans and animals. It is quite clear from Gen. 1.29-30 that the editors of Genesis 1 envisage the primal condi-tion as vegetarian: humans, beasts and birds are given only green plants and fruit as food, and thus one might infer that violence between the species would be unnecessary.

But while it may be possible to interpret the verb 'rule' in the posi-tive sense of 'care for the weak', as evidenced in Israelite royal ideol-ogy, the imperative to 'subdue' the earth excludes a purely peaceful interpretation. Thus, the representation of even this utopian begin-ning is marked by a significant tension, which probably betrays the realities of daily experience in the ancient world.

Up until modern times, there have been many societies in which the threat presented by wild animals is a constant danger. This was espe-cially true in ancient Israel, and one can find many prophetic judg-ments, for example, which draw on this fear. The theme is taken to almost comical lengths in Amos 5.19 where a day of judgment is compared to serial encounters with the face of death:

> It will be as if someone fled from a lion and met a bear,
> entered the house and rested his hand on the wall
> only to have a serpent bite him.

Conversely, prophetic announcements of hope often entail the utopi-an removal of such threats, such as in Isa. 65.25 where the lion finally turns to eating straw and the serpent to eating dust (cf. Gen. 3.14). The first creation story reflects the tension between, on the one hand, these primal and eschatological utopias and, on the other hand, the day-to-day reality of a threat to human beings from wild animals. In this connection, it is important to note than in the hymn to leviathan in Job 41, it is specifically said that the great beast of the sea cannot be subdued (Job 41.9) and that 'he is king over all the children of pride' (Job 41.34). In short, the book of Job contests the idea that humankind can ever be fully successful in being kings over all the earth.

The prophecies of Hosea are particularly relevant to this discussion since that book uses strikingly similar vocabulary to Gen. 1.27-28 when it suggests that Israelite violence and faithlessness have brought death to 'the beasts of the field, the birds of the heavens, and the fish of the sea' (Hos. 4.3). The point of this text is that the wholesale destruction of other species is an image of horror for the prophet; it is evidence of wrongdoing. In Hos. 2.18, the security of a new covenant with Yahweh envisages not only the end of war, but also a covenant with 'the beasts of the field, the birds of the heavens, and the creatures that move on the earth'. In other words, a holistic vision of human restoration entails the removal of both threats of war and threats from the natural world. Hosea's vision of peace in human society is integrally linked with a return to ecological utopia, and this is characteristic of prophetic hope (cf. Gowan 1986: 97-120).

The first creation story concludes with a reference to a divine rest on the seventh day, after the primal utopia has been brought to birth, and that day is declared holy (Gen. 2.3). There is no keeping of the Sabbath in Genesis, but the practice is secretly inscribed here on the cosmic order. Although the Sabbath usually had an anthropocentric focus, in the rest of the Pentateuch it accumulated implications which spread outward into the wider created order. Deuteronomy 5.14, for example, envisages a rest for domesticated animals, not just humans.[8] The Jubilee legislation in Leviticus 25–26, which extrapolates from Sabbath principles, envisages the land itself as having rights. This Priestly legislation of Leviticus makes a more relevant comparison, perhaps, than Deuteronomy, since the first creation story in Genesis is usually ascribed to Priestly circles. It is all the more striking, then, that Leviticus should suggest that a human exile was necessary to ensure 'that the land might enjoy its Sabbaths' (Lev. 26.34-35). In short, the divine rest on the seventh day of creation underwrites an interlinked

---

8.   Since wild animals are beyond human purview, it hardly makes sense to ascribe anthropocentrism to the Deuteronomic Sabbath law. Similarly, one would presume that the Leviathan of Job 41 rests at will, regardless of human initiatives.

set of land and animal rights, and it is not just a warrant for a narrowly human practice.

The Second Creation Narrative

The editors of Genesis have juxtaposed a second creation story which potentially undermines any human supremacy which might have been envisaged by Gen. 1.27-28. Genesis 2.4-5 returns the reader to the time before plants were made, and displaces the anthropocentric perspective of the first story by saying that 'there was no human to work the land'. Not only does this form of words place the needs of the land before those of the human; there seems to be a deliberate irony in the Hebrew text since the word for 'work' (*abad*) is otherwise most commonly translated as 'serve', in the sense of 'work for'. A more pointed translation would be: 'there was no human to serve the land'. The same vocabulary is used in Gen. 2.15: 'And Yahweh *Elohim* took the human and put him in the Garden of Eden to serve it and to take care of it', effectively reversing the vocation to rule and to subdue the earth. The irony is heightened in Gen. 2.7 where the human is created with materials from the earth: 'And Yahweh *Elohim* formed the human (*adam*)[9] from the dust of the land (*adamah*) and breathed into his nostrils the breath of life.' The wordplay between *adam* and *adamah* is manifest, but beyond the wordplay lies the potentially subversive claim that the human is derived from soil.

This subversive hint becomes relevant to our understanding of the further wordplay in 2.23 where the human (*adam*) says, 'She shall be called woman (*ishah*), because she was taken out of man (*ish*)'. Some interpretations of this speech suggest that it contains an implied claim to gender superiority in that the woman is represented as deriving from the man; her role as co-creator with the divine is displaced by giving a chronological priority to the generative capacity of the male. (It makes no difference to this claim whether this was in some sense

---

9.   *Adam* is a generic term throughout Gen. 3, but it has a specific referent indicated by the definite article '*the* human'—the character in the story. Strictly speaking, *adam* is semantically vague in the same way as the word 'animal' is vague in English: 'animal', for example, does not distinguish between 'cats' and 'dogs', and *adam* does not distinguish semantically between male and female, as indicated by its use in Gen. 1.27. But just as, in context, the word 'animal' can refer to a particular cat or dog, so *adam* can refer to a particular man, as it does in Gen. 2.23. One wonders, however, whether gender is meaningful before the creation of woman.

the author's 'intention' or whether the speech is an unconscious product of patriarchal ideology.)

Two features of the narrative undermine any such claim to gender superiority by the male. First, Eve's speech in Gen. 4.1 ('With Yahweh I have made[10] a man') is a peculiar form of words, partly because the use of *ish* to describe a child is unusual; it normally is used with reference to adults. The use of this particular word has a point, however, if Eve's speech is read as an ironic retort to the man: you claim to have made *ishah*, but I have made *ish* (so Pardes 1993). Secondly, the seeds of deconstruction have already been planted before Eve's speech in Genesis 4, since the male logic could also be applied to the claim that the human was made from soil (Gen. 2.7; 3.19): if the man is superior to the woman, because woman was taken from man, then the land is superior to the man, because man was taken from soil. If chronological priority provides status, then on this score both humans have a lesser status than the land.

We should notice here that the animals also were formed from the land. The vocabulary in Gen. 2.19, where the animals are created, is the same as in Gen. 2.7 where the human is created. The question of status is by no means self-evident in this narrative, since it envisages the possibility that the human's 'helper' might come from the animals (Gen. 2.20). Commentators have made much of the idea that the act of naming the animals is an act of dominance, and this is clearly one function of naming, especially, for example, when pejorative social labelling serves to make a claim of superiority. However, the act of naming something can also be construed positively, for example, when some fresh experience can be expressed in language (like Hagar's naming of God in Gen. 16.13), or when naming is an act of resistance to ideological dominance (like Eve's naming of Cain, which subtly resists Gen. 2.23 by claiming that she has made *ish*). Not all naming has the same social function. If we take the narrative on its own terms, the human's naming of the animals cannot have had an evil intent, since humankind has not yet acquired the knowledge of good and evil; the naming of the animals seems rather to be a celebration of diversity. Similarly, the human's naming of woman in Gen. 2.23 marks the celebration of intimacy which is then reinforced in

10. The verb here, *qnh*, is ambiguous in classical Hebrew; it can mean both 'making' and 'possessing'. Umberto Cassuto (1961: 198-201) convincingly argued that this text makes best sense if *qnh* is taken in the sense of 'making', as do the uses in Gen. 14.22, Deut. 32.6 and Ps. 139.13.

Gen. 2.24 by the idea of being 'one flesh'. The fact that Gen. 2.18-21 describes a quest for a 'helper' (*ezer*) does not count against this interpretation. Elsewhere in the Hebrew Bible the *ezer* is frequently God (e.g. Pss. 33.20; 115.9-10), and the fact that the human needs an *ezer* is a sign of lack, not of superiority.

According to the second creation narrative, then, the human belongs to the same kinship group as the animals in the sense that they all descend from the land. In the genealogical terms suggested by the introductory formula in Gen. 2.4a ('these are the generations of the heavens and the earth'), the land is the parent. But there is a special intimacy between the man and the woman which differentiates them from the animals, and this is expressed by having Yahweh *Elohim* build the woman from a part of the man (Gen. 2.22). In Genesis 2, at least, there is no 'ruling' to be found, only a descent group.

There are indeed more ironies arising as the second creation story unfolds. If the first creation story is concerned to affirm a likeness between *Elohim* and humankind, the second creation story denies it. Contrary to many traditional interpretations, the first humans are mortal from the beginning: although the tree of life introduced in Gen. 2.9 receives hardly any attention at all, it appears again in Gen. 3.22 when God contemplates the possibility that an evil humanity might *acquire* immortality. This can only mean that death was part of the original created order, and in this sense the humans are clearly unlike God. Admittedly, the humans possess the knowledge of good and evil after eating the forbidden fruit, and this is construed as a likeness to divinity, but this likeness was not part of the divine intention. Indeed, the possession of such knowledge was initially put forward by the snake (who speaks nothing but the truth) as simply a seductive possibility: 'You will be like *Elohim*, knowing good and evil' (Gen. 3.5).

In Gen. 3.22, God resolves to keep the humans from getting any closer:

> And Yahweh *Elohim* said, 'The human has now become like one of us, knowing good and evil. He must not be allowed to reach out his hand and take also from the tree of life and eat, and live forever.'

This humbling of the humans is pointed up by the fact that although they must first eat the fruit of a forbidden tree to gain wisdom, the talking reptile has wisdom to start with. The serpent is said to be *arum* ('shrewd'), and this is precisely the word used in the book of Proverbs to speak approvingly of the prudent (e.g. Prov. 12.16, 23; 13.16; 14.8, 15, 16; 22.3; 27.12). There are other resonances with Proverbs as well.

In Gen. 3.6, the forbidden fruit is said to be 'desirable' (*nechmad*) for 'gaining wisdom' (*haskil*), and outside this narrative, *nechmad* only occurs in Prov. 21.20 to describe desirable food in the house of the wise; *haskil* appears in Prov. 16.23 and 21.11 with clearly positive connotations (cf. Mendenhall 1974). To fall prey to a wise reptile which 'creeps upon the earth'—as the RSV translates the phrase in Gen. 1.26 and 28—is a cutting humiliation. While one can barely conceive of the first humans dominating the seas and the heavens, one might imagine that subduing the land animals was slightly more realistic. But Genesis 3 dashes even that notion; one which creeps upon the earth wins out.

In order to understand the nature of this forbidden wisdom, critics have explored the traces of mythological motifs which are now opaque to the reader of the final text. The goddess Ishtar from ancient Mesopotamia was pictured holding a 'tree of life' from which four rivers flowed (cf. Gen. 2.10-14), and Ishtar's priestesses apparently dispensed divine favours through sacral prostitution. The *Epic of Gilgamesh* associates this cultic practice with the getting of wisdom, suggesting at one point that sexual knowledge makes a mere man 'like a god' (Gardner 1990). In the Sumerian myth *Enki and Ninhursag*, the marriage of the main characters takes place in the land of Dilmun, a garden of the gods which figures in several Mesopotamian narratives (Wallace 1985). But contrary to these ancient parallels and to some traditional Christian interpretations of the Eden story, the final editors did not see the forbidden fruit as providing sexual knowledge, since sexuality is already presumed by Gen. 2.24: 'Therefore a man (*ish*) leaves his father and his mother and clings to his woman (*ishah*), and they become one flesh.'

So what kind of wisdom is dangerous and should properly have belonged to God alone? The negative light thrown on wisdom in Genesis is arguably to be seen more precisely as a critique of *royal* wisdom. There is, for example, a close verbal resonance between the second creation story and 2 Sam. 14.17, 20 where the shrewd woman of Tekoa ironically flatters king David by referring to his godlike wisdom: 'The king is like an angel of God in discerning good and evil.' The expression 'knowledge of good and evil' (Gen. 2.9, 17) is also used to characterize political wisdom in 1 Kgs 3.9, where Solomon asks God for wisdom in a dream. The connections to royal material are indeed reinforced by the only other use of Eden motifs in the Hebrew Bible—Ezekiel 28, where the king of Tyre is indicted for imagining himself to possess divine wisdom (Ezek. 28.2). He did indeed possess wisdom, Ezekiel suggests (Ezek. 28.12, 17), but pride, violence and dishonest trade (Ezek. 28.16-18) led to his expulsion from 'Eden, the garden of God' (Ezek. 28.13).

Thus, the strongest intertextual links within the Hebrew Bible suggest that the negative view of wisdom in the Eden narrative can be explained by the same hypothesis which we used to interpret the 'image of *Elohim*' in Gen. 1.27-28: the final editors of Genesis were covertly anti-monarchic. This reading does not exclude the possibility that the editors have used pre-existing sources which were already anti-monarchic in tone; that may well be so. But the juxtaposition of the two creation stories has heightened the theme to such an extent that every attempt at hierarchy has been destabilized. If the first creation story deconstructs a royal 'image of *Elohim*' by democratizing it, the second creation story undermines any 'royal' aspirations which humankind may have had by satirizing the human failure to rule over even the creatures who 'creep upon the earth'. The only kind of 'rule' spoken about in Genesis 3 is the lamentable patriarchal rule of male over female (Gen. 3.16), a symptom of alienation which befits the new-found royal knowledge. It is a symptom of alienation which characterizes life outside the garden of Eden, and in this sense, male rule is a sign of distance from God, not likeness to God. Monarchic wisdom seems to distort the primal vision of an interconnected created order, and the aspiration to be like God is inherently dangerous.

Hermeneutical Questions

This reading of Genesis 1–3 shows how the juxtaposition of the two creation stories is highly ironic. Some literary critics would simply stop at this point and celebrate the deconstruction of a hierarchical text. But, for some of us, there are two questions left over. First, is there any sense in which this reading might overlap with the intentions of the editors of Genesis? And secondly, has the imposition of ecological norms simply replicated the basic problem with which we began—that of failing to hear another voice? It might be argued, for example, that the voice of a classic text has been shouted down by a reader who imposes his own prefabricated, egalitarian norms.

The first question can really only be answered by a more comprehensive reading of the book of Genesis. Space does not permit a full discussion of the issues, but I have argued elsewhere that the final text of Genesis exhibits highly ironic patterns of editing in every section of the book.[11] The final editors, presumably writing in the period of Persian domination, have restructured the traditions in ways which relentlessly undercut any pretensions of hierarchy—whether these pretensions are based on genealogical superiority, moral qualities, ethnic election or claims to divine revelation. On my view, the editors have deliberately juxtaposed their materials in a manner which can be described as 'intentional hybridity'.[12] What is envisaged here is *neither* an organic hybridity wherein the complex prehistory of cultural elements is entirely unknown, *nor* a serial addition of traditions, simply motivated by antiquarianism. Rather, intentional hybridity is a blending of two or more voices, without compositional boundaries being evident, such that the voices combine into an unstable symphony—sometimes speaking univocally but more often juxtaposing alternative points of view such that the authority of the dominant voice is put into question. Hybridization takes the focus off particular editorial additions and allows a more 'holistic' consideration of the texts, except that this notion of holism is post-structuralist to the extant that it expects complexity and contradiction, not unity. In the case of Genesis, the overriding ideologies have been juxtaposed with so many traces of otherness that the dominant voices can be deconstructed by audiences who have ears to hear.

This style of interpretation might be seen as the invention of a deconstructive reader whose concerns are entirely different from the theological and social intentions of the ancient editors. There are indeed forms of deconstructive criticism which advocate the 'free play' of textuality, but deconstruction is construed differently within postcolonial theory. My purpose has been to trace the patterns of incongruity in the text of Genesis and to suggest that these patterns point to an ancient editorial agency which is contesting the privileged grasp of colonial power in the Persian period. The agency of resistance is not seen as the product of a pure, egalitarian and consistent consciousness (cf. Bhabha 1994: 187). On the contrary, the text of Genesis seems to reveal a hybrid intersubjectivity, not necessarily perspicuous to itself, incorporating diverse cultural elements both from within Israelite tradition and from outside it. Older literary sources may

11. See Brett (2000). The present essay revises and expands portions of chapter 2.

12. The term is borrowed from Mikhail Bakhtin (1981: 358-61), who argued that the deliberate juxtaposition of different voices is potentially subversive of dominant ideologies. See further, Young (1995), and the concept of 'double-voiced revisionism' in African American literary criticism (Gates 1988).

well have been used without any knowledge of the origins of such sources. Against extreme forms of postmodernism that would deny hybrid subjectivity any agency at all, I would follow Homi Bhabha (1994: 171-97) in arguing that some kind of agency is necessary in any resistance to a dominant culture.

Having said all that, I do not believe that the editors of Genesis were motivated by anything we might recognize as an ecological critique of the dominant culture. There are traces in the text which are relevant to our concerns, but these hardly constitute a coherent, ecological theology. The theological hermeneutics which provide perhaps the most helpful analogy derive from feminism, and in particular, from the feminist models which have given up trying to find 'feminist consciousness' in the Bible but which nevertheless begin with the prophetic *principles* of social critique which are clearly evidenced in biblical material.

My hypothesis is that the editors of Genesis deliberately undermined the hierarchies of their day, mainly in response to the effects of Persian colonial administration. In the process, they have produced a text which potentially subverts the 'species supremacy' which lies behind the ecological crisis. As part of a living tradition of theological reflection, we are free to build on their initiative and apply it to our own life and context. What we now need to resist is the instrumental model of rationality which has colonized modern minds and reduced the earth to an object of exploitation (Plumwood 1998–99). And in spite of the hermeneutical difficulties involved, Genesis 1–3 still provides a model of ecological interconnectedness in which human beings are genealogically related to the earth. Fundamentally, we belong to a single kinship system. As Alasdair MacIntyre has suggested, a living tradition is 'an historically extended, socially embodied argument, and an argument precisely in part about the goods which constitute that tradition' (1981: 207). It is incumbent upon those of us who relate to biblical tradition to realize the ecological potential that the creation narratives offer, even if that potential is expressed in an ironic mode.

'Beloved, Come Back to Me': Ground's Theme Song in Genesis 3?

Shirley Wurst

Is Silence Golden?

How can you understand what someone is saying if you do not understand their language? How can you read silences in an ancient text? How can you give the silenced and marginalized subject-in-the-text a voice and agency?

In an earlier unpublished paper, I developed a strategy for reading the voices of women silenced, marginalized and treated pejoratively in the Hebrew Scriptures. The strategy, which I called a 'fleshly reading practice', is designed to put flesh or body—and, hence, voice and agency—into the text. It uses a constellation of potential sources of knowledge that inform each other, and me as the reader of the silences: my own located knowledge and experiences; historical and contextual information; knowledge acquired through reading and self-reflexivity; and sociocultural knowledge of the world in the text. The practice is subjective, and is informed by my own location in my own discursive spaces. It is one way of giving voice and agency to a character silenced and marginalized in the text.

An aspect of the Earth Bible Project that particularly excites my interest is the principle of voice. This principle is integral to my project in this paper, because my understanding of voice revolves around the nature of subject status and agency. When we silence subjects, we take away their ability to speak their locations, to tell other people how they construct themselves and their reality. We make them objects, unable to say how they are, why they are, who they are. Seeing them as objects enables us to construct and manipulate them and make them be what we want, be how we want them to be.

In the text of Genesis 3, the problem of silences is complex. There are numerous silences in the text—in fact there are more opportunities to be spoken than to speak, in this text. My focus in this paper is the ground, the *adamah* (אדמה), who, in traditional readings of the text, is 'cursed' because of what humans have done.[1]

> To the human YHWH, God said:
> Because you have listened to the voice of your woman
> and have eaten from the tree about which I commanded you, saying
> 'You are not to eat from it',
> cursed be the ground because of you.
> With painstaking labour shall you eat from it, all the days of your life.
> Thorns and sting-shrub let it spring up for you,
> when you seek to eat the plants of the field!
> By the sweat of your brow shall you get bread to eat,
> until you return to the ground,
> for from it you were taken.
> For dust you are, and to dust you shall return.[2]

Like many Western readers, I had accepted the view of contemporary mainstream commentaries of the meaning of the Earth story[3] in Genesis 3. The man and woman in the text—the husband and his wife[4]—have been disobedient, and they are now being punished by God. Genesis 3.8-24 describes their punishment in a genre evocative of the ancient world of jurisprudence.[5] The woman will endure painful childbirths to remind her of her part in the 'first sin', and both she and her descendants will engage in a life-and-death 'love–hate' relationship with snakes. All women will be ruled—be under the headship and discipline of their husbands. In his turn, because the man obeyed his wife (literally, because he listened to her voice) he will have to work hard with his hands, sweating profusely, to grow enough food to survive. The ground, once fertile and bounteous, will now produce 'good' growth only grudgingly. Instead, weeds and thistles—plants not suitable or desirable for human consumption—will grow profusely! The final punishment, included in the words of God to the man, is mortality. Humans, according to biblical scholars

---

1.   Although I do not have time to pursue the point in this article, Gen. 8.21b, where God promises 'I will never again curse the ground because of humankind', is an interesting intertext for Gen. 3.17b.

2.   My translation here and later in the chapter uses insights from Fox's 1983 translation.

3.   'Earth' is capitalized to emphasize that this is a reference to the planet.

4.   Because I am giving the traditional reading, I am using the sexist terms endemic to this discourse.

5.   Trible (1978) is an example of a scholar who sees this section of the text mimicking an ancient Near Eastern trial/court scene; many of the terms come from the vocabulary associated with ancient Near Eastern jurisprudence.

in the mainstream 'malestream'[6] tradition, are cursed to die in this text because one man listened to one woman and did what God had explicitly told him not to do!

For me, as for most readers educated within this androcentric and phallocentric tradition—a perspective in which the world is seen from the perspective of humans, and men in particular—death was a punishment, and something I feared. For people immersed in the individualistic tradition that dominates contemporary Western society, my death was the end of me and my world. It threatened my ego; it challenged me to do something to ensure I would not die with my body! If I was wise and made the most of my potential to take action, the essential me could live on—in my children, in the things I had done and the marks I had made in the world while I was alive.

As many contemporary ecologists cynically assert, the human inheritance of Western rationalism and unbridled consumption—human being and taking action—may well be the death of all life on this planet! Suzuki and McConnell's text *The Sacred Balance* (1997) is a timely contemporary reminder of the interconnectedness of all living things, and of the consequences of forgetting this web of connections and counterbalances.

It is my contention that, even though this text in the Hebrew Scriptures has many traces of androcentrism—perhaps phallocentrism—it also has traces of other traditions. In this paper, I will focus on the connections the text inscribes between humans and the ground and other living creatures; in this text the Earth community is indissolubly linked by their common origins—they all come from the ground.

In the process, I will draw on other silences inscribed in the text, silences relating to the goddess traditions, and the traditions focusing on the ground, the soil, as sacred. I share the view of other feminist scholars that these remnants have been silenced and pilloried by a 'jealous' and chauvinistic Yahwist patriarchal monothesim, seeking, in the construction of this text, and in its discourse and rhetoric, to make an inalienable place for itself in the world.

---

6.   'Malestream' is a term, first used by Mary O'Brien (1981: 5), to talk about androcentric perspectives. She defines 'malestream' as 'subject matter [that] reflects male concerns, deals with male activity and male ambitions and is *directed away from* issues involving, or of concern to, women'. I use it to denote the patriarchal and androcentric mainstream characteristics of the Western culture in which my work is situated. It refers to a perspective that is predominantly 'male-identified'.

Listen to Me—I'm your Kin!

The Earth story in Genesis 2–3 sets out to show how humans and animals are made, how Earth is filled with living, growing plants and other living things, and how God ensures this thriving 'paradise' will be looked after and protected.

As the text demonstrates, a relationship between humans, *adam* (אדם) and the ground, the *adamah* (אדמה), is announced at the beginning of this story of the creation of life on Earth as we know it.[7] In Gen. 2.5, both the ground and Earth are naked—there are no trees or grasses, no plant life. According to the text, this lack has two causes: there is as yet no rain—a term that implies no seasons—and there are no humans to 'till the soil'.

The Hebrew term translated 'till/work', *abed* (עבד), has several key nuances. It denotes working the soil, cultivation; but it is also the term for service, and is linked with worshipping a god. The integral human role implied in this term involves working with and serving the soil. Humans are to cultivate the soil—to break its surface, introduce rich humus and manure, air, and facilitate its pursuit of its potential: to sprout grasses of the field. Trible (1978: 85) notes the term 'till' 'connotes respect, indeed reverence and worship'.

Later in Genesis 2, the ground cooperates with God in producing the first trees (Gen. 2.9). The word 'cooperates' is appropriate, as the verbal form used in this context—a hiphil—is understood to involve the joint action of both the subject and object of the verb; in this context, God is the agent, and the ground, as the object of God's agency, is a co-agent. For the action to occur, both God and the ground have to act.[8] It is interesting to note in passing that the text implies that the tree of life and the tree of the knowledge of good and bad are also co-products of God and the ground's activity.

In Gen. 2.15, God is depicted as placing the *adam* in this planted garden. The text however adds another role to the one introduced in the opening verses. Now the *adam* has a second role—to 'watch' the garden. The Hebrew term, *shamar* (שמר), is often translated as 'guard, protect'. The concept denotes careful and close observation—this is

---

7.   Trible (1978: 80) observes that the 'very words that differentiate creature from soil indicate similarity... Yahweh God makes distinctions that result not in oppositions but in harmony. A punned separation articulates unity.'

8.   On the notion of co-creators, see Fretheim (1992); Welker (1991–92) also talks about the notion of shared activity in Gen. 1; my understanding of the role of the hiphil verbs in this section of Genesis was stimulated by his observations.

attentive and protective tending. Used together, these terms imply reverence for the ground—the soil that produces the food for the human who works and watches. The picture: a mutual nurturing. As Indigenous Australians observe, 'we look after our mother Earth just as she looks after us'. This is a reciprocal custodianship. In this text, an understanding of reciprocal care is underlined. Trible notes that

> [t]o till the garden is to serve the garden; to exercise power over it is to reverence it. Similarly, to keep…the garden is an act of protection (cf. 3:24) not of possession. The two infinitives, to till and to keep, connote not plunder and rape but care and attention. They enhance the delight of the garden. By the same token they give to the earth creature the joy of work (1978: 85).

In this Earth story, the human comes from the ground, and the food the human consumes is produced by the ground; the ground is unproductive without rain—the natural processes and seasons over which humans have no control—and the close and careful tending of humans. Humans serve the ground so the ground can serve humans.[9] It is a mutual dependence, an interdependence—neither party in the partnership is complete, able to reach its potential and live fully, without the other.[10]

In the next section of the Genesis Earth story, the text implies there is a flaw in the paradisical perfection now in existence—what has been heralded as 'good to the highest degree' (Hebrew *tob*/טוב) in the previous Earth story (Genesis 1.1–2.4, esp. 2.31b) is now perceived, by God, to be 'not good'. And the problem is seen from the perspective of the lone human, by a God who created humans 'in our image'. The God who is 'in cooperative being' recognizes that humans, in God's 'image', also need to be more than one!

In one of the first of many subtle jokes in this Jewish text, this beneficent jokester of a creator is depicted as testing and tantalizing

---

9.   Although this text does not say humans are to eat what the ground produces, Gen. 2.9 observes that God 'made grow every tree that is pleasant to the sight and good for food'; in Gen. 2.16, the human is given permission to 'freely eat of every tree of the garden'. Strictly, then, the human is an orchardist rather than a farmer/agriculturalist!

10.   Although readers might see this as 'irredeemably anthropocentric', and treat this section of the text with judicious suspicion, as I am trying to read the text's silence, I am content to take this as part of the Earth story 'set up' in this section of Genesis. In my reading, this material is essential background for understanding how this text presents the relationship between ground and human, and the links that bind together all members of Earth community.

the tastes and judgment of this new groundling,[11] this 'earth being' or 'earthling'[12] made from ground/earth—a human from the humus—and linked indissolubly with it. Wild creatures, who also come from the ground, are all paraded before the *adam* to see if any can be embraced as a suitable partner for a human. The text is ambiguous: does God mistakenly believe humans and animals can be intimates? Or does God realize that although humans and animals can be close companions, their relationship will never result in 'one flesh', a reminder for the *adam* of the paradox of closeness without intimacy.

The human passes the test; the human recognizes that although all the creatures presented for inspection are made from the ground, of one substance with human beings, sharing the breath of life and agency,[13] there is not one that meets the human need for intimate companionship. There is no 'fitting helper', or 'helper corresponding', for the *adam*. When an *ishah* (אשׁה), a woman—a being so like this groundling that she is recognized as 'bone from my bones' and 'flesh from my flesh'—is brought to the *adam*, she is embraced with delighted exclamations! The text is redolent with the joy and relief of recognition, of a potential oneness!

Everett Fox's translation (1983: 12) captures the mood in the Hebrew effectively:

> The Human said:
> This-time, she-is-it!

The Earth story in Genesis 2 demonstrates that humans are formed from the ground; we are ground's kin.[14] Perhaps this understanding is reflected in Ps. 139.15: 'My frame was not hidden from you [YHWH]

---

11. See Korsak (1993: 40): 'We will make a groundling'.

12. Korsak (1993: 48) observes that the word *adam* (אדם) occurs 28 times in Genesis 1–5, and *adamah* (אדמה) occurs 16 times; she chooses 'groundling' and 'ground', arguing that 'ground' is a more appropriate translation for *adamah* (אדמה) than 'earth', which she reserves as a translation for *erets* (ארץ).

13. Trible (1978: 91) notes that the texts describing the creation of the human, and the creation of animals, are virtually synonymous. She observes that 'with the sole omission of the word dust...the line that reports the creation of animals (2.19) is identical to the line that reported the creation of the earth creature'.

14. Ps. 139.15 presents an even clearer picture of the how humans are 'from the ground': 'My frame was not hidden from you [YHWH] when I was shaped in a hidden place, knit together in the recesses of the earth' (Jewish Publication Society 1988). Elaine Wainwright's paper on Matthew (2000: 162-73) talks about the 'kindom of God' as God's dream for Earth community, a dream that is realized in the person and activity of Jesus Christ.

when I was shaped in a hidden place, knit together in the recesses of the earth.'

Animals and plants also come from the ground. A possible reading of God bringing the animals to the human as potential partners is that God saw the kinship between them, too; it was only when the human did not resonate with any animal that God decided to create a more suitable partner: a female human being.

Indigenous Australian Earth stories are enriched with an understanding of this connection that binds humans to their place on Earth. They have a piece of ground that is 'their place'—for some traditional Aboriginal people, this connection was made concrete by this being the place where their afterbirth was buried.[15] It is also the place where they will be returned to their mother–lover, Earth.

Indigenous Australians are also connected—through their human kinship, and their ground kinship—with other species that 'come from' the ground. Each Aboriginal person has a place in the Earth community, a network of reciprocal family relationships with human, animal and plant kin. These connected individuals share a spiritual and physical essence. In the primordial times of Aboriginal Australian Earth story, the ancestors of all species came from the ground, moved over the ground, laid down the patterns of life, aspects of human and other living beings' cultures on Earth, and the patterns of the landscape, and returned, like all living things, to the ground. As is the case in the Genesis creation stories, in Aboriginal Australian understanding all living beings come from the ground and are destined to return to the ground.

What is implicit in this Earth story in Genesis, and explicit in Aboriginal Australian peoples' understanding, is that humans and other living species have never left the ground. They, and the ground that gives birth to them and nurtures their lives, are connected by physical, emotional, spiritual and material connections both practical and imminent, and mysterious and transcendent. As Diane Bell (1998: 262-78) observes, this is implicit in Ngarrindjeri language, where body, *ruwa*, and land, *ruwe*, have the same stem.[16] Bell (1998: 264) observes that in 'this metaphor of land and body, we have another way of thinking about the relationship of individual sites to the larger area of the land in the region'.

For people in the Western cultural tradition, David Suzuki and Amanda McConnell (1997: 77) make the same connections.

15. See Salevao 2000: 221-31.
16. See also Bell 1998: 622-24 nn. 1, 3, 4.

> One way or another, we are Earthenware. These stories [creation sto-
> ries] tell us the truth: the soil is the source of life. Throughout the ages it
> has been treated as precious, even sacred, because of the gifts it gives us.

In a chapter called 'Made from the Soil' (1997: 76-104), they demonstrate that 'Earth is the planet we live on and the material we live
from'.

I'm Innocent; Why Are You Blaming Me?

So, how can we understand the ground's subject position and agency
in this Earth story in Genesis 2–3? What is the ground's response to
these events? How does the ground deal with the curse? Does the
ground remonstrate: 'Hang on, I didn't do it. I'm innocent! Don't
blame me!', following the pattern of the other subjects given a voice in
the text?

As is apparent from the Hebrew Scriptures' text, the ground is
subjected to a curse. Like the snake, who is also cursed by the Lord
God running the court proceedings in the garden, the ground is not
given a chance to voice a defence.[17] Both humans admit they ate from
the tree they had been forbidden to eat from (Gen. 3.11b-13); however,
when they are invited to explain their actions, they also attempt to
project most of the blame onto a more culpable co-perpetrator. The
adam blames the 'woman whom you gave to be beside me' (Gen.
3.12a), subtly blaming God as well as the woman for his lapse; the
ishah claims that the snake 'enticed' her.

The scene is set for another exculpatory statement by the snake,
who we already know is implicated in the focal event. Contrary to our
expectations, the snake is not allowed to voice an opinion. The snake
is judged guilty without any defence, and suffers an immediate consequence:

> Because you have done this,
> cursed be you from all the animals and from all the wild living-things
>   of the field;
> upon your belly shall you crawl and dust (*apar*) shall you eat all the
>   days of your life.
> I will put enmity between you and the woman (*ishah*), between your
>   seed and her seed:
> they will strike at your head, you will strike at their heel.

---

17.   Norman Habel, in a conversation, suggested that the snake in this text represents non-human creation. That both the non-human animal representative and
the ground—the material source of both life forms—are cursed because they were
there underlines the androcentric nature of this text on at least one level.

The Hebrew syntax suggests the curse is about separation rather than degree—the snake will be separated from other animals rather than cursed more than they are. Furthermore, this consequence is forever. The curse involves a brutish vengeance, an ancient Near Eastern feud of mythic proportions. Humans—the offspring of the woman[18] —will hit out at snakes, and they will hit back! However, as Korsak (1993: 51) observes, this curse is 'merely that it [the snake] should be a serpent'.

In an interesting subtle twist, the snake perhaps has the last laugh— the dust it is forced to eat is ultimately what humans are reduced to, in the cycle of mortality. Ultimately, the snake wins the feud, consuming the enemy as part of its everyday existence: it eats the dust that humans become!

Several recent feminist interpretations of Genesis 2–3 have observed that the snake's treatment is probably a polemic against the indigenous Canaanite religions of the land. In these traditions, snakes are familiars of the goddess, and symbolize eternal life—snakes shed their skin, and, because they live both on and under the ground, control both the above-ground world of the living and the underground world of the dead.[19] Hayter (1987: 104) observes that

> the snake plays a prominent role in the literature and cults of the ancient world...the serpent was associated with the fertility cult—with

---

18. She is about to be given a name that describes who she is, her place in the world: she is Chavva, the mother of all living. I adopt Fox's translation (1983: 16): 'Havva/Life-giver', rather than the usual English translation, Eve, to underline that her name is connected with her role as birthing mother/life-giver. However, I prefer the spelling *Chavva* to Fox's *Havva*. As Korsak (1993: 41) observes, the 'connection between "Eve" and "living" is not apparent to the reader without reference to a footnote, which gives Hebrew *ḥawwâ* and *ḥay'*—she is talking about the usual practice with English translations of the Hebrew Scriptures where the translators 'traditionally relegate this connection to footnotes'.

19. See Schüngel-Straumann 1993; Westbrook 1990; Joines 1975. Schüngel-Straumann (1993: 67-68) observes that the 'serpent is a heavily symbolic animal in the positive as well as in the negative sense...a symbol of life as well as death... The latest interpretation of the serpent as a symbol of the Canaanite fertility cult, which also symbolises the Canaanite Baal and his sexual potency, seems the most convincing'. She also notes that the 'Tree-Serpent-Goddess belonged together as a fixed motif' (Schüngel-Straumann 1993: 68-69). Westbrook (1990: 127-28) observes that the image complex 'of the goddess, her serpent, and the mystical tree of life and wisdom' is 'metaphoric of existence seen as cyclic...controlled by the great goddess who is at once the womb and tomb of all that lives. Included in the goddess's cycles of existence, of course, are the human generations which ebb and flow in their turn.'

the worship of Astarte and Baal...enthralment to the fertility cult, far
from generating life, led to death... To heed the serpent's voice, to follow the deceptive enticements of nature religion was to dislodge Yahweh, the creator and life-giver.

The snake, a mundane reptilian version of the fiery phoenix, cheats
death by ever-renewing itself and leaving its skin—its mortal shell—
behind. In this ancient view of snakes, they also implicitly win the
feud: in Gen. 3.17 humans are condemned to mortality!

Because they have done things they were explicitly told not to do,
we are expecting the 'talking to' both the woman and man receive.[20] If
the snake gets a damning indictment that has no escape clause—and,
incidentally, there is no indication in the text that the snake has done
other than it was created to do: it is the 'shrewdest of all the wild
beasts', easily capable of 'duping'[21] a human being who is open to
debate and discussion, and the nuances of words and their meanings—then these two should really have 'the book thrown at them'.

I was surprised when I discovered, contrary to traditional interpretation and popular understanding of this text, that neither the woman
nor the man are cursed directly.[22] The woman is informed that her
labour will be unceasing, and that one of her core roles, having children, is going to be a fairly challenging experience; she will only risk
the pain and potential death because she is sexually entranced by her
partner.[23] In the period in which Hebrew Scriptures were written and
edited into the form we now have access to, childbirth was a

---

20. The Hebrew form *lo tokal* (לא תאכל)—the negative particle לא plus an imperfect verbal form—demonstrates this as a prohibition that lasts for all time.

21. TANAKH translation.

22. Although contemporary translations are careful to note that neither the
man nor the woman is cursed, that this is a general understanding of the text is
demonstrated by Hayter (1987: 106-107), and even more explicitly by *IDB* (1962:
750), in the section under the heading 'curse': 'As a retributive or preventative measure, curses are found to be levelled against...woman, who experiences pain in
childbirth...and man who must exert himself to wring existence from the earth';
and Mays (1988: 88): 'The divine judgement begins with a curse on the serpent...
The curse of the woman involves the pain of child bearing... The curse on the man
involves disharmony with the earth.'

23. I am following the argument and translation of Meyers (1988, 1993). See
esp. Meyers (1988: 95-121); see also Meyers (1988: 118), for her translation: 'I will
greatly increase your toil and your pregnancies; [Along] with travail shall you
beget children. For to a man is your desire, and he shall predominate over you.'
See also Meyers 1978; 1983.

risky business; many women died giving birth; many children did not survive their first few years of life.[24]

Yet, women continued to go to any lengths to have children; as the stories in Genesis demonstrate, this is partly because, in the patriarchal system, a woman's life was bleak without children. As Rachel says to Jacob, 'Give me children, or I shall die' (Gen. 30.1). Ironically, her words come to haunt her—she dies giving birth to her second son (Gen. 35.16-19).[25]

Carol Meyers argues convincingly that life in the 'land of milk and honey' was arduous and back-breaking. The soil was poor, the rainfall low and unpredictable, and much sweat was expended in eking a living from the soil in the Palestinean highland regions (Meyers 1988). The man's predicament, like the woman's, reflects the reality of life in that period. Both will be involved in hard labour, and will produce through sweating and intensive effort! In fact, their 'punishment' is to be human, just as the snake's 'curse' is to be snake!

The pronouncement directed to the man is surprising in yet another respect. We might be perturbed that he is castigated for listening to his woman's voice, but not that he is told off for breaking a strongly worded prohibition without scarcely a thought: we are merely told 'he ate' what he was given; in the Hebrew text, the action is even more terse than in English: yokal (יאכל).

However, there is no preparation in the text for the opening words of God's pronouncement: 'Cursed be the soil on your account' (Gen. 3.17b). Up to this point, each pronouncement has followed from the story—the snake is the last blamed and the first dealt with; the woman, the second to be interrogated—'What is this you have done?' (Gen. 3.13)—is dealt with next; the man, who is the first whose actions are placed under scrutiny, is saved till the end.[26]

The ground, however, has not been implicated in the 'crime'; the adamah could justly remonstrate, 'Me? What have I done!' At worst, the ground could claim, 'I was an innocent bystander. I couldn't not be there. You can't blame me'.

The text, however, is silent. Neither the ground, nor the guilty

24. See Meyers (1988) for an extended discussion of the 'everyday existence' exemplified in Gen. 3.16-19, focusing on the experiences of women in particular. Some of her arguments are summarized in her article (1993).

25. Ironically, in the light of this text, she dies as the result of a curse pronounced on her by her partner, Jacob (Gen. 31.32). For an interesting discussion of this event, see J. Williams (1982: 42-66 [51]).

26. See Trible (1978: 121) for her analysis outlining and demonstrating the chiastic structure of this section of the story.

humans, remonstrate, or ask the question that is silently shouting to be heard!

So, what is going on? How can we make sense of this extremely ground-unfriendly action on the part of this benevolent creator—and, so far in the story, righteous judge? How can we explain this aberrant activity? How can a just God be so unjust? Is this a text that demands a warning, 'Beware, this text is not ground-friendly'? How can this text be counter-read? How can the ground's voice, silent is the text, be included? Can we counter-read the androcentrism in this text?

Curse Me, Not my Child

Although the text sets up a series of 'I did it—but X did it more than me', and 'You made me immovable—I had to be there!' is a sustainable objection from the ground, and we can readily insert an ecojustice counter-plea into the text: 'I did nothing—you can't blame me!', I think there is another way of reading the ground's voice in this Earth story.

The key to my reading lies in the early scenes in this 'drama', this Earth community event. The final verse of the 'judgment' confirms the plausibility of my reading:

> Cursed be the ground (*adamah*) because of you,
> With painstaking labour shall you eat from it all the days of your life.
> Thorn and sting-shrub let it spring up for you,
> when you seek to eat the plants of the field!
> By the sweat of your brow shall you get bread to eat,
> until you return to the ground (*adamah*),
> for from it you were taken.
> For dust you are (*apar*, עפר), and to dust (*apar*) you shall return (Gen. 3.19).

The human is 'earthenware' (Suzuki and McConnell 1997: 77), an 'earthling' (Trible 1978), a 'clod' (Bal 1987: 113). The *adam*'s essence is underlined by the name Adam, just as the woman's name, Chavva, underlines her central characteristic: she gives life; she is a 'life-giver'.[27] The name shows where the groundling comes from, and what characterizes the essence of this 'earth creature' (Trible 1978: 107)—the *adam* is human from the humus. The earth/ground, the red *adamah*, is the progenitor of *adam*.[28] Westbrook (1990: 126) notes that

---

27. Fox (1983: 16) makes this translation and connection.

28. Korsak (1993: 44) observes: 'It may be said, in passing, that there are many details in this version of Genesis that lend themselves to an ecological interpreta-

the woman is also 'born of the matter of which she consists—the dust from which the man was crafted':

> Thus a chain of existence is forged: The ground (*adamah*) gives existence to the man (*adam, ish*) who gives birth to the woman (*ishshah*), 'because she was taken out of man' (*ish*), later to be known as *Eve* ('living', hence 'the mother of all living'), who in her goddess form is the earth or ground (*adamah*) (Westbrook 1990: 126).

Perhaps Westbrook's final observation also explains why the woman, who was not in existence when the prohibition was given to the *adam*, is punished as severely in the text; it also explains her castigation in many traditions as the one who brought sin into human existence. As the mother of all living, she symbolizes Earth goddess, the ground. Joines notes that the 'common Semitic word for serpent, *hawwa*, [is] from the same root as the word for life' (1975: 2-3; citing Morgenstern). As she also observes, this is the name given to the woman in Gen. 3.20: 'the first woman is called *hawwa* because she is the mother of all living'.

The essential nature of the human condition is underlined in Gen. 3.17. Humans come from the ground and return to it. And, as this text shows—contrary to Western and traditional understanding—this return to the ground is a release from hard labour! Unlike the usual Western interpretation, which sees death as a punishment, this is a return to which we belong—the embrace of our mother–lover, the ground. This is a homecoming!

It is my contention that this mother, the *adamah*, like other mothers in Genesis, will do just about anything for her child. She, like Rebekah, says, 'Your curse, my son, be upon me!' (Gen. 27.13b). Maternal sacrifice is a theme in Genesis: mothers die giving birth, offer to die for their children, die when their children die,[29] and risk death to have a child.[30]

---

tion. The literal character of [Everett Fox's] translation creates an immediate contact with the Hebrew source, which itself conveys a sense of oneness about the universe, a connectedness, as seen here, between animal and human for instance.'

29. Is the demise of Sarah a self-willed death because she knows Abraham has taken their long-awaited son to Mount Moriah, to sacrifice him to God? We hear no more of her after this incident; her death is reported in the next chapter.

30. Tamar is accused of adultery by her father-in-law and the father of her unborn child; at the time she 'tricks' Judah into sleeping with her, she takes items that will identify him to protect herself from just this eventuality (Gen. 38). See J. Williams (1982: 42-66) for a discussion of what he calls the 'arche-mother: the mother of Israel's beginnings'.

In Genesis 3, YHWH is depicted as the patriarchal father, meting out deserved punishment to his disobedient children. Williams (1982: 58), in his discussion of the 'arche-mother' in 'Israel's beginnings', asserts that in the 'mother's role as mediating agent we see the unfriendly aspects of the world as a range of hostile male authority figures: father, father-in-law, king, and God'.[31] The disappointed 'father' God—the text does not actually tell us how God feels about the 'punishment'—informs these 'naughty' children of the consequences of their actions.

Breaking the relationship with God has a ripple effect on all their other relationships—they have already demonstrated, paradigmatically, the broken relationships between themselves as partners—and perhaps between themselves and the animals, represented by the snake. God sees the consequences, and the need for consequences. In her essay in this volume, Carol Newsom observes that this is a 'fall into anthropocentrism'; I would add androcentrism and gynocentrism: both human collaborators in the 'fall' place themselves at the centre of their world, projecting their participation-as-guilt onto someone else. In agreeing to let the ground be cursed because of human actions, God participates in this blame-by-projection.

The ground–mother can see another way—but it has a cost for her! This generous 'Earth' mother, who acted with God to produce humans, now acts to protect their precious creation. The *adamah* asks to take the brunt of the 'curse' on herself, and diminishes the ripples, by grounding the curse in herself. God agrees. The ground, like the other mothers in Genesis, wears the curse of her children's destructive behaviour. Perhaps, like all mothers, she believes she is able to shield her children from the consequences of their actions. Perhaps, like Rachel, she will die to give her children life!

Instead of nutritious grasses and trees that are beautiful to look at and produce edible fruits,[32] 'thorn and sting-shrub'[33] will 'spring up' from her. Because the relationship between her 'children' has been disrupted by her children's actions, the bond between herself and her offspring is no longer naive and straightforward. She will produce plants that will be useless for human consumption; not even her other Earth children—goats and camels—will choose this unpalatable fodder! The curse does not diminish her fertility; the plants will still

31. Williams (1982: 55) also observes that in stories of 'arche-mothers' in Genesis, a 'common thread…is that the hostile reality is "male"'.

32. Fox's translation: 'desirable to look at and good to eat' (1983: 10).

33. Fox's translation (1983: 16).

'spring up' from her—they will not, however, be suitable for human consumption.

In effect, this curse is also ironic: the ground is cursed to be ground as we know it! And, instead of living in a land flowing with all good fruits, the humans will live in the world as we know it—the food humans produce will be gained through 'painstaking labour…all the days of [their] life' (Fox 1983: 16).

Another subtle irony of the curse on the ground—this action by the God-judge-in-the-text subtly recognizes the ground as subject!

Westbrook (1990: 126) notes that the ground is revered as the goddess, the mother of all living; this explains why the ground, like the snake, is cursed: both represent powerful symbols of the indigenous Canaanite religions that cannot be tolerated in the new regime of Yahwist monotheism.[34] This text, then, perhaps merely reflects the anti-indigenous monotheistic and narrow rhetoric of the writers.

If, as feminist scholars have suggested, this text is a parable of human life at the time it was written, it is also a parable for our time. As ecologists have demonstrated, the ground and other members of the Earth community are still bearing the curse-consequences of human actions!

The failure of the human 'children' to take responsibility, to attempt to restore the balance, is a significant silence in this text. At best we are left with the brief but redolent restoration of the intimacy between the man and the woman. 'The human [*adam*] called his wife's name Chavva/Life-giver! For she became the mother of all living [*Chay*]' (Gen. 3.20; translation Fox 1983: 16). Her name also hints at the goddess she epitomizes: Astarte, the mother of the gods!

Contrary to his earlier eagerness to implicate the woman—and through her, God—in his predicament, the man now focuses on the woman as gift, and giver. She is the one who gives birth to children. Her ability to give birth represents one of the ways a corporate society, like that of ancient Israel, understood living forever. In Israelite patriarchal terms, a man lives on forever through his children! In this explicitly phallocentric text, she is the means by which he escapes mortality!

To some extent this 'renaming' retrieves the broken relationship apparent in Gen. 3.12. In this text there is, however, no reconciliation with the others who are also human kin: the snake and the ground.

---

34. Habel (1965) also explores the indigenous imagery in Gen. 3. See also Hayter (1987).

Conclusion

The ground, the mother who gives us life and sustains us, is still taking our bad behaviour on board and trying to deal with its consequences. Surely it is time that we, the errant children of the ground, start being responsible; it is time we started reciprocating the love our mother–lover shows us. 'Yes, we did it. And this is what we are going to do to make things right again, to restore relationship, to restore the sacred balance.'

The ground, our mother–lover, is crying out to us from the silent spaces in this text. Like a loving parent, despite our errant behaviour, the ground welcomes us upon our return. She is the epitome of the loving parent celebrated in the parable of the prodigal son (Lk. 15.11-32). Like a human mother, the ground celebrates our living by integrating us totally back into the 'ground community's life'.

Like a lover, she invites us to come to her, and find welcome relief in her embrace. She takes us into herself, and returns us to community! She brings us back to where we belong. In our return, our homecoming, we are integrated with our mother–lover in a way that no human intercourse can manage! In our final ground embrace, we become one 'flesh'!

Suzuki and McConnell, in their chapter demonstrating that humans are 'made from the soil', assert that the soil is alive,[35] and that nothing is lost in this return! They demonstrate how this exchange operates, using our contemporary understanding of the cycles in nature (1997: 80).

> Petals, leaves and stems fall from a plant to become compost for the seeds of the plant—death turns into life, grows up, feeds life and dies again, returning to the workshop underground to be restored to life.

We, too, return in our dying.

The irony is that we have never been separated. The connections of the ground's mother-love have kept us grounded. We become one again with the ground when we are enclosed in the soil's embrace, as

---

35. (1997: 80-81): 'Soil organisms comprise a major portion of the total diversity of life. In this dark, teeming world, minute predators stalk their prey, tiny herbivores graze on algae, thousands of aquatic microorganisms throng a single drop of soil water, and fungi, bacteria and viruses play out their part on this invisible stage. In their life and death these organisms create and maintain the texture and fertility of the soil; they are caretakers of the mysterious life-creating material on which they, and we, depend absolutely.'

we are reintegrated physically into the ground, our mother–lover, from whom, like the *adam* in Gen. 2.7, we have been separated as living beings. In our reintegration with the ground, we give our lives, our being, for the Earth community's ongoing life. This is the cycle of all living: we are all born, separated from our mother, we live independently but always in connection, and when we die, we return to our source, we return to our nurturer, our mother, our lover.

What the ground is also saying to us, in the silent spaces of our humdrum contemporary reality, is that every action has a reaction, that our behaviour has implications for other members of the Earth community.[36] While the ground takes on our curse in Christlike self-sacrifice, we are also experiencing the consequences of our actions. Even a loving mother cannot protect us forever from the consequences of our bad behaviour!

Suzuki and McConnell (1997: 102) demonstrate that this reciprocal connectedness has implications: '[t]he interconnectedness of all things on Earth means that everything we do has consequences that reverberate through the systems of which we are a part'. They also see signs of human recognition of these links (1997: 103).

> Earth's old wisdom is beginning to be heard again…the soil is returning to its place at the centre of human life. Its productivity and health are a crucial link in the chain of life upon which we depend. Without exaggeration we can say the soil is the ground of our being; along with water and air it is the stuff that life helped to make, maintains and depends on absolutely.

The text of Genesis 2–3 seems to be reminding us that although we always belong to the ground, we most completely are one with the ground when we return to our origins, when we are 'grounded' through our death and decomposition.

However, implicitly this text also underlines—as does the parable of the prodigal son—that even though we abuse our mother-ground, like any loving parent, we are welcomed back with open arms when we return.

We need to attune our ears to hear the voice of the ground, the voice Indigenous peoples around the world are trying to share with us. Though the ground and the Earth community have been cursed because of what we have done, because we are inextricably connected

---

36. The point is made succinctly by Suzuki and McConnell (1997: 103): 'Without exaggeration we can say the soil is the ground of our being; along with water and air it is the stuff that life helped to make, maintains and depends on absolutely.'

to the other members of the Earth community, the curse rests on us, too. We are part of the Earth community; we cannot live outside that connection.

Or, perhaps we just need to recognize that we are corporate beings, and that we only have our place on the ground, on Earth, as a consequence of all our ancestors—our human and non-human kin—who are 'dead in the ground' before us. As José Arcadio Buendía, a character in Gabriel García Márquez's *One Hundred Years of Solitude* (1978: 19), observes, a 'person does not belong to a place until there is someone dead under the ground'.

Alienation and 'Emancipation' from the Earth:
The Earth Story in Genesis 4

Gunther Wittenberg

Introduction

How did it happen that we humans became alienated from the Earth? This question has been debated by many ecologists, scientists, philosophers and theologians. The answer to this question is indeed of great significance for our attempts at reorienting ourselves as humans within and as part of nature and not above and removed from it. Many have singled out the scientific discoveries of the sixteenth and seventeenth centuries and the subsequent Industrial Revolution as the time when the close relationship broke down (see. esp. Merchant 1982); others see the roots of this separation much earlier.

In this essay I want to explore whether the Bible can contribute to this debate. Does it deal with the problem of alienation and separation from the Earth with all its disastrous consequences? And if so, where does it see the crucial point of departure when humankind became alienated and separated from the Earth? A reading of Genesis 4 from the perspective of the Earth will reveal how this alienation took place. Separation does not happen at once, but it is a process, it is a story that unfolds. Instead of being part of the Earth 'as a community of interconnected living things which are mutually dependent on each other for life and survival' (principle of interconnectedness), human beings becoming autonomous, standing on their own, opposed to and removed from the Earth, seems to become the norm. How this happened is told in Genesis 4. But I will also try to show that for the biblical author alienation is not the last word on our human relationship with the Earth, but that at the end of the chapter there is a faint hope that the broken relationship with the Earth may be restored.

Although most scholars have split up Genesis 4 into several units and interpreted each one separately, I plan to read this narrative (Gen. 4.1-26; 5.29) as a literary whole and as the continuation of the Earth story of Genesis 2 and 3. It is not a story with two actors, Yahweh and

Cain (or humankind), but with three, the Earth entering the stage at its turning point.

Alienation from the Earth: Genesis 4.1-16

The Earth story in Genesis 4 starts with the earthling *ha adam*, whom Yahweh had created out of the Earth, *ha adamah*. Although in Gen. 3.19 God had announced that humans would return to the Earth from which they had been taken, the earthling and his wife do not die as yet but have to make their living in the new surrounding outside the garden of Eden from which they had been banished. That is the setting of the story as it starts to unfold.

The man knew his wife and she bore a son; Eve, the mother of all living, takes the initiative and names him Cain. Cain is the firstborn with all the rights and privileges attached to that status. The exact meaning of the name given by Eve is not clear. 'Every word of this little sentence is difficult' (von Rad 1978: 103). The verb *qanah* can have two meanings. The more common one is 'acquire, buy' (e.g. Gen. 25.10; 33.19). Although its usage for the birth of a child is unusual, a majority of scholars have chosen this option (von Rad 1978: 103; Wenham 1987: 101). Considering the context of Genesis 2–3 dealing with creation Cassuto (1961: 196) and Westermann (1984: 290) opt for the latter meaning of 'create' (Gen. 14.19, 22). Considering the progression of the storyline Westermann's explanation seems to be the most probable. He sees in the sentence explaining the name of Cain a cry of triumph. It corresponds with the jubilant cry of welcome of the woman by the man in Gen. 2.23 (Westermann 1984: 289). Eve sees in her newborn baby the future man and she boasts that just as Yahweh created *ha adam*, the earthling, from the womb of the Earth, so Eve has now created from her womb her son Cain. Creation has gone on and was ongoing, even beyond Eden, because after Cain Eve conceived again and bore her second son, Abel.

Genesis 3 had ended with a question: how would the two human beings who had been banished by God from the garden of Eden manage to live on the Earth which had been cursed by God (Gen. 3.17-19)? The drama of the Earth story unfolds in the narrative of the two brothers. When they grew up Abel became a *roeh tson*, a keeper of sheep, while Cain as the firstborn took up the profession of his father and became an *obed ha adamah*, a tiller or server of the soil.

Some commentators (e.g. von Rad 1978: 104) have seen in the professions of the two brothers the basic division of early society into nomadic and settled communities. This collective interpretation seems to suggest itself especially in view of the similarity of Gen. 4.2 and the other part of the genealogy in Gen. 4.17-21 where the ancestors of other professions are mentioned. But the narrative context is more important. The land outside the garden is arid. To obtain produce from the soil is only possible with a lot of toil and sweat. As farmers in the subsistence economy of the arid areas of Palestine, Adam's family could not rely wholly on dry-land cultivation, they had to rear sheep and goats on the desert shrubs as well. The differentiation in two different professions arises naturally from the given geographical context. However, it is not the distinction between the two professions that leads to deadly conflict and ultimately murder, but the offering to God which two brothers make of their produce.

Westermann (1984b: 294) has emphasized that the offering of the two brothers mentioned in Gen. 4.3-5a has to be understood in the context of their occupations. Without God's blessing no produce of field and flock was possible. Within early society it was unthinkable that the produce could be accepted without an offering, a gift of acknowledgment and thanks to God. Both Cain and Abel therefore brought an offering from the firstlings of their produce. But God accepted only the offering of Abel. 'Cain and his offering' God did not even look at (Gunkel 1969: 43).

Many commentators through the ages have asked why God rejected Cain's offering and how Cain knew about it? According to Westermann (1984: 296) an offering that is 'regarded' by God tells us something about the produce. The Earth that had been cursed yielded only a meagre harvest. Cain, therefore could only bring 'some produce of the land', while Abel, in contrast could offer the choicest animals from his flock, 'firstlings' and their 'fat portions' (Wenham 1987: 104). Cain realized that in spite of his hard labour his harvest was not blessed, while the animals of his younger brother Abel were thriving. Yahweh's curse on the ground seemed to have fallen on him. If his offering was not accepted he himself must have been rejected as well. Hot resentment rose up in him and 'his face fell' (Gen. 4.5).

The next scene consists of a dialogue between God and Cain. 'Why are you angry, and why has your countenance fallen?' Yahweh asked Cain. This question shows that God considers Cain's anger unnecessary and unjustified. A legitimate reason for feeling rejected does not exist (Drewermann 1976: 126). Cain needs to accept his position as the firstborn of Adam who has to follow in his father's footsteps and become a tiller of the Earth, even if it means that the Earth which Yahweh has cursed will never bear for him as abundantly as for Abel and his flock. God is getting Cain to face reality, the reality of existence outside of Eden.

The meaning of the next verse (Gen. 4.7) is obscure. According to Crüsemann (1980) this text takes up a central theme of the Paradise narrative in Genesis 2: *knowledge of good and evil.* 'Knowledge of good and evil' does not refer to any theoretical knowledge, but it refers to the ability to determine what is good and beneficial or evil for oneself (Steck 1970: 34-35; Crüsemann 1980: 61, 67). In Gen. 2.9; 3.5, 7 the emphasis is on the act of knowing and being able to distinguish between good and evil by eating from the forbidden fruit. In Gen. 4.7 the *doing* of what is beneficial or evil and the consequences of the act are central. The same terminology is again used in the two sections framing the story of the Flood (Gen. 6.5; 8.21). This shows the significance of the passage for the whole 'Yahwistic'[1] narrative (Crüsemann 1980: 64).

When Cain brought an offering he wanted to do what was beneficial for himself. He wanted to secure God's blessing for his toil on the Earth. But he did not succeed. His offering was not accepted, blessing was not secured. This is the reason for God's comment: 'If you intend what is good and beneficial and you succeed, you will be proud (literally 'a lifting'). But if this does not happen, then sin like a wild animal crouches in front of the door and threatens to attack you.' According to the author sin threatens where Cain, and with him other human beings, wishes to evade the negative consequences of his deeds (Crüsemann 1980: 66). It is here where God calls for vigilance and the mastery of sin.

In Gen. 4.8 the words that Cain said are missing. 'Let's go to the field' found in some ancient versions are an addition. Instead, the author states concisely and to the point. 'Cain rose up against his brother Abel and killed him.' According to Wenham (1987: 105) this is the central scene. But Westermann (1984: 304) claims that the author, by cutting down the descriptive elements of the story to the bare minimum of the murder, has succeeded in shifting the central focus of the action onto the following scene. Yahweh confronts the murderer with a question which is very similar to the question he asked Adam in Genesis 3. But instead of asking, 'Where are you?', God now asks, 'Where is your brother?' Cain is called to face up to his responsibility for his brother. But he dismisses the question jokingly with a lie: 'Does a shepherd need a keeper?' Cain may have thought that he

---

1.   I retain the traditional terminology although the existence of the Yahwistic source has been called into question (cf. Rendtorff 1976; Crüsemann 1981).

could cover up his deed because he had removed the evidence, but God now confronts him directly with the indictment: 'What have you done? The voice of your brother's blood is crying to me from the ground *(min ha adamah)*.'

It would seem that in this central passage there are only two actors in the drama, Yahweh and Cain, but the pointed reference to the *adamah*, which is used three times in this context and then again in the response of Cain in Gen. 4.14 shows that another player has entered the stage, the Earth. A key concept of the whole of the 'Yahwistic' primeval history is *adamah*, the fertile soil, on which crops can grow and which alone can sustain life. This *adamah* is the realm where human life and work take place (Gen. 2.5). At the same time it is the stuff from which all animals and humans are made and to which they will ultimately return. It is the stage of all the great cycles, of life, death, decomposition, decay and new life. The *adamah* appears here as a living organism which has 'opened her mouth' and has gulped the blood of Abel down her throat (cf. the identical phrase used in Num. 16.30, 32; Deut. 11.6). Blood-filled it cries out aloud against the abomination of the crime. (The third guiding principle for an ecojustice hermeneutic, the principle of voice, is clearly enunciated in this passage.) Finally, the Earth reacts to the murder by withholding 'her strength', her fertility (Westermann 1984: 306).

To the Western mindset that considers the Earth mainly as the material for ruthless exploitation irrespective of the consequences, the conception of the Earth as a living organism that has the capacity to deny the arable soil its power to produce belongs to 'the realm of magic' (Westermann 1984: 306). Only recently this ancient conception 'that the entire living pelt of our planet, its thin green rind of life, is actually one single life-form with senses, intelligence and the power to act' has gained wider acceptance (Pedler 1991: 13).[2]

Because the Earth is the third player in the drama, the key term in Yahweh's curse is the ground *(ha adamah)*. Cassuto (1961: 218-19) notes the close parallel between 'your brother's blood' and 'from the ground' at the end of Gen. 4.10, and the reverse order in Gen. 4.11: 'from the ground' and 'your brother's blood'. He paraphrases the statement as follows: 'Your curse shall come upon you from the ground, just as the cry of your brother's blood came to me from the ground' (Cassuto 1961: 219). The sentence in Gen. 4.12 then spells out the details of God's curse. So far Cain could make a livelihood by tilling the soil (Gen. 4.2), albeit only after hard toil. He even could make

2. Pedler points to the Gaia hypothesis of James Lovelock.

an offering from its fruit. But from now on this link with the Earth will be broken (Cassuto 1961: 221). Because he gave it the blood of his brother to drink, it will now refuse to give him fruit when he 'tills' *(ta abod)* the soil. Von Rad (1978: 106) notes that Yahweh's punishment of Cain goes far beyond the punishment of Adam in Gen. 3.17. Cain's relation to the mother Earth is disturbed much more deeply. 'It is so shattered that the Earth has no home for him.' As a 'vagrant and a wanderer', alienated from the Earth, he must now spend the rest of his life.

The deep sense of alienation is poignantly expressed in Cain's lamentation. Cain's outburst, 'My punishment is greater than I can bear', suggests that life under the curse is worse than death. Genesis 4.14 describes the nature of the alienation: to be driven away from the arable soil *(mey al peney ha adamah)* is to have all relationships broken, first of all with Yahweh (cf. also Gen. 3.10) and then with the protective bonds of the family (cf. Gen. 3.24 with the same verb) (Coats 1983: 65). If Cain must be a fugitive living far away from God, it means that his life will no longer be protected. Anybody can kill him. But God reacts to this plea by putting a mark upon Cain thereby placing his life under strict protection: 'Whoever kills Cain will suffer sevenfold vengeance.'

Cain has to leave God's presence and on his wanderings he comes to the land of Nod where he settles. *Nod* is related to the verb *nud,* which had earlier characterized his existence (Gen. 4.14). 'He who had been sentenced to be a *nad* settles in the land of *nod.* The wanderer lands up in the land of wandering' (Hamilton 1990: 235). Nod is further defined as 'east of Eden', a phrase that recalls Gen. 3.24, but whereas Adam and Eve were banished from the garden to an arid *adamah,* Cain is banished from the soil itself. But how is such an existence, alienated from the Earth, at all possible? The next section of the Earth story will give an answer to this question.

'Emancipation' from the Earth: Genesis 4.17-26

The following section records the genealogy of Cain. In Gen. 4.17 the identity of the builder of the city is considered a problem by many scholars. According to the Masoretic Text (MT), Cain built the first city and named it after his son Enoch, but scholars (Cassuto 1961: 229; Westermann 1984: 327; Coats 1983: 61; Wenham 1987: 111) have argued that Cain cannot be 'a tiller of the ground' (Gen. 4.2) and a 'builder of a city' at the same time in one genealogy. The first city builder therefore has to be Enoch.

There can be no doubt that this proposal would eliminate also some textual problems and would better fit the context of the genealogy in Gen. 4.1, 17-26. But the author was not primarily interested in the genealogy as such, although he made use of this traditional material. The progression of the story was more important to him. Von Rad (1978: 110) makes the point that the conscientious reader must have 'some power of discrimination with this narrator, first for the peculiarities of each individual tradition, and secondly for the chief ideas that the narrator himself wants to express when he combines so many traditions into a whole'.

This has important implications for the understanding of this story. While Westermann (1984b: 327) regards the founding of the first city as reported in the genealogy Gen. 4.1, 17 'as the first achievement of civilization' and claims that 'Israel did not regard the foundation of cities and urban civilization as something a priori negative', but rather 'as a very positive part in the history of humankind' (1984b: 328), this assessment is only possible if the genealogy is separated from its literary context. If we consider the progression of the story a completely different picture emerges. In the whole of the 'Yahwist' primaeval history (Gen. 2–11) we can detect a very strong anti-city bias (cf. for more details Wittenberg 1995). This is not only clear in Genesis 11, but also emerges from a careful analysis of the Table of Nations in Genesis 10, where the strong men in the genealogy of Ham are the founders of city-based empires (cf. Wittenberg 1991). This anti-city bias is also underlined by changes brought about by the author in his traditional material. They serve not only to link the genealogy with the Cain and Abel narrative, but more specifically to identify the murderer Cain as the founder of the city with all its momentous consequences.

The building of the city seems to contradict God's judgment that Cain should be a fugitive and a wanderer. Hamilton (1990: 238) asks how we can explain the shift in Cain's lifestyle. Could it perhaps be an act of defiance? But he rejects this possibility, because nowhere in Genesis 4 does God state his displeasure with Cain's urban enterprise. But this is not a valid objection, because, as we shall see presently, God does not react to the boasting of Lamech either, although it poses a direct challenge to God's prohibition of blood vengeance. It is a characteristic of the genealogy of Cain that God is silent. Cain and his descendants have separated themselves from God, they have become 'emancipated', autonomous, no longer concerned about the commands of God. At the same time they have also become 'emancipated' from the Earth. In a conscious choice Cain frees himself from the existence of a vagrant and a wanderer by building a city. He also frees himself from the burden of having to till the soil. City culture allows him to become independent of the drudgery of the life of a peasant. By building the city Cain demonstrates that his life of wandering away from the Earth is no longer a concern for him. He has found a new security within his own city walls. Genesis 11.4 is almost an exact parallel. There the people are afraid of an existence like Cain's and therefore decide to build a city 'otherwise we shall be scattered abroad upon the face of the whole earth' (compare the formulations in Gen. 4.14 *gerashta...me al peney ha adamah* with *pen naphuts al peney kol ha arets.*)[3]

In Gen. 4.20-22 the descendants of Cain are depicted as the ancestors of prominent urban crafts. The narrator therefore presents Cain not only as the founder of a city but as the ancestor of city culture as such (Wallis 1966: 134). Because these new city dwellers are 'emancipated' from the Earth they are no longer directly dependent on the *adamah*. Tubal, also mentioned in Ezek. 27.13 as owner of copper mines, was most probably a guild of well-known smiths and welders of bronze and other metals (Wallis 1966: 134). The double name Tubal-qain firmly links him with the first of the line, Cain (Coote and Ord 1989: 79). Yabal, 'the father of those who live in tents and raise livestock' does not refer to nomads, but those raising and tending livestock for urban stock owners (Wallis 1966: 134; Coote and Ord 1989: 79). Jubal is identified as the ancestor of the musicians, again an urban craft characterized by its restlessness and lack of attachment to the soil.

Cain and his descendants had considered that it was good and beneficial for them to become autonomous and 'emancipated' from the Earth by building the city, but they still needed to eat and their food ultimately had to come from the soil, the *adamah*. How could they secure their food supply? It was only possible by violence, only by extortion, exploitation and oppression of the peasant populations producing the food. The city, from its inception is therefore linked with violence. This is shown by Lewis Mumford (1966: 40-69) in his book *The City in History*. He claims that the early city, almost from the beginning, was based on violence, war and aggression on a scale unknown to palaeo-neolithic village communities. Mumford believes that it was the introduction of kingship that produced an overall change and led to the emergence of cities in the true sense of the word. With the king in command of its entire manpower, the city

---

3. The use of the term *erets* for 'Earth' is more appropriate here because it is not only restricted to the arable land, but applies to the whole Earth.

became a permanently mobilized standing army, held in reserve. Royal power measured its strength and divine favour by its capacities 'for pillage, destruction, and extermination' (1966: 65). The author of the primaeval history basically stresses the same point.

It is consistent with the path chosen by Cain that one of his descendants, Lamech, is the prototype of a violent city king. While Cain accepted the judgment on murder by Yahweh, for Lamech violence and murder became the source of boasting (Drewermann 1976: 165). By boasting in front of his two wives Adah and Zillah, Lamech stresses his right to do as he pleases. He even challenges Yahweh who had prohibited revenge by consciously referring to his judgment (Gen. 4.15), and claims the right of exacting his own revenge not only sevenfold but seventy-sevenfold on anyone standing in his way. 'I have killed a man for my bruise, a boy for my injury' (Gen. 4.23). By placing *ish* and *jeled* in parallelism the narrator emphasizes the youthfulness of Lamech's victim: 'in order to draw out the utter illegitimacy of the act. The picture is of the strongest man in the society killing one of the weakest men in society, a mere boy' (Coote and Ord 1989: 80).

Coote and Ord (1989: 80) make the following comment:

> City culture emerged from Yahweh's attempt to dampen the revenge element by putting a protective mark on Cain. By this point in the story, revenge has instead gone rampant. Royal culture is supposed to suppress endemic revenge. In this *exposé* of royal urban culture, urban culture is exposed as the worst fosterer of revenge of all.

In all this it is remarkable that Yahweh does not say a word. Also the Earth which was drinking so much blood is not mentioned at all. That does not mean that Yahweh condones the violence. Rather, it is an ominous sign. Humankind has become so alienated from the Earth and from Yahweh that Yahweh no longer speaks to them. They are ripe for the Flood.

Hope of a New Relationship with the Earth: Genesis 4.25-26; 5.29

The short list of the descendants of Seth in Gen. 4.25-26 is not an originally independent genealogy (Westermann 1984: 338; cf. also von Rad 1978: 112) nor a bridge passage inserted by an editor to connect the genealogy of J (the Yahwistic material) in Gen. 4.17-26 with that of P (the Priestly material) in Genesis 5 (Coats 1983: 68, Wenham 1987: 98), but, as Miller (1974) has shown, consciously created by the author of the story out of a stock genealogy of ten generations still preserved in Genesis 5. The purpose was to create a contrast between two genealogies, the one starting with Cain and leading to the destruction of the Flood, the other starting with Seth and leading to Noah and the future human race, kindling the hope that the disastrous decisions of Cain—which broke all relationships, not only within the human family but with God and the Earth as well—would not be repeated.

The parallelism of the two genealogies is striking in the two sons of Seth and Cain respectively. *Enosh* is a synonym for *adam*, human. He would be the founder of the *human race* belonging to the line of Seth; just as *Enoch*, which means 'to consecrate the founding of', who is closely linked with the first city, is the inaugurator of the branch of humankind that would end in the Flood (Cassuto 1961: 246; Coote and Ord 1989: 78). The antithesis between the descendants of Cain and the descendants of Seth is also implicit in the statement in Gen. 4.26b: 'At that time people began to call upon the name of Yahweh.' Cain had moved away from Yahweh's presence (Gen. 4.16) and Lamech had openly challenged Yahweh's statute (Gen. 4.15) and placed himself, in making his decision over human life and death, in Yahweh's place. As a result the relationship was totally broken. Yahweh no longer spoke to them. But now among Seth's descendants the relationship is restored. People began again to worship Yahweh. Considering the context of the story the extensive discussion in scholarship concerning the beginning of the Yahweh cult seems misplaced. The text is not concerned with the beginning of the specific worship of Yahweh as a datum of the history of religions, but with the story of a progressive restoration of broken relationships that comes to its culmination in the healing of the breach with the Earth under Noah.

There is general agreement among scholars that the statement about Noah in Gen. 5.29 belongs to J although it is now part of the genealogy of Adam in P. There is, however, no unanimity regarding which genealogy it originally belonged to, that of Cain or of Seth. According to the genealogy recorded in P, Noah was the son of Lamech. But due to the rearrangement of the lists by J, Noah could no longer be the son of Lamech. The explanation of Noah's name would have been totally out of place in his mouth. Lamech as a brutal city king would not have been concerned about the soil (*adamah*) that Yahweh had cursed (a clear reference to Gen. 3.17), nor would he have hoped for some one to 'bring relief from our work and from the toil of our hands'. He would not have toiled himself as a tiller of the ground, but would have let others work for him. The Cainite genealogy in J has to end with Lamech (cf. also Drewermann 1976: 164). It is therefore clear from the context that Noah has to be the son of Enosh in the genealogy of Seth.

The explanation of Noah's name, '*This one shall bring us comfort from our work*', does not fit the root *nuach* 'to rest' but alludes to the root *nacham* 'to comfort' (Cassuto 1961: 288). The progression of the story shows that the work of comforting does fit Noah very well, because he was the first to plant a vineyard (Gen. 9.20) (Drewermann 1976: 169). This statement has been elaborated by the addition 'arising from the ground which Yahweh has cursed' *(min ha adamah)*. The reference to Yahweh's curse on the ground in Gen. 3.17 at the end of the chapter that deals with progressive alienation of humankind from the Earth, though rather awkward stylistically, is crucial for the narrator. Here at the end of this section of the Earth story the name of Noah gives rise to the hope that the relationship of humankind with the Earth might be healed (in the original text Enosh, the human, would have said these words).

Genesis 5.29 clearly points beyond itself, to the Flood narrative and the new beginning after it. There is hope of a restored relationship between humankind and the Earth because there is one, Noah, who found favour *(chen)* in the sight of Yahweh (Gen. 6.8). In what way was Noah righteous *(tsaddiq)* before God so that God decided to save him in the Flood? 'According to the Old Testament the *tsaddiq* "righteous person" does justice to a relationship in which he stands' (von Rad 1978: 120). Nothing is mentioned about his relationship with other humans apart from the great hopes attached by others to his name. His relationship with God was right because, as a member of the family of Seth and Enosh, he worshipped Yahweh. But all these relationships are not specifically mentioned by the narrator. He places the emphasis on one particular relationship, Noah's relationship with the Earth. Noah was a man of the soil, an *ish ha adamah* (Gen. 9.20). Because he was a man of the soil, he was chosen by God to cultivate the Earth after the Flood. It was Noah who as a first act after the Flood built an altar to Yahweh. Yahweh then gave the solemn promise: 'I will never again curse the ground *(adamah)* because of humankind... As long as the Earth *(erets)* endures, seed time and harvest, cold and heat, summer and winter, day and night, shall not cease' (Gen. 8.22). The rhythm of the seasons with all the chores characteristic of the life on the land will endure. Life can now start anew. It is no wonder that Noah was the first to plant a vineyard, which reminds us of the trees that God planted in the garden of Eden.

Conclusion

The remaining chapters of the primaeval history show that although the descendants of Cain were wiped out by the Flood the spirit of Cain lived on among the descendants of Ham the son of the righteous Noah. Alienation and 'emancipation' from the Earth reappeared with the great city and empire builders (Gen. 10) and the people who built the city and the tower of Babel (Gen. 11). The Earth story in Genesis 4 teaches that right relationship between humans and fellow humans, with God and the Earth, ultimately rests on a decision: a decision for separation from the community of interconnected living things and domination as seen in the path taken by Cain and the builders of the first cities with concomitant violence against fellow human beings and the Earth; or a decision for a close relationship with the soil as taken by Noah. For a new ecojustice hermeneutic this means that only by deciding to become again 'people of the land' and recognizing mutuality and interdependence with all creatures of the Earth will there be a chance of overcoming the environmental crisis. The choice is ours.[4]

4.   How wrong choices can lead to the break up of the bond between humans and the Earth has been shown by Vandana Shiva (1991) in her brilliant case study on the impact of the Green Revolution on the agriculture of India. Farmers in the rural areas are 'exploited by the needs of the urban elites for cheap food and raw material. The Green Revolution strategy was in fact a strategy for creating cheap food surpluses for the growing urban/industrial centres' (1991: 178). The conscious decision for 'improving' the food production in India by introducing the hybrid 'high yielding varieties' of wheat and rice and farming not with nature but against it led to the breakdown of a stable and balanced relationship between the rural population and the Earth. 'Ecological breakdown in nature and political breakdown of society were consequences of a policy based on tearing apart both nature and society' (Shiva 1991: 24).

Ecojustice: A Study of Genesis 6.11-13

Anne Gardner

Introduction

The Earth (*erets*) was destroyed (*tishacheth*)
in the view[1] of God[2] and the earth (*erets*) was filled with violence
(*chamas*).
[12]And God saw the earth (*erets*) and behold it was destroyed (*nishchath*)
for all flesh had caused the destruction (*hishchith*) of his way upon the
earth (*erets*).
[13]And God said to Noah 'The end of all flesh comes before me for the
earth (*erets*) is filled with violence (*chamas*) because of[3] them and behold
I will destroy them (*mashchitham*) with the earth (*erets*)'.[4]

In the space of three verses the word 'earth' (*erets*) appears six times, a
form of the verb 'to destroy' (*shachath*) appears four times, and 'all
flesh' (*col basar*) and 'violence' (*chamas*) twice each. Such repetition
throws the spotlight upon the earth, upon its state of being as well as
upon the role played by 'all flesh' in filling it with 'violence' (*chamas*).
Despite this the earth has not been the focal point of scholarly discussion; rather the focus has been the 'violence' of 'all flesh'. It is
hoped that the present essay will go some way to remedying this situation and contribute to an ecojustice reading of the text.

Links with Genesis 1

Genesis 6.11-13 is part of what has previously been identified as the P
account.[5] Whatever criticisms there may be concerning the documen-

---

1.   Literally 'in the face of'. usually translated as 'before'. Here. 'in the view of'.

tary source theory both in general[6] and in relation to the flood story in particular,[7] Gen. 6.11-13 links in linguistic usage and thought with an earlier P narrative, the first story of creation (Gen.1.1–2.4a). That the writer of Gen. 6.12-13 framed his narrative in line with Genesis 1 is clear: in a deliberate contrast he picks up the pattern of Genesis 1 and reverses it. The original 'And God said...and God saw' now becomes 'And God saw...and God said'. Further, Gen. 1.31, 'And God saw all he had made [including the earth] and behold it was very good', is provided with a shocking counterpart by Gen. 6.12: 'And God saw the earth and behold it was destroyed' (cf. Westermann 1984b: 416). In addition, in Gen. 6.13 God tells Noah that the 'end' is coming for all flesh, contrasting with the 'beginning' of Gen. 1.1.

In Genesis 1 the earth was brought into being by God in two stages: (1) on the second day, as part of the lower firmament it was separated from the upper firmament (Gen. 1.6-8); (2) on the third day, the waters of the lower firmament were gathered together and the dry land appeared which God called 'earth' (*erets*) (Gen. 1.9-10). Immediately afterwards, still on the third day, at God's command the earth brought forth seed yielding grass and fruit trees with their own internal seed (Gen. 1.11-12). Both the earth and its produce were perceived as 'good' by God (Gen. 1.10-12) (cf. Habel [ed.] 2000: 11).

The Earth as 'Destroyed' in Genesis 6.11, 12

It has been posited that 'earth' (*erets*) in Gen. 6.11-13 should be understood as 'civilization' (Zipor 1991: 367). This is unlikely because of the strong links with Genesis 1, where the earth is defined as a physical entity—as dry land which is a habitat, a source of life and of food upon which all land creatures were dependent (cf. Gen. 1.24, 29-30). What had happened in the meantime that this same 'earth' (*erets*) should be described as 'destroyed' (from the verb *shachath*)? In what

---

6.   A discussion of the documentary source theory and the views of its opponents appears in Knight (1985: 263-96).

7.   Westermann (1984: 395-98) delineates the J (Yahwist author) and P narratives in the flood story and discusses the differences and relationship between them. Wenham (1987) questions the putative separate nature of these sources, pointing out that it is only when they are combined that they present an account of the flood that resembles the Mesopotamian versions. The difficulty of assigning some passages to one source or another with absolute certainty is apparent to the present writer. Nevertheless, this paper will presume the existence of both sources, deal with P passages first and only consider J passages in a secondary way.

way was it destroyed? These are questions which need to be answered if Gen. 6.11-13 is to be understood.

The frequent translation of *shachath* as 'corrupt' (Gen. 6.11, 12) does not convey in modern English idiom the true import of the Hebrew (although it did in the days of King James!). It is clear from the occurences of *shachath* in the forms in which it appears in Gen. 6.11, 12 that physical, rather than moral or metaphorical, destruction is intended, but as the commentators have not reached this firm conclusion it is necessary to peruse the evidence.

The same form (niphal perfect) of the verb 'destroy' (*shachath*) which appears in Gen. 6.12 also appears in Jer. 13.7 and 18.4. In Jer. 13.1-7 the prophet is instructed by God to put on a linen girdle but not to get it wet. He is then told to go to the 'Euphrates'[8] and to hide the girdle in the hole of a rock. After some time Jeremiah is ordered by God to retrieve the girdle and when he does so it is *nishchath*. The text makes the meaning of *nishchath* absolutely clear when it adds 'it [the girdle] was profitable for nothing' (Jer. 13.7; cf. Jer. 13.10). In other words the physical state of the garment had been so altered that it could no longer serve its original purpose. The other occurence of the niphal perfect of *shachath* concerns a clay vessel made by a potter (Jer. 18.4). The vessel was *nishchath* 'in the hand of the potter' so much so that he had to make another one.[9] This text, like Jer. 13.7, deals with an item which is ruined *physically*, which cannot fulfil its intended function. By analogy, the earth in Gen. 6.12 is ruined to the extent that it cannot fulfil its original purpose either (i.e. as a source of life, habitat for, and sustainer of, land creatures).

In Gen. 6.11 the niphal imperfect form of the verb *shachath* ('destroy') appears. There is one other occurence of it in conjunction with 'earth' (*erets*). The particular text is Exod. 8.20 (Hebrew; 8.24 ET) and it is necessary to investigate it closely as the biblical text and its commentators do not specify whether *erets* should be understood as 'civilization' or as the physical earth. Exodus 8.20 (24) reads, 'the earth was destroyed because of a swarm'.[10] Most English translations add

---

8.   According to Bright (1965: 96), the reference is more likely to be to Parah, north east of Anathoth, Jeremiah's home town, than to the Euphrates river which is about 350 miles away. In Hebrew Parah and Euphrates sound very similar.

9.   Cassuto (1964: 53) also refers to Jer. 18.4. However he reads the whole incident of the clay vessel as a parable that indicates in the flood story that God would annihilate humankind and then remake it.

10.   The word *arov*, translated as 'swarm', is related linguistically to the noun *erev* ('evening') and its verbal form which appears in Isa. 24.11 with the meaning of 'darken'. This suggests that the primary meaning of *arov* is 'something which

'of flies' but this goes beyond the Hebrew text which does not define the creatures involved. The word *arov* ('swarm') occurs only in Exodus 8 (seven times) and in Pss. 78.45; 105.31. All these texts refer to one of the plagues of Egypt, indeed, presumably to the same plague. In none of them is a specific creature indicated.[11] Exodus 8.17 (Hebrew; 8.21 ET) says that as well as settling upon Pharaoh, his servants, the people and the houses, the swarm was also upon the ground (*erets*). If the identification of the 'swarm' as insects is correct, what damage, if any, can they do to the ground or the land in a physical sense? Investigation of this matter revealed that 'several species of flies are pests of agricultural and horticultural activities' (Hadlington and Gerozisis 1988: 113); indeed they can be 'pests of fruit and vegetable production' (Hadlington and Gerozisis 1988: 45). A number of other species of flying insects can also cause devastation to agricultural production: termites, which can damage trees and crops; moths and butterflies, usually admired for their beauty, produce young ones whose 'voracious appetites make them loathesome in the eyes of the farmer' (Hadlington and Gerozisis 1988: 45), and some species of bees and wasps can be 'foliage eaters' (Hadlington and Gerozisis 1988: 47). Locusts, whose destruction of vegetation is well known, have to be excluded from the present plague as they are cited specifically in connection with a later plague (Exod. 10.12-19). It is apparent that flying insects, other than locusts, can impose physical degradation upon the produce of the earth and there is every reason to take the claim of Exod. 8.20 (24) that 'the land was destroyed because of a swarm' in a physical, rather than a metaphorical, sense.

By analogy with its appearance in Exod. 8.20 (24), the niphal of *shachath* in Gen. 6.11 posits physical destruction of the produce of the land. This coheres with what was discovered about the earth in Gen. 6.12, namely, that it had suffered physical destruction in some way.

All Flesh and the Destruction of his/its Way

Genesis 6.12 posits that the earth had been destroyed because 'all flesh had caused the destruction of his/its way upon the earth'. Before proceeding to a delineation of what God required of his crea-

darkens', hence the translation 'swarm' as a swarm of flying creatures that does darken the daylight.

11.   Later tradition attempted to elucidate the matter: the Septuagint supplied 'dog flies'; R. Nehemiah in *Exodus Rabbah* uses 'gnats and mosquitos'; while Josephus, R. Judah in *Exodus Rabbah* and the Targum suggested a 'mixture of birds and beasts'. Cited under the heading 'Plagues' in *EncJud* XIII.

tures, the term 'all flesh' needs to be discussed because some commentators, ancient and modern, limit its applicability to human beings (cf. Westermann 1984b: 415; Lewis 1968: 93). In the P account of the flood story 'all flesh' appears elsewhere in Gen. 6.17, 19; 7.21; 9.11, 15-17. Genesis 6.17 defines 'all flesh' as those creatures who have 'the breath of life' and reiterates God's intention to destroy them. The following verses (18-21) are God's instructions to Noah as to who and what should be taken on the ark to avoid total annihilation: as well as Noah and his family, two of every kind of land and air creatures (specified as every living thing of all flesh), as well as food for all concerned were to be included. Genesis 7.21, which echoes 1.21-27 of the creation story, says, 'And all flesh died which moved upon the earth, including birds, cattle, beasts, all creeping ones who creep upon the earth and all mankind [*sic*]'.

After the flood God promises, in 9.11, 'I will never again cut off all flesh by the waters of a flood'. The previous verses, 9.9-10, talk about the establishment of a covenant with Noah and his seed (9.9) and with every living creature which was in the ark (9.10). The last two occurences of 'all flesh' (Gen. 9.15, 17) concern the rainbow as a sign of the covenant made in the above passage.

In every occurrence in the P narrative of the flood, 'all flesh' includes all sentient beings of land and air.[12] This indicates, with reference to Gen. 6.12, that animals and birds as well as humankind had gone against the way of life prescribed for them by God. The 'way' for all creatures is specified in Gen. 1.28-30 and so an investigation into the meaning of 'the destruction of his/its way' necessarily entails looking at that text. Further, Gen. 9.1-7 modifies the specifications of Gen. 1.28-30 and as Frymer-Kensky (1977: 152) asserts, throws light on the causes of the flood. Forward references to Gen. 9.1-7 therefore are necessary also.

How Did Non-Humans Transgress the Way?

A directive was issued to 'every beast of the earth and every bird of the air and everything which creeps upon the earth' in Gen. 1.30 that they may have 'every green herb as food'. In other words, no dispen-

---

12. Westermann (1984: 416) disputes that a decision can be made concerning the meaning of 'all flesh' from its occurrences in P, believing that Gen. 9.15 indicates animals only. This is unlikely, for God, addressing Noah, makes a covenant between 'you and me' and 'all flesh', which surely applies to human beings other than Noah as well as to non-humans.

sation was given to eat meat and thus no permission granted to attack or kill other creatures (cf. Rashi, cited in Skinner 1930: 159). That non-violence of all creatures was viewed as the ideal can be seen in Isa. 11.6-8 where normally predatory creatures such as the wolf, leopard, lion, bear and asp live in peace with defenceless beings such as a lamb, kid and a child. It is asserted that this will be the situation when 'the earth is full of the knowledge of the Lord'.[13] This ideal is echoed in Isa. 65.25.

Interestingly, in connection with the meaning of 'his/its way' in Gen. 6.12, Isa. 65.2, prior to a list of human wrongdoings, specifies that they are effected by people 'who walk in a way not good, after their own thoughts'. In other words, not in the way specified by God.[14]

Non-humans could have transgressed against God's way as specified in Gen. 1.30 by eating foodstuffs other than vegetation. This would have required feeding on dead bodies or killing other creatures. By analogy with the murdered Abel's blood crying to God from the ground, this would have caused pollution. Certainly 'all flesh', including non-humans, is indicted in Gen. 6.13 with 'filling the earth with violence'. Another possibility is that non-humans were unrestrained in their eating of vegetation and thus caused the destruction of vast areas of once fertile land.[15]

How did humankind go against God's prescriptions for it? In Gen. 1.28-29 God instructs humans

> [28](a) Be fruitful and multiply
> (b) Fill the earth and subdue it
> (c) Have dominion over the fish of the sea
> and over the birds of the air
> and over every living being that lives on the earth.

---

13. Interestingly, in the J account, enmity between the snake, the woman and their respective seed in Gen. 3.15 resulted from disobedience to God.

14. Sacks (1990: 55) has an extended discussion of the meaning of 'the way'. As Cassuto (1964) points out, 'way' in Gen. 6.12 links with Noah walking with God (Gen. 6.9). It is interesting that Isa. 65.2 also links 'walk' and 'way'.

15. Later Jewish tradition, in the interests of defending justice, speculated why non-humans were killed in the flood. Lewis (1968: 132) cites R. Azariah who, upon the authority of R. Judah, asserted that the animals were destroyed because they had interbred across species. A similar thought appears in *Jub.* 5.2; 7.24; *1 En.* 7.5 and *Midrash Tanhuma Noah* 12, as pointed out by Kugel (1997: 118). Kugel also draws attention to the contrasting view of Philo in *Quaest. in Gen.* 2.9, who asserted that the animals were destroyed because they were part of the general body of creatures and when their head (humankind) was cut off, so they too died.

[29](d) I have given you every herb
bearing seed upon the face of the whole earth
and every tree in whose fruit its seed is contained
as food for you.

The division between the precepts is set out here in four stages. It is necessary to emphasize this as many commentators: (1) read the first half of precept 'b' ('Fill the earth') with the previous instruction ('Be fruitful and multiply'); and (2) discuss the second half of precept 'b' ('subdue it') with what follows ('Have dominion'). In other words the earth story has been virtually ignored. The four precepts address four different spheres:

(a) humans;
(b) the earth and humankind's relationship to the earth;
(c) non-human creatures and humankind's relationship to them;
(d) the gift of herbs and fruit as food.

To repeat the question posed above: in what ways did humans disobey God's instructions encompassed in this passage? It is clear from the only other P narrative in Genesis prior to the flood that humakind fulfilled the first prescription: it was fruitful and did multiply (Gen. 5.1-28, 30-32). The second prescription, 'Fill the earth and subdue it' is usually taken by commentators to:

(1) refer to humans filling the earth with themselves;
(2) to subduing the earth or its produce in a harsh way.

As these clauses are of prime importance in a paper dealing with the perspective of the earth a review of them is necessary.

The notion that 'fill the earth' is a further reference to human multiplication is argued by analogy with Gen. 1.22 where God instructs water and air creatures, 'Be fruitful and multiply, fill the waters'. This is correct, but it needs to be stressed that humans are being ordered to spread throughout the earth which would put them in a better position to 'subdue it'.

The 'subdue' (*kabash*) of Gen. 1.28 implies force or subjugation of the earth. In his chapter in this volume, Norman Habel gives a summary of the occurences of the verb in the Hebrew Bible and concludes that an ecofriendly meaning of the term in Gen. 1.28 is not possible. G. Auld (1998: 63-68) very ably draws attention to the fact that the subjugation of the earth was seen as a quite unremarkable statement by commentators until recent years. He then shows, in quite an amusing fashion, some of the unsuccessful attempts of scholars to wriggle out of the full implication of the word by positing some form of agricultural domination. Auld himself suggests that the word 'subdue' may have accreted to Gen. 1.28 from Josh. 18.1, which is part of the conquest tradition. This is an attractive thesis and may be correct in terms of vocabulary usage, but Joshua is unlikely to be the origin of the concept as the tradition of the earth being subjugated appears in Ps. 8.7 (Hebrew; ET 8.6) also, although it is expressed in different words. There God puts everything 'under his [humankind's] feet'. The date of Psalm 8 is unknown but it is possible that it comes from the pre-exilic period (cf. Craigie 1983: 106). This would exonerate Joshua from what appears to the ecoconscious person to be a blight upon the landscape of Genesis 1.

The question must be posed: if humans were given the remit to subdue the earth, what were they subduing? It was not plant life, for herbs and the fruit from trees were only given to humans for food *after* they were told to 'subdue' (Gen. 1.29). The earth itself was perceived by God to be good (Gen. 1.10, 12) so why is the heavy artillery to be brought in against the earth, for such is the implication of 'subdue'. The answer may well lie in the power or spirit of the earth itself, a power/spirit which was made manifest in the nature religions of the surrounding nations where the earth, or aspects of the earth, were deified.[16] Scholars have long seen in the non-naming of the sun and moon in Genesis 1 an attempt to strip these luminaries of any godlike status which they enjoyed in other cultures (cf. Skinner 1930: 25; von Rad 1972a: 55-56),[17] but to my knowledge it has not been suggested before that the subjection of the earth was for a similar reason. That a polemic against the power of the earth and the heavenly bodies was in play in Israel can be seen from other texts which stress God's lordship over heaven and earth (e.g. Gen. 14.19, 22; Pss. 108.6 [Hebrew; ET 108.5]; 148.13). Genesis 1.28 then advocates a suppression of the voice of the earth, in the interests of the supremacy of the God of Israel.

The biblical statements made in the aftermath of the flood will be explored now to see what light they shed on the failure of humans in terms of the second precept, 'Fill the earth and subdue it'. There are two statements in Genesis 9 which relate to and partially repeat Gen. 1.28ab. They are Gen. 9.1 and Gen. 9.7. The former repeats Gen. 1.28ab, 'Be fruitful and multiply, and fill the earth', but omits the permission

16. For future information cf. Ruether (1985: 36-44). There is also a polemic against goddess worship in Gen. 3 cf. Gardner (1990).

17. Habel, in this volume, emphasizes the function of the heavenly bodies as light-givers for the earth rather than their non-naming as indicative of a polemic against their adoption as deities by other cultures of the time.

to 'subdue'. The latter, Gen. 9.7, 'Be fruitful and multiply; bring forth abundance in the earth and multiply therein' matches the first clause of Gen. 1.28 but differs thereafter: 'fill' is replaced by 'bring forth abundance', and 'subdue' by 'multiply'.[18] The verb *sharats*, used for 'bringing forth abundance', is ambiguous: it can refer to people increasing in number (Exod. 1.7) or to an increase in the produce of the natural environment (Gen. 1.21; cf. Gen. 1.20). It is likely that both aspects are included in Gen. 9.7 and if this is so, it would suggest that after the flood humans were given a new precept: to increase the earth's natural produce. This notion is given support by Noah planting a vineyard in the immediate postdiluvian period (Gen. 9.20, a J passage).[19] It also implies that prior to the flood the produce of the earth was *de*creased. It is noteworthy that in Gen. 9.7, as Gen. 9.1, permission to subdue the earth was withdrawn!

Humankind's third prescription in Gen. 1.28 is to 'have dominion over the fish of the sea and over the birds of the air and over the cattle and over every creeping thing which creeps upon the earth'. As many commentators have noticed, 'have dominion over' (*radah*) implies kingly rule (e.g. Westermann 1984: 159; Wenham 1987: 33; D.T. Williams 1993: 59-60). There can of course be good kings who care for their subjects and bad kings who exploit those under their dominion. In Genesis the remit of kingly rule is given to humans 'made in the image of God' (Gen. 1.26), a statement which serves to qualify the nature of the rule. Two texts from elsewhere in the Hebrew Bible make it clear that the dominion of a godlike king would create (1) harmony with the physical earth (Ps. 72.3); (2) the non-violence of other creatures (Isa. 11.6-8). This does not exclude the godlike king exercising the harsher aspect of his dominion in cases where the safety or

18. The Lucianic recension of the Septuagint reads *radah* as 'have dominion over' in place of *rabah* 'multiply'. This is a possibility as the two words are similar and there may have been a scribal error in the Hebrew. In support of this it could be claimed that 'multiply' crept in because it appeared in the first clause of Gen. 9.7. If so, a better parallel with Gen. 1.28 would be created. The matter is complex though and it is just as likely that *rabah* 'multiply' and *radah* 'have dominion over' appeared by analogy with Gen. 1.28.

19. Scholars have expressed puzzlement as to why Noah was said to plant a vineyard. They tend to assume that it has been included only to introduce the subject of Noah's drunkenness and the differing treatment of him by his sons; e.g. Skinner (1930: 183). Brueggemann (1982: 89) subscribes to the notion that Gen. 9.20 provides the context for what follows. He then adds, 'Almost in passing, verse 20 identifies Noah as the one who cares for the earth...it...suggests that Noah fulfils the mandate given to the first man (1.28)'. This suggests that Brueggemann views 'subdue' in an agricultural light.

freedom of his subjects was threatened; Ps. 72.9 has the king's enemies licking the dust, whereas in Isa. 11.4 the ruler 'will slay the
wicked'. In connection with Gen. 1.28 it implies that human beings
were to live in accord with God and to direct non-humans, protecting
the weak and overruling other creatures who would harm them in
some way.

As 'the earth was destroyed (or ruined)' prior to the flood (Gen.
6.11, 12), it is implied that humankind had not fulfilled its remit;
instead it had 'destroyed its way'. It would seem likely that human
beings failed to act in accordance with the second two prescriptions of
Gen. 1.28: they did not *fill* the earth with *themselves in a way which promoted the welfare of the earth*. Instead, in a supreme irony, they *filled* it
with *violence* (Gen. 6.11, 13). They did not exercise the desirable form
of dominion over other creatures. It may be that they allowed them to
denude areas of the earth of vegetation and took no steps to prevent
their slaughter of other creatures for food. It may even be that human
beings themselves transgressed the precept of Gen. 1.29 and instead
of being herbivores became carnivores, eating 'the flesh' of other
species. In fact there may be a pointer in the direction of the latter
misdeed: the exclusion of eating blood (Gen. 9.4), in the opinion of
Frymer-Kensky (1977: 152), suggests a limitation on what had been
the practice prior to the flood. The other prescription after the flood
against the shedding of blood concerns the blood of humans.

Chamas ('Violence') Filled the Earth

The blood taboos may well contribute to the notion of 'violence'
(*chamas*) with which all flesh filled the earth (Gen. 6.11, 13) prior to the
flood. It is clear, however, that *chamas* can not be limited to human
violence, for although a number of biblical appearances of the word
do relate to bloodshed, for example Judg. 9.24; Joel 4.19 (3.19), many
do not. A number of scholars have undertaken an analysis of the
occurences of the word *chamas* ('violence') in the Hebrew Bible and
their conclusions vary from the specific to the general: Harland (1996:
44) thinks that it concerns social crimes and he sees murder as the primary cause of the flood; Frymer-Kensky (1977: 150-54) relates it to
wrongs committed in the absence of laws and the resulting pollution
of the land; Haag (1975), in a thoroughgoing analysis, also emphasizes
the socio-ethical aspects but adds 'all *chamas* is ultimately directed
against Yahweh'; Speiser (1964: 51) sees *chamas* in general terms as
'lawlessness'. Cassuto (1964: 52) concludes that it 'signifies generally
anything which is not righteous'. He has been criticized for this (cf.

Wenham 1987: 171), but essentially he is correct. His view finds a reflection in Prov. 16.29 which reads, 'A man of *chamas* entices his neighbour and leads him into the way not good'. *Chamas* and 'way not good' are virtual parallels. *Chamas* should then be considered as the opposite of the path God had intended for God's creation. It is a violation, a deviation, a breaking of God's plan. As such it is parallel in meaning to 'the destruction of his way' which appears in Gen. 6.12. Frymer-Kensky (1977: 152; 1983: 409) is right to posit that laws were the antidote to humankind's evil inclination (Gen. 6.5) which led to *chamas*. That individual acts were not specifically prohibited at the time of creation suggests that God expected human beings (and non-humans) to be able to regulate their behaviour in an internal way, conforming to their having been 'made in the image of God' (Gen. 1.26). That they were unable to do so is clear.

At a later time it would be seen by the prophets Jeremiah and Ezekiel (and possibly Hosea) that the laws themselves did not work and they hoped for a new internal regulator of human behaviour (cf. Frymer-Kensky 1983: 412), in other words, what had been expected in the beginning.

All Flesh Is Destroyed 'with the Earth'

In Gen. 6.13, because of all they have done, God vows to destroy all flesh (according to the majority of translators) 'with the earth' (*eth ha arets*). It has been questioned whether the Hebrew text is corrupt at this point, for the previous two verses have posited that the earth has already been subjected to destruction. How can it thus be destroyed again? Various emendations have been proposed to overcome this difficulty (cf. Cassuto 1964: 57-58; Westermann 1984: 417; Zipor 1991: 366-69), while other scholars have attempted to comprehend the text as it stands. As Cassuto (1964: 58) points out, the latter is the most popular option. It has recently been defended by Harland (1993) who, by retaining 'with the earth', is forced to concede that the earth is destroyed a second time. He makes this intelligible by positing that the second destruction consists of the breaking down of the boundary between the dry land and the water. That Harland is correct is evidenced by Gen. 1.10 where in the second stage of the creation of the earth the waters were gathered together and the dry land appeared. As the flood story makes clear, the dry land *dis*-appeared (Gen. 7.11). Against those critics who cannot accept that Gen. 6.13 indicates that God will destroy the earth with all flesh, it should be noted that in Gen. 9.11 God promises, 'There will not be again a flood to destroy the earth'. That particular verse contains no possible ambiguity: by using the key words 'destroy' (*shachath*) and 'earth' (*erets*) which also appeared in Gen. 6.13 it provides corroboration of God's intention. Nevertheless the earth was not annihilated, for when the waters were subsiding, a mountain became visible (Gen. 8.5) and vegetation was in evidence, as the dove sent out by Noah returned with an olive leaf (Gen. 8.11). The flood then allowed the earth to rest and heal itself, and its produce to regenerate.

The Precept of Kabash *('Subduing') Is Withdrawn*

Genesis 6.11-13 shows that all creatures failed to respect the integrity of each other and of the earth (the principle of intrinsic worth). In the case of the earth, this may have come about in part because God, with the intention of overcoming any deification of the earth as happened in nature religions, had earlier given humankind permission to sub-due it (suppression of the voice). That God realized that such a pre-cept led to exploitation (a failure to uphold the principles of intrinsic worth and interconnectedness) is signalled by the withdrawal of such permission after the flood (cf. Gen. 9.7). Even with the precept to 'subdue' in place, if humans had followed God's 'way' (Gen. 6.12) the earth would not have been degraded. To use the language of myth, the failure to treat the earth as 'thou' (cf. Frankfort *et al.* 1946: 12-15) in an 'I–thou' relationship (the principle of intrinsic worth) resulted in the destruction of the environment. Another way of expressing the same truth would be the precept, put forward by Jesus of Nazareth and Hillel the Pharisee, 'Do unto others as you would have them do unto you', widened to include the earth (and non-human life forms).

The biblical story of the causes of the flood (Gen. 6.11-13) in its interplay with Gen. 1.26-30 and God's instructions in the aftermath of the flood clearly show that the earth and its integrity must be respected. It is apparent that permission to 'subdue' the earth had led, in part, to its abuse.[20] Such permission is withdrawn after the flood, a

---

20. It may be that the J source can amplify our knowledge of the ways in which humans failed in their duty towards the earth because (1) it relates the story of Cain and Abel (Gen. 4.2-16) which reflects the conflict between shepherd and pas-toralist (in general terms a pastoralist could exclude the shepherd from his land and its produce, and the shepherd could allow his flock to trample the pastoralist's crops); (2) the building of cities with Enoch (Gen. 4.17; city building requires the clearing of land and thus the removal of vegetation and natural habitat; it may involve forced irrigation so that more food could be produced for urbanites; this would result in salination of the land; further, cities produce large amounts of

detail which has not previously been noted by those concerned with the earth.

The Implications for the Present Time

The failure, prior to the flood, to respect the principles of intrinsic worth and interconnectedness are being repeated in the modern age. To give just a few examples: an injudicious removal of trees without replacing them has led to soil degradation, changes in rainfall patterns, global warming and all that that threatens; stripping areas of natural vegetation without concern for the preservation of flora or habitat for fauna has led to the irrevocable loss of some species and, as humans have now discovered, to their own personal cost, potential sources of medicines have been eliminated; contamination or pollution of the earth or its rivers has caused loss of species but also a reduction in the ability of the earth to sustain habitat or provide sustenance for its creatures. Survival of all life forms is dependent upon a healthy earth and healthy waters: to destroy them is ultimately to threaten one's own species.

waste which, if disposed of in an improper way, render the landscape unsightly or contaminate the ground); (3) mining is implied with the narrative of Tubal-Cain, a worker and instructor in brass and iron (cf. Sawyer 1986) (mining can exploit the earth by disturbing the natural vegetation and habitat; further it produces materials which can be forged into the instruments of war, cf. Rashi, cited in Skinner 1930: 119, a violent pastime that could further degrade the land). In a fascinating Hamito-Semitic philological study, Oduyoye (1984) compares the pre-history related in Genesis with myths/legends that have survived in Africa. He sheds much light on the truncated stories of the Bible.

Mixed Blessings for Animals:
The Contrasts of Genesis 9

John Olley

Introduction

Animals in the richness of their variety have been included in the occupants of the ark, a diversity of which we are reminded in the description of those who came out of the ark (Gen. 8.17, 19). The completeness is emphasized by the repeated *kol*, 'all' (seven times in the two verses). One can only assume that this plentiful diversity is seen as good and is to be maintained.

Yet the first reference to animals in Genesis 9 is to 'the fear and dread' of Noah and his descendants that 'shall rest on every animal of the earth, and on every bird of the air, on everything that creeps on the ground, and on all the fish of the sea' (Gen. 9.2). This time 'fish' are included along with the diversity represented in the ark. Strengthening this is the statement, 'into your hand they are delivered (*natan*) —every moving thing that lives shall be food for you; and just as I gave you the green plants, I give (*natan*) you everything'. As in Genesis 8 there is comprehensiveness, with 'every' (*kol*) as the first and last word of the food statement, but now the sole beneficiary is humankind. Have animals been kept through the flood simply to be human food supply, ruthlessly treated by humans?

A qualification follows, accountability for 'life/blood', required of animals and of humans. What does it mean that animals and humans seem to have accountability?

Read sequentially, the passage takes another surprising turn. Genesis 9.8-17, the passage that records the first covenant in Genesis, involves not only Noah, as might have been expected from the foreshadowing in Gen. 6.18, but explicitly and repeatedly involves 'every living creature' (Gen. 9.10 [twice], 12, 15, 16, 17). A form of the root 'life' occurs six times. There are not two covenants, one with the dominant (important?) Noah, and a lesser one with other 'life'. Rather there is one covenant made equally with both; in fact, once it is simply described as between God 'and the earth' (Gen. 9.13).

How is the juxtaposition of these features to be interpreted? Is it significant that, while the covenant is made with Noah *and* all life, God addresses only Noah and his descendants? Above all, how might this chapter be read when looked at from the perspective of animals? Animals can rightly feel slighted by the lack of attention they receive from commentators. At times there is complete neglect, reflected in the chapter heading supplied in editions of the NRSV and NIV, 'God's Covenant with Noah'. Brueggemann observes that 'we are only beginning to notice and appreciate the accent on nonhuman creatures in the creation theology of the Old Testament', although significantly his comment is in a footnote and in the body of the text he seems to have difficulty recognizing animals as 'covenant partners with Yahweh' (1997: 454). Brueggemann's confession could well be applied to others. The traditions of writing commentaries mean that most writers have to say something, but the comments are usually brief, albeit at times saying no more than the obvious! Some will be cited later.

Animals—A Contrast to Near Eastern Parallels

For many parts of Genesis 1–11 ancient Near Eastern material provides helpful contexts for seeing features of the biblical text. Well-known flood narratives include references to animals in the boat: in *Atrahasis* both domestic and wild creatures are explicitly included, 'Clean (animals)... Fat (animals)... The winged [birds of] the heavens. The cattle (?)... The wild [creatures (?)...]' (3.2.32-37); and in the late Assyrian recension, '[Creatures] of the steppe, all the wild creatures of the steppe that eat grass' [DT 42 (W)] (Lambert and Millard 1969: 92-93, 128-29). These quotes however are the only mention of animals in *Atrahasis*.

Similarly, in the *Epic of Gilgamesh*, the sole reference (other than the sending out of birds) is in the command, 'Aboard the ship take thou the seed of all living things', and the act, 'the beast of the field, the wild creatures of the field... I made go aboard' (11.27, 85-86; Speiser 1969: 93-94). In all of the extant Near Eastern material I have found only one mention of animals after the flood: in the *Eridu Genesis* Ziusdra is made 'preserver, as king, of the name of the small animals and the seed of mankind' (Jacobsen 1997: 515).

Given other features of Genesis 1–11 that stand in contrast to contemporary accounts, it seems most likely that the amount of attention given to animals after the flood is intentional. There is more here than an afterthought or appendage that says simply 'animals were in the ark so they are included afterwards'!

A Priestly Concern?

With Genesis 9 being commonly identified as P (Priestly) material, the possibility of links with similar material is raised. Firmage sees a concern for diet, as in Genesis 1, linking with the food laws in Leviticus and with sacrifice: 'meat was a delicacy. Every time one made a sacrifice, one thanked God for the privilege of eating meat' (1999: 102 n. 16; also 1999: 105). In the significant longer prohibition of the eating of blood, Lev. 17.10-16, the blood is linked with sacrifice ('the blood makes atonement'), although reference is not only to domestic animals (the 'ox, lamb or kid' of Lev. 17.3) but also to animals and birds that can be 'hunted' (Lev. 17.13). In an earlier article Firmage sees Genesis 9 as humans taking 'a step up', becoming more like God, with the 'culmination of a progression in holiness' coming in Leviticus 11 so that clean animals are 'like those which God "eats" (in the form of sacrifices)' (1990: 196-97).

In Genesis, however, there is no hint of any restriction as to the 'living creatures' that can be eaten; nor, in keeping with an assumed Priestly view that sacrifice was not instituted until Sinai, is there an association with sacrifice, other than the present narrative juxtaposition following Genesis 8. (In Gen. 6–8 the 'clean/unclean' distinction is nowhere explained, and there is just one single reference in a narrative context to link with sacrifice, in Gen. 8.20.)

The association with the parallel in Gen. 1.28-30 (P) is obvious, but what do the differences convey? Can 'fear and dread' really be 'a step up'? The phrase now sets humans and animals apart, whereas, as Barth points out in Genesis 1, 'men and animals—irrespective of the dominant position of the former—are associated in the same necessity, the same support and the same permission and command' (1958: 211).

The attention given to 'covenant' (seven times in Gen. 9.10-17; probably a deliberate literary feature and an argument against layers in the text), is seen to be typical of P, especially the phrase, 'eternal covenant'. While elsewhere the covenant sign is linked with human actions (Gen. 17.7, 13, 19: circumcision; Exod. 31.16: Sabbath; Lev. 24.8 and Num. 18.19: the offerings to be brought and eaten by the priests; and Num. 25.13: unilateral promise [reward?] to zealous Phineas regarding his descendants being priests), here

> God binds himself unilaterally…and includes humankind and all other living beings as well…shaken neither by natural catastrophes of any sort nor—and this is most important for P—by the transgressions, corruption or revolt of human beings (Westermann 1984: 473).

One can agree with Westermann's comments, yet it must be said that apart from the emphasis in this passage upon 'covenant', the inclusion of animals in an 'eternal covenant' has to be seen as a characteristic of this passage alone.

Human Appetite and Human Violence

Still, Firmage's analysis is in keeping with a number of commentators through the centuries who have seen little sympathy for animals in this passage. In this case, the key words have become 'God blessed' (Gen. 9.1) and the double use of 'give' (Gen. 9.2-3). Animals are freely given to humans at their pleasure for the enrichment of their diet.

Luther, in his usual bold language, explains that the provision is 'to make up, as it were, for the great sorrow that pious Noah experienced during the flood... Accordingly, ...dumb animals are made subject to man for the purpose of serving him even to the extent of dying' (Pelikan 1960: 133-34). The mediaeval Jewish commentator Ramban had also seen meat eating as a response to Noah, 'because of his role in their [the animals'] rescue from the flood' (Firmage 1990: 204; Firmage says Ramban is unique). The modern Cassuto follows Ramban in seeing a link with Noah's actions, but as only a 'permission', the prohibition on eating blood serving 'in a sense, to remind us that rightly all parts of the flesh should have been forbidden' (Cassuto 1961: 58-59, 1964: 126).

There have been other voices who have placed more emphasis upon the restriction of Gen. 9.4: 'Only, you shall not eat flesh with its life, that is, its blood.' Sometimes, when reading the flood narrative as a whole, attention is drawn to the statement that human behaviour has not changed: as before the flood, 'the inclination of the human heart is evil from youth' (Gen. 8.21; compare Gen. 6.5), noting in Genesis 6 the focus on human 'violence' (Gen. 6.11, 13). The emphasis shifts now to God's 'permission' as a concession, seeking to lessen the inevitable effects of human 'evil desires' (recognizing that the heart is where decisions are made). 'This might conceivably be intended as an outlet for his violent impulses' (Alter 1996: 38). Is this comment a reflection in the light of ancient and modern cultures that exhibit the (male) propensity for the 'sport'(!) of hunting?

Westermann rightly recognizes the tension in the passage, between the delivering into human hands and 'the good will of the creator toward every living being', between the 'gift of blessing' (the verb 'give') and the 'possibility of taking life'. Yet, in commenting on P's linking of the two prohibitions of Gen. 9.4 and 9.5, he highlights 'the danger of blood-lust...of killing for the sake of killing' (1984: 462-63).

Surprisingly, some see even the draining of blood as positive. Most recently Walton and Matthews, linking with the blood sacrifice, see 'recognition that they have taken the life with permission and are partaking of God's bounty as his guests. Its function is not unlike that of the blessing said before a meal in modern practice' (1997: 30). However, as I have already noted, although Leviticus 17 relates to sacrifice, there is no link explicitly made in Genesis 9. Have commentators read too much from other passages and not heard the distinctive emphases of this passage itself? Just as readers have used Gen. 1.28 to justify exploitation, has the thrust of Genesis 9 been similarly subverted for human ends, focusing on 'I give' but neglecting the context?

It cannot be fortuitous that there is a close linking of permission to eat flesh and strong statements about human killing. Is there not in the foreground of this section a strong recognition of human violence and the need for divine sanctions? If the eating of flesh is so positive, why is there the juxtaposition of the statement about human killing of humans as well as animals? It is this explicit link with violence that enables the reader to link with the earlier statements on human 'evil' while the non-mention of sacrifice disallows that link.

Is there not also in the statement about 'blood' the awareness that somehow something is not right? One can compare the kind of sensitivity in the prohibition on taking both a mother bird and her young or eggs (Deut. 22.6-7), and in the traditional interpretation, at least since Philo, of not boiling a kid in its mother's milk as an inappropriate mixing of symbols of life and death (Exod. 23.19b; the link with possible Canaanite fertility practice is now questioned with reinterpretation of Ugaritic material, e.g., Milgrom 1985). The tragic awareness that somehow the relationship is less than it should be is also reflected in the strong words, 'fear and dread'.

'Fear and Dread'

Before the flood animals 'came to Noah', but now the relationship has dramatically changed. There is more here than the 'rule' of Gen. 1.28; after all, throughout the ancient Near East it was the theory (if rarely the practice) that rulers are to act for the benefit of their subjects. A clear expression is in Hammurabi's self-praise in the prologue to the code that he named:

> to promote the welfare of the people...to cause justice to prevail in the land, to destroy the wicked and the evil, that the strong might not oppress the weak (Meek 1955: 164).

'Fear and dread' are very strong words. Their use elsewhere in the MT (Masoretic Text) show a limited range of contexts.

The two roots *yare'* and *chatat* occur together in only 17 verses (none in a commonly recognized P context). The great majority occur in military settings: being '(not) terrified' of the fearsome might of opponents (Deut. 1.21; 31.8; Josh. 8.1; 10.25; 1 Sam. 17.11; 2 Chron. 20.15, 17; 32.7; Jer. 30.10; 46.27); two in 1 Chronicles (22.13; 28.30) match the Deuteronomic wording. Three deal similarly with 'fear' of physical violence (Isa. 51.7; Ezek. 2.6; 3.9). Only in one case is the object Yahweh (Mal. 2.5, referring to Levi, possibly alluding to the terrifying events of Num. 25). As many have seen in Gen. 9.2 an extension of the royal language of Gen. 1.28, the imagery of the remaining verse, Jer. 23.4, provides a striking commentary: instead of 'shepherds' who are not caring for 'my flock', Yahweh 'will place shepherds over them who will tend them, and they will no longer be afraid or terrified'. For subjects to be 'afraid and terrified' is not right! It is a sign that there is something terribly (literally) wrong in the relationship.

Extending the search to instances of *chatat* alone shows the same kind of distribution. Overwhelmingly it is 'terror' of an enemy, brought about through might and destruction. One instance stands out in its environmental wholeness. Woe is announced for the marauding enemy, there is a reversal of 'terror':

> For the violence done to Lebanon will overwhelm you;
> the destruction of the animals will terrify you—
> because of human bloodshed and violence to the earth,
> to cities and all who live in them (Hab. 2.17).

In line 2 the NRSV, like most commentators, follows the interpretation of the Septuagint, that is, the terror will (re)turn upon the Babylonians. Although the MT has the 'animals' as the object and thus has even more focus on the terror caused to animals, in both interpretations judgment is clearly pronounced on the Babylonians for their cruel rule which has affected all of nature. The broad sweep—Lebanon, wild beasts, humans, earth—argues against seeing animals simply as a symbol for other nations, as in Dan. 4.7, 9, 11 (so against Delcor 1964: 420). After noting passages where Isaiah speaks against the arrogant despoliation of the forests of Lebanon by Assyria and Babylon (Isa. 14.8; 37.24), Eaton comments that the 'Hebrew prophets were sensitive to the ruthlessness of these operations, leading as they eventually did to the complete destruction of the forests'. (As I write debate continues in my home state concerning government policy that destroys old-growth forests.) He continues: 'The terror and havoc wrought among the wild beasts of the mountains, massacred in their own rightful domain, also impresses Habakkuk as an injustice' (1961: 105). The language that reminds the reader of Genesis 9 reinforces the judgment on human arrogant self-centred violence towards the non-human partners of the earth community.

God's Covenant of Life

After the repeated statements relating to killing in Gen. 9.1-7, Gen. 9.8-17 is striking in the repeated references to 'life' and to 'flesh' (sometimes linked with 'earth'):

verse	MT	NRSV
10	kol-nepesh ha-chayyah	every living creature
	kol-chayyat ha'arets	every animal ['living'] of the earth
	kol-chayyat ha'arets	—(at end of verse)
11	kol-basar	all flesh
12	kol-nepesh chayyah	every living creature
15	kol-nepesh chayyah bᵉkol-basar	every living creature of all flesh
	kol-basar	all flesh
16	kol-nepesh chayyah bᵉkol-kol-basar 'ᵃsher 'al-ha'arets	every living creature of all flesh that is on the earth
17	kol-basar 'ᵃsher 'al-ha'arets	all flesh that is on the earth

While the word *basar* is used in Hebrew (as in many languages) both for all creatures (including humans) and for 'flesh/meat', it does provide a striking contrast that 'flesh' can be eaten (with restriction) in Gen. 9.4, but repeatedly 'flesh' is to be kept alive in Gen. 9.8-15. Is there a deliberate intertextuality between the two sections? Is one modifying the other?

Another repeated feature is the close association between Noah and the animals. Not only is the covenant made by God with both Noah and all creatures (four times: Gen. 9.9-10, 12, 15, 17) but Noah is also reminded that the animals were 'with you' (three times: Gen. 9.10 [twice], 12). The double inclusions of the section (Gen. 9.9-17, and 9.12-17) are instructive: the opening (Gen. 9.9-10) explicitly lists 'you, your descendants after you, every living creature' (with the 'creatures' being further classified); the secondary start, the 'sign of the covenant' (Gen. 9.12), involves 'you and every living creature'; but the conclusion (Gen. 9.17) is simply 'all flesh that is on earth'. There is no separation or hierarchy; rather, there is a bonding together on 'earth'.

Further, semantically the bond is even closer than commonality of being 'on' earth. 'Earth' is used alone as the object of God's action in

Gen. 9.11, 13, 14. When the covenant 'between me and...' is given its shortest statement as to the other partner, it is simply 'between me and the earth' (Gen. 9.13). All are together *with* the earth. The animals may be described as 'with you', but that is parallelled with 'upon the earth'. They may have been 'with' Noah in the ark, to be delivered with him, but now they are not bound to him. That is the ending of Gen. 9.10 (omitted in NRSV), and also the double ending of Gen. 9.16, 17.

It may be countered that the words are addressed only to Noah—the animals are not addressed. The announcement of the covenant is made 'to Noah and to his sons with him' (Gen. 9.8). The anthropocentric and patriarchal character of the author is apparent. This could be read as simply reflecting and reinforcing male human dominance.

Yet the words that are spoken are unequivocally egalitarian. This suggests that the words are spoken to men, because 'this is what men need to hear'! This is a similar reading to that suggested by Goldingay regarding Genesis 2 and 3 as he imagines Eve saying, 'After all in our culture it's mostly men who read the Bible, and this story gives them something in which they can see themselves mirrored, so that they can be self-critical' (1996: 41). The cry of all creatures apart from men is that the voice of God will be heeded and the commonality affirmed.

That the covenant is with all 'flesh', with 'the earth', is rarely commented on. Brueggemann in his insightful theological commentary on Genesis discourses at length on the covenant passage. He draws attention, following Bernhard Anderson, to the turning point in the flood narrative of Gen. 8.1: 'But God remembered Noah and all the wild animals and the livestock that were with him in the ark.' But then he simply says, 'God remembered Noah. God remembered' (Brueggemann 1982: 85). His theological focus is on God and chaos, especially as experienced by humans, by the people of God. As is so often the case, animals are an appendage, words are used but no attention is paid to them. But in God's 'remembering', in Gen. 8.1 and in Gen. 9.15, animals are included equally. Again, Barth affirms the continuing close link between humans and animals: as in Genesis 2 both are 'formed of the earth' and each becomes 'a "living creature"', so also 'man [*sic*] and beast are linked in weal and woe in the story of the Flood' (Barth cites Gen. 7.21-22; 9.10, 12, 15; 1958: 246).

The focus on the animals and the earth, and no longer just humans, is seen by van Wolde as a feature of transformation in the narrative of the flood:

> While at the beginning of the flood story the bad behaviour of humans was the inducement for God's decision to sweep away all life on earth

by a flood, at the end of the flood story he decides that the bad behaviour of humans will no longer have that influence on the continuation of life on earth... This is affirmed by the sign of the covenant: a
bow that arches the whole earth (1998: 38).

Another factor in her argument is the shift she observes from 'all
the days of his [the human being's] life' (Gen. 6.5) before the flood to
'days of the earth' (Gen. 8.22) after the event.

Her remarks require some qualification if, with Harland (1996: 31)
and Wenham (1987: 171), and against Westermann (1984: 416), 'all
flesh' in Gen. 6.12, 13 is seen to include animals (as is the case in Gen.
6.17, 19; 7.15, 16; 8.17; and importantly in 9.11-17). Thus animals are
included in the observation that 'all flesh had corrupted its ways
upon the earth' (Gen. 6.12). That animals are included is strengthened
by their accountability in Gen. 9.5: 'There is no reason why the animals should not be seen as having some moral responsibility given
the statement of 9:5 that animals are liable for punishment' (Harland
1996: 31; see also 202). Biblical writers were far more aware of violence
among animals than city-dwelling modern scholars!

This gives added point to God's promise never again to 'destroy'
the earth (*shachat*, piel: Gen. 9.11, 15), a clear allusion to the decision to
'destroy' in Gen. 6.13 (hiphil), Gen. 6.17 (piel), because the earth was
'corrupt' (niphal: Gen. 6.11, 12) for 'all flesh' had 'corrupted' (hiphil:
Gen. 6.12). The link between 'corruption' and 'destruction' is clear in
Genesis 6; now in the covenant, in Genesis 9, the nexus is broken. The
question as to how human (and animal) violence is ultimately to be
overcome is not the issue here—but it does surface on numerous
occasions throughout the Bible. Somehow the 'whole creation' is to be
set free (Rom. 8.20-22).

There is a clear indication that God gives to animals more dignity
and importance than simply the value they have for humans.
Although Linzey does not refer to Genesis 9, the 'covenant' adds
significant support to his statement:

> We must view creation from God's perspective and not our own. The
> worth of every creature does not lie in whether it is beautiful (to us) or
> whether it serves or sustains our life and happiness. Only if we can save
> ourselves from an anthropocentricity can we begin to construct an ade-
> quate theology of animals (Linzey 1993: 513).

Or more simply, 'To recognize animal rights is to recognize the intrinsic value of God-given life' (Linzey 1991: 909), to which the covenant
adds, 'the intrinsic value of God-promised continuation of life'.

Genesis 9 is general in its statements about creatures—it is 'all-inclusive' (*kol*, meaning 'all', 'everything', occurs 19 times!). One must go to other passages to look at specific treatment of and attitudes to domestic and wild animals as objects of care and interest by God apart from human benefit (e.g., Job 38–39; Ps. 104; the participation of animals in the Sabbath): 'the biblical world view is not so much anthropocentric as theocentric' (Tucker 1997: 17).

There is a contrast between Genesis 1 and Genesis 9. In the creation narrative there are many similarities between animals and humans, with God expressing concern for both, although humans are to 'rule'. But Genesis 9 faces the reality of self-centred human violence, and as happens in any situation of oppressive rule, the subjects experience 'fear and terror'. Animal life can only continue if there are some limitations and sanctions; ultimately continuation of human and animal life and of the earth depends upon God's 'covenant' made equally with all parties.

The final focus of the flood narrative is not the reality of human violence to animals and to one another, but the promise of God given unilaterally to the 'earth' and all who live on it. Human readers of the text are encouraged to look beyond their own interests ('food') and to look at all creatures as partners in God's covenant. God is concerned for the well-being of animals and enters into covenant with them. It is God's intention to keep together the rich biodiversity of the earth.

The Voice of the Earth:
An Indigenous Reading of Genesis 9

Wali Fejo

Personal Background

As background to my paper, it is probably helpful for readers to know something of my origins. I am an Indigenous Australian, from the Larrikia country around Darwin. The trails of my ancestors reach into Arnhem Land in Northern Australia. I belong to this land; the land is my mother, my provider, my keeper.

My people are the original custodians of the land in this part of Australia. We look after the land as we look after a mother. And the land looks after us like a mother. From the land comes our law and our life, our stories and our strength. Our own land is also within us and binds us to the place where we live. Even when we are displaced or taken away and seem to have lost our roots, the land stays within us. The task is to find ourselves by finding the land within and making the connection with our country. We are 'heirs' of the land, spiritually, just as Christians say they are heirs of Christ. Wherever I go I have a piece of land within me.

My personal dreaming (totem) is connected with Nungalinya, 'Old Man Rock'. The physical form of that rock is revealed at low tide off the shore near Darwin. I and the rock and the crocodile have the same spirit, the spirit of our common ancestor, the Old Man himself. That rock does not stand in isolation; it is linked physically and spiritually with Uluru, the great red rock at the centre of Australia, the centre of the Earth. Every rock is an extension of Uluru.

The land is alive. I can talk to the land or the Earth, just as God does. The Earth is a means of communicating with my ancestors, my people, my God. I make my spiritual connections through the land. God, the Creator, is present in the land. When I die I return to my land, my God. I do not escape the Earth and go to heaven as many missionaries tried to tell us.

Sad to say, when the Europeans came they messed up our land, desecrated it, polluted it and caused it great suffering. As custodians of the land we used to look after the land according to our traditional law. Before the Europeans came, there was plenty of bush tucker, medicine and life in the land. Now the Earth cries with the pain of pollutants from mining that kill trees, cause cancer in the land and sickness in the soil. Where is the medicine we need to heal the Earth?

The many injustices inflicted on the land and the Indigenous peoples of the land hurt us deeply. The land has been giving, forever giving. My people have been giving, forever giving. The land cries out. The ancestors cry out from the land, like the blood of Abel. The Europeans are forever taking. When will they give something back?

For us, the rainbow was always an assurance of food, plentiful food. It was the sign of the Creator Spirit speaking with us, promising us food. The Creator spoke through the rainbow. What does God say through the rainbow today? What does God say through the rainbow in the Bible? I will now read again what European readers have called the flood story and listen to the Earth as I read the story. For this is really a story about the Earth, the land.

Earth Revealed

I first want to refer to the account of how the land was first revealed in Gen. 1.9-10 as outlined by Norman Habel in the first essay of this volume. The land, like the Dreaming, has always been. The Earth, like the Creator, has always existed. In the beginning the land was covered with waters until the Creator spoke. When the Creator spoke the Earth was revealed, emerging from beneath the waters (Gen. 1.9-10). When the Creator spoke the Dreaming happened: all kinds of life emerged from the land and covered the Earth, forms of life with which humans have kinship, both physical and spiritual (Gen. 1.11-12, 20-21, 24-25). For an Indigenous Australian's visual portrayal of this revelation, see the paintings of Jasmine Corowa in *The Rainbow Spirit in Creation: A Reading of Genesis One* (2000).

The land that appeared is more than matter. The land is alive with people, with ancestors, with life, with God. God was—and still is—in the land. So when God said, 'let the land be seen', God was also saying 'let me be seen so that you can see'. The Earth is the first and primary medium of God's self-revelation. When the Earth was revealed, the Creator filled the Earth with Dreaming and from the Dreaming emerge all life forces, all creatures—including trees, animals and rocks.

Earth Violated

The violation of the Earth by human beings is the reason for the flood. When humans fill the Earth with violence (Gen. 6.11), they violate the Earth and the Earth becomes corrupt. The violence of nuclear explosions, nuclear mines and nuclear waste is one modern example of how the Earth is violated and corrupted. And this violation is personal; the Earth as a living reality is hurt by these human actions. The Earth suffers. And God suffers.

Why does God suffer and grieve in Gen. 6.5-7? First, because the human beings God has created from the Earth have become evil and have filled the Earth community with evil. God also suffers because this evil violates the sacred, the Earth where God is present. The 'sorry' of God is the deep hurt God feels because of a deep hurt in the Earth.

Earth Concealed

Why then does God choose to send a flood and destroy life on the Earth? If the Earth is where God is and the home of all God has created, why does God destroy this precious place? Because it is sick—corrupted by human evils—and in need of healing. The Earth needs to be healed so that it can be renewed and unpolluted life can again replenish the land. The flood is the cleansing, the covering. God covers the hurt earth with water, just like we place a cut finger in our mouths to cover it with moisture from our bodies. God removes the old to make way for the new.

When the Earth is concealed by water, the situation returns to the way it was in the beginning of the Dreaming (Gen. 1.2). The Earth is beneath the waters again. God is beneath the waters again. God is not at a distance on some cloud watching the flood with an expression of justified anger. God is in the Earth. God experiences the flood, the death of life on Earth. The suffering of God in the flood anticipates the suffering of God in the crucifixion.

The flood is like the fires which we Indigenous Australians once used to light in order to burn off part of the land. The surface is burned and the debris is removed to stimulate new life in the land. The spider, for example, stays alive and spins her web again. Life returns because life is in the land.

Noah finds favour in the eyes of the Lord (Gen. 6.8). Noah is all our ancestors, including our Indigenous ancestors. Noah is our ancestor who made boats and crossed the waters. The ark represents the Earth community; all species are preserved for the future and blessed with the power to multiply on the Earth again. The ark is the symbol of our hope amid this ecological crisis, this flood of pollutants.

Earth Revealed—Again

The ark lands on a rock called Mt Ararat. As the water recedes the rock appears. The rock is like Old Man Rock, the rock of my Dreaming. Mt Ararat is also like Uluru, the rock at the centre of the Earth, the rock of God's presence. The ark lands on the first rock of the Earth to be revealed after the flood. We can also say that the ark lands on God, because God is there, in the rock, too.

When the Earth community in the ark touched base with the Earth, everything made connection with God again, with the Creator in the Earth. God, within the Earth, felt the touch of living creatures again. When the ark made contact, the interconnection between all creatures, God and the earth was re-established (Earth Bible ecojustice principle two). God's invitation to touch the Earth and experience that interconnection is an invitation to touch God. That interconnection between all things is fundamental to the fertility process. Without the Earth there is no connection: no fertility, no life, no divine presence.

Voice from the Earth

The covenant with all living creatures in Genesis 9 is the voice of God speaking from within the Earth to Earth's creatures. The covenant reflects God's concern for the Earth, a deep respect for the Earth as a subject of permanent worth. This covenant honours all life on the Earth, not just human life. Through this covenant a close interrelationship between humans and other living things, including the Earth itself, is reaffirmed.

Traditional interpretations of this chapter in Genesis have tended to focus on the content of God's promise never to destroy the Earth with a flood again. Just as significant is the fact that God is making a covenant with creatures other than humans. God's covenant with all living things means that God relates to the animals, birds and other creatures on Earth as living subjects, not simply as mindless objects (Earth Bible ecojustice principle three). God makes the same personal promise to kangaroos and crocodiles, to turtles and beetles as to human beings.

For Indigenous Australians this personal covenant relationship confirms their experience of Dreaming relationships, living bonds with particular species who share the same spirit as particular individuals or groups. I have the same living spirit as crocodiles and turtles. They are my Dreaming. They have the same promise from God as I do. My covenant as custodian for my land is to preserve these particular species on Earth. God's covenant is to preserve all species. God's voice from the Earth is spoken to all life, a bond that lasts forever.

Voice of the Earth

The content of God's promise is to reveal God's purpose for the future of the Earth (Earth Bible ecojustice principle four). God will never again 'destroy' the earth by covering it with water. The Earth will always be seen—and that means God will always be seen. The Earth will always be there for me and my ancestors, for me and my descendants. I will always have a place to belong, before and after death.

Unfortunately, human beings are often bent on destroying the Earth through acts of greed and violence. They hurt the Earth and make it tremble deep within. When the Earth trembles we can hear the voice of the Earth. We must be open to hear the voice of the Earth, not in human language but in the Earth's own language. The language of Earth is like the body language of humans. Earth communicates in its own distinct way.

In words consistent with the promise of Genesis 9, the Earth says, 'I am still intact. I am still reachable.' The Earth speaks through the rain and the storms, the trees and the rivers. 'Listen. Stop. Let's have a normal conversation about life together.' But when humans start killing life on Earth, polluting the Earth, hurting the Earth, the voice gets louder. The Earth quakes as it feels the hurt of ecological disasters. The voice rises from the Earth. 'I won't let you destroy the Earth.' The same voice rises from this text, 'I won't destroy the Earth', and that means, 'I won't let you destroy the Earth'.

The Rainbow of Earth

The rainbow reveals just how intimately God is related to the Earth. The rainbow is the living expression of God's promise to the Earth community. The rainbow is an assurance for humans to see that God has done something remarkable. The rainbow is the sign, a clear communication from God about God's relationship with Earth, another expression of the voice of God rising from the Earth.

The rainbow, however, is not only for humans to see. Just as God once saw the Earth at creation and found it 'good', so God sees the rainbow and 'remembers' the promise made with the Earth. 'I will remember my covenant' (9.15). God sends the rainbow from the Earth into the sky for all to see, even God. 'I will see it and remember the everlasting covenant' (9.16). The rainbow points to a God who not only creates and makes covenants with creation, but also one who remembers the responsibilities that come with a covenant relationship.

The rainbow in turn points to our responsibility to be partners with God, custodians of creation. That means reconnecting what is broken on Earth. The rainbow comes from the Earth and returns to the Earth as a symmetrical arc, reflecting all the delicate colours of the Earth. The rainbow is also a reminder to us of the balance in creation that we called to restore.

The balance in creation is reflected in the seasons, the pattern of rain, wind and clouds that God promises to maintain (Gen. 8.22). My people seek to maintain that balance in creation in song, ceremony and dance as we relive the story of a particular place where the Creator Spirit is present for us. Each place is different but, at the same time, an integral part of the harmony of creation. As we move from place to place we must adapt and allow ourselves to be 'welcomed' in a new place. Among our people, a formal welcome means a promise of sharing: 'in this place what's mine is yours'. It is not only the people who welcome you; the land in this place also welcomes you as one who belongs. Such a welcome implies respect for the land and the ecological laws of the land in any given place. God has welcomed us to this place, this Earth. The rainbow is the sign of that welcome. In response we ought to show respect.

The Rainbow Spirit

For many Indigenous peoples in Australia the rainbow is more than a meteorological phenomenon. The rainbow is a revelation of the Rainbow Spirit or Rainbow Snake emerging from within the Earth. The theological significance of the Rainbow Snake for some Indigenous Australian Christians is outlined in a book by the Rainbow Spirit Elders entitled *Rainbow Spirit Theology*. All the colours of the Rainbow Snake appearing in the sky come from the ground. The Rainbow Spirit is like a chameleon—it changes colour as it crosses the land: the red of the centre, the gold of the beaches, the green of the rainforests. The colours of the land also reflect the colours of all the peoples on this land—and all the colours of the Earth itself.

The Creator Spirit and the Rainbow Snake are modes of the same God within the Earth, whose face we see reflected in the face of the Earth—like the face of a parent reflected in the face of a child. And Old Man Rock, my spiritual piece of Earth, my Dreaming, is another expression of the same sacred presence. As Indigenous peoples, we not only see God as the Rainbow rising from Earth into the sky, but we also smell God when we smell the Earth. We touch God when we touch the Earth. God is as close as the ground on which we walk.

The Earth Connection

The covenant promise in Genesis 9 highlights the close interconnection between me, God, the Earth and all life. God bonds personally with all parts of creation in one embracing covenant. This text makes the expression 'Earth community' a vivid reality. Humans belong with all flesh—all life—to the Earth as a community. And as an Indigenous Australian I know I belong to a specific piece of the Earth that is also within me no matter where I go. I am forever connected physically and spiritually with my land and through my land with the whole Earth community.

As interconnected members of the Earth community, we have a responsibility to listen to the voices of others in the community. We listen to the land, to the Earth, to our own Dreaming species. We hear the injustices, the disharmony, the hurt. The cries keep rising in our hearts until the noise is almost unbearable. As Indigenous peoples who know and feel this deep connection with the Earth, the suffering of the Earth is not an academic concept—it is reality we hear and feel and see and experience.

The rainbow is the promise of healing, of God's remembering. The rainbow is also the sign of covenant responsibility. We need to heed this sign like all the signs from the Earth. It is like the sign of the honey fly, a very tiny fly that signals the beginning of the rainy season and fertility. This fly is tricky. Unlike the honey bee that flies direct to its hive, the honey fly takes an indirect and devious path home. Only those who watch the sign carefully find the honey.

Postscript

I want to thank Norman Habel, Shirley Wurst and the Earth Bible Team for enabling me to express my insights in relation to this text orally, and for the formulation of these insights into specific wording printed above.

The Earth Story as Presented by the
Tower of Babel Narrative

Ellen van Wolde

Come, let us make a trip. Let us climb a tower, the highest tower ever built. Come, let us have a look at the Earth Story from the perspective of the Tower of Babel narrative. A careful reading of Gen. 11.1-9, its main story line and actors, will be our guide, so that we will be able to view the landscape from the top of the tower. The intention is to make visible how the tower is part of its environment and how the narrative in Genesis 11 forms a unity with the Earth Story in Genesis 1–11. The motivation of this guided tour in primaeval time and place is to offer a point of reference in the readers' actual attitude towards the earth.

The Main Story Line of the Tower of Babel Narrative

The story of the Tower of Babel in Gen. 11.1-9 opens with two descriptive clauses (indicated by *wayyehi*). The first paints in one brush the condition of the whole earth: 'The whole earth had one language and the same words' (Gen. 11.1). Against this background, the actions of the following verses will take place. This series of events starts with a description, too: 'It occurred as they migrated from the east, that they came upon a plain in the land of Shinar and settled there' (Gen. 11.2). A chain of narrative verbal forms indicates the main line of the action: 'they came upon, they settled, they said to one another, YHWH came down, YHWH said, YHWH dispersed, they stopped'. The last verse (Gen. 11.9), however, stands outside the narrative chain, and opens with 'therefore'. Here the narrator communicates more directly with the reader: 'Therefore it was called Babel, because there YHWH confused the language of the whole earth; and from there YHWH dispersed them abroad over the face of the whole earth.' The framework of the story is thus formed by Gen. 11.1 relating the story to 'once upon a time' in the past, and Gen. 11.9 relating the story to the present time of the narrator and reader. This is the setting of the first and the last verse within which the actions of the characters function:

1. the whole earth	is one language
9. YHWH confuses the language	of the whole earth
9. YHWH disperses them	over the whole earth

The framework concerns the condition of 'the whole earth' (כל־הארץ). Usually the human beings are the speaking, listening and communicating persons. It is significant that the text refers to language and calls the earth its subject, as if the earth is able to speak. This sign points at the earth as the main subject; actually, the narrative has 'the whole earth' (כל־הארץ) as the first word and as the last word: the earth forms this text's frame of reference.

The embedded story (Gen. 11.2-8) begins with a subject that is neither introduced nor described in more detail than 'they'. The reference is undoubtedly to the people, but it is striking that they are not presented with a personal or collective name, but with an undifferentiated third-person plural: 'they came upon', 'they settled'. In one single verse, which the narrator presents in his own words, although the perceptual perspective is YHWH's, these 'they' are 'human beings' (בני האדם): 'YHWH came down to see the city and the tower, which the human beings had built' (Gen. 11.5). These human beings are characterized by their building activities; the alliteration in the words *bene* and *banu* (בני and בנו, cf. 'big boys build big buildings') shows their strong tie. After the narrator has established this relationship, in the rest of the text, that is both in the discourse (or character's text) and in the narrative (or narrator's text), the human beings are merely referred to as 'they' or 'them' (Gen. 11.6-8). In short, unlike the framework of Gen. 11.1 and Gen. 11.9, in which 'the whole earth' occurs three times, the narrator, with one exception in which he emphasizes human beings and their building for themselves, presents the active subjects as 'they' and thus as subjects that are not marked or specified like the earth.

Within the narrative, three direct discourses are embedded. The first two discourses have 'they' as the speaking subject, and these 'they' speak to one another: 'Come, let us make bricks, and burn them thoroughly' (Gen. 11.3) and 'Come, let us build ourselves a city, and a tower with its head in heaven, and let us make a name for ourselves; so that we shall not be dispersed over the face of the whole earth' (Gen. 11.4). These discourses include four mutual exhortations, which all have one aim: 'so that we shall not be dispersed over the face of the whole earth'. This is the only time in the discourses that the subject of the narrative framework 'the whole earth' (כל־הארץ) recurs: the people want to ensure that they will not be dispersed over the entire earth. In opposition to being scattered over the entire earth the humans set up an 'us'-oriented action: 'not us over the entire earth'.

In the third discourse in Gen. 11.6-7, YHWH is the speaking subject:

> Look, they are one people, and they all have one language; and this is only the beginning of what they will do; nothing that they propose to do will now be impossible for them. Come, let us go down, and confuse their language there, so that they will not understand one another's speech.

YHWH's speech is presented in a form analogous to that of the human beings: verb forms in the first-person plural. 'Let us' is preceded by the hortatory word 'come'. Both YHWH's speech and action are opposite to those of the human beings. They did want one name and did not want to be scattered over the entire earth (Gen. 11.4). YHWH, however, expresses the need for many languages (Gen. 11.6) and the will to confuse their words (Gen. 11.7). YHWH actually disperses them over the face of the whole earth (Gen. 11.8), and confuses the language of the whole earth (Gen. 11.9).

In short, in the framework of the story, the changing situation of the earth is referred to. This change is brought about by the action and the spoken text of the characters in Gen. 11.2-8. Here, the humans strive for more unity of place and language, as is depicted by one surface area, one city, one tower and one name. However, YHWH subsequently strives for plurality or non-unity: not one language but many languages, not one place, but dispersion over the entire earth. With this second series of actions by YHWH, the final situation is established: a multiplicity of languages and people, dispersed over the entire earth.

A Tower and a Name

Usually, Gen. 11.1-9 is associated with *hybris*: the building of the tower is considered to be an expression of the human desire to become divine (Skinner 1930: 229; Fokkelman 1975: 14-20; Sasson 1980; Couffignal 1983; Wenham 1987: 239-42; Vogels 1992: 11-37). The primary basis for this has been the tower with 'its head in heaven' (מגדל ראשו בשמים).

The word 'tower' (מגדל), occurs in the Hebrew Bible either as a general term for a high and fortified building or as a toponym. In the first meaning, this high building is very often associated with a city (or a vineyard, cf. Isa. 5.2), in which the tower is made for defence purposes. To express its defensive power, the tower is often preceded by adjectives like 'high' (Isa. 2.15), 'great' (Neh. 3.27) or 'powerful' (Judg. 9.51; Ps. 61.4; Prov. 18.10). The function of a tower is to defend people against attackers (Judg. 9.51-2). Its essence is dissociation: the enclosed people are dissociated from the outsiders. The second meaning as a toponym is the consequence of its first meaning. A tower is the visible sign of the autonomous and impressive power of a city (cf. Jud. 8.9). That is why many cities are called after their tower: Migdal-El (Josh. 19.38), Migdal-Gath (Josh. 15.37), Migdal-Eder (Gen. 35.21), Migdal-Sichem (Judg. 9.46, 49). A tower represents a city par excellence.

The term 'head in heaven' (ראש בשמים) in combination with towers or large edifices does occur elsewhere in the Hebrew Bible as figurative language to describe edifices of impressive high proportions, impossible to attack. For example, in Deut. 1.28 it is stated that 'The people are greater and taller than we; the cities are great and fortified up to heaven'. Deuteronomy 9.1 shows a similar thing: 'Hear Israel; you are about to cross the Jordan today, to go in and dispossess nations larger and mightier than you, great cities, fortified up to heaven.' Consequently, the term 'head in heaven' (ראש בשמים) expresses the mightiness and fortified character of the tower and has no connotation whatsoever with God (cf. von Rad 1972b: 149; Gowan 1975: 27-28; Hamilton 1990: 261-72).

This is confirmed by the use of the term 'heaven' (שמים) in Genesis 1–11, which does not refer to the place where God lives, but to a part of the universe created by God. This universe consists of two parts: heaven or the firmament separating the waters above, and earth, the dry stuff in between the waters below. Whereas the heaven is populated by heavenly bodies, sun, moon and stars, the earth is populated by animals and human beings. The heavenly bodies do not procreate or multiply, the earthly bodies do procreate and multiply in order to fill the earth. In this view, the human beings are exclusively linked to the earth, and not to the heaven (see Genesis 1).

Therefore, one might conclude that 'a tower with its head in heaven' has nothing to do with divinity or the desire to become godlike. The building of the tower and the city expresses the desire of these human beings to dissociate themselves from the earth and to concentrate on each other ('us') in their enclosed and fortified area.

This is confirmed by another aspect in the text. All human actions are horizontally oriented: they move to the east, to the land Shinear, to a plain, and the direction of their movements becomes increasingly closely identified. Finally, they settle 'there' (*sham*, שם) on this spot where they want to build a city and a tower, which indicates an even narrower focus of place. There they express their ideal: by remaining in this place and according themselves a name (*shem*, שם), they will not be dispersed over the entire earth. The earth is not given a name, but the city and the tower are. The unity of language evidently leads to a desire for a single spot, and to a desire for a single name. The one place is actually represented by the one name: one place (*sham*, שם) stands for one name (*shem*, שם). In response to this striving for one place and one name, YHWH comes into action and sets himself in motion. YHWH expresses his opposition in word and deed: in Gen. 11.7, YHWH expresses his intention of confusing their language 'there', and thereupon he disperses them there 'from there' (Gen. 11.8). The result is obvious: instead of one place and one name for the human beings, the place has received a name; 'her name' (*shemah*, שמה) is Babel. And the word *shemah* (שמה) shows how the one language and the one place come together in that place, since, in this word, there is both the *a*-sound of *sham* and the *e*-sound of *shem*. The name Babel carries the same connotation: it is a single name that expresses confusion and non-singularity.

Whereas the Christian tradition associated with Gen. 11.1-9 has focused one-sidedly on the *hybris* of humanity, the human sin against God, and the desire to penetrate the divine realm, the Jewish tradition from a very early date onwards, has read Gen. 11.1-9 as a story about the variety of languages on the earth and the dispersion of human beings over the earth. Cassuto observes:

> Although the construction of the tower occupies an important place in the narrative, it is not the main subject. The principal theme is the dispersion of mankind over the face of the whole earth, a matter that God purposed and that was ultimately fulfilled in accordance with the Divine will, notwithstanding human attempts to obstruct it... Hence I did not put at the head of this narrative the usual title 'The Tower of Babel' or 'The building of the Tower of Babel'; I used instead the expression customarily employed in Jewish literature, 'The Story of the Generation of Division', which best fits the intention and the content of the text (1961: 226).

The (Jewish) horizontal orientation can therefore replace the (Christian) vertical orientation.

In one respect, however, both the Christian and the Jewish traditions need to be corrected. Both traditions are 'human-centred' in their interpretation of this story. This begins already with their exposition of Gen. 11.1. Though the text speaks of the language 'of the whole earth', almost every exegete refers to the languages 'of all people'. Sarna (1989: 81), for example, who stands in the Jewish tradition,

states: 'This episode does not contain the names of individuals. A key
expression, repeated five times, is "all the earth" for the entire human
race is presumed to be sinful.' Although he first recognizes that this
story does not mention people's names and that the text five times
mentions the words 'the whole earth' or 'all the earth' (כל־הארץ
'all the earth'), he nevertheless equates these words with 'the entire
human race'. Wenham (1987: 240), a Christian exegete, speaks of the
irony of the text, with reference to Gen. 11.5: 'With heavy irony we
now see the tower through God's eyes. This tower which man
thought reached to heaven, God can hardly see!' But this irony fades
when one realizes that the people think the concern is with the
building of a city and tower, while, in fact, YHWH is concerned with
the earth and the dispersion of human beings over the earth. In Gen.
11.1-9, the dispersion is not only presented as a punishment: differentiation, from the point of view of the earth, is a necessity (cf. Anderson
1978; Kikawada 1974: 32; Turner 1990: 30-33). The obstacle to dispersion, the single language, is removed because YHWH discovers its
consequences with respect to the earth: 'Look, they are one people,
and they all have one language; and this is only the beginning of what
they will do; nothing that they propose to do will now be impossible
for them' (Gen. 11.6). The dispersion of the people is entirely in line
with the earth's interests.

Genesis 11 in relation to Genesis 1

The primaeval history presented in Genesis 1–11 is often read as a
description of the earliest history of humankind, but this text is less
human-centred than is generally supposed. The main theme of the
story of creation in Gen. 1.1–2.4a concerns the creation of heaven and
earth, and the network of relationships between the creatures in the
created universe. In this network, humankind is only one factor, an
important factor indeed.

The immense attention usually paid to Gen. 1.26-28 requires some
additional comment on the place of the human beings in this network.
Very often, one of the first arguments used to underline the human-
centredness of the story is the fact that, in Genesis 1, the human being
is made as the last creature. It is generally inferred from this that the
human being is the climax of creation: in this creature, creation reaches
its culmination, possibly even its goal. A similar thing occurs in the
story of paradise (Gen. 2–3), where the woman is made as the last
creature. Then of course, one has to infer that is the creation finds its

climax and ultimate end in the female creature! Illogically, usually the opposite conclusion is drawn.

The second and main argument of human rulership is based on the content of Gen. 1.28. The opening of the divine commands to the human beings in Gen. 1.28 starts with God's blessing, which is very similar to the blessings to the animals in Gen. 1.22. In Gen. 1.28a, the first assignment human beings receive is to be fruitful, multiply and fill the earth. It is exactly the same as the one given to the animals in Gen. 1.22. The only difference is that the human beings are asked to fill the earth, while the fishes have to fill the sea, and the birds the air. Earlier in the story, in Gen. 1.16, God has directed the heavenly bodies, moon and sun, and given them the task to *mashal* (מֹשֵׁל), to exercise dominion over the day and the night on earth. This word denotes a ruling activity as strong as the words *kabash* (כבשׁ) and *radah* (רדה), used for the human beings in Gen. 1.28. It is astonishing, though, that after reading in Gen. 1.16 of the sovereignty of the sun and moon over the days and feasts on earth, people conclude that these planets are at the earth's service. Reading Gen. 1.28 or Gen. 3.16 (with the same word *mashal*, מֹשֵׁל, expressing the relationship between man and woman), one draws the conclusion not that the human beings are at the earth's service, but the earth is at the humans' service (and the woman at the man's service)! Some deduce from Gen. 1.28 that God commands the human beings to subject the earth to their will and to make it the object of their desires (Rendtorff 1979; Turner 1990: 33-35).

The structure of Genesis 1 makes it clear, however, that the assignment of dominion both to the planets and to the human beings is an expression of reciprocal relationships between the created phenomena: the planets fulfil their ruling function in relation to light and life on earth, and, analogically, the human beings fulfil their ruling function in relation to the earth and the animals on earth. This management is both *relative* (as we can infer from the restricted human dominion over birds and fishes, over lions and microbes) and *relational*, because it is based on interdependency. As sovereigns of the earth and the animals, people are at the same time dependent on the sun, the air, the waters and the plants of the earth. Dominion and dependency go hand in hand and are actually part of all existent phenomena. A network of created phenomena is therefore built up by these relationships and the story sometimes stresses one aspect and sometimes another. One cannot just read one aspect of the complete network and ignore the other parts (van Wolde 1996a).

The third argument in favour of a human dominion over the earth is based on Gen. 1.26-27, in which it is said that the human being is created after God's image. In fact, (s)he is the only creature that God does not make 'after its own kind', but 'in our image' and 'after our likeness'. The possessive pronouns connected with 'kind'—everything is created and is to procreate after 'his' or 'her' or 'their' kind (*min*, מין)—indicate that the plants and animals refer back to these creatures themselves. They are distinct from the possessive pronouns belonging to 'image' (*tselem*, צלם) and 'likeness' (*demut*, דמות): these pronouns do not refer to humankind but to God. This contrast in possessive pronouns is an indication that the human being, unlike the other creatures, does not find a point of reference in himself or herself, but in God.

The word *tselem* (צלם), image, was studied thoroughly by Barr (1968). He discusses a group of Hebrew words that may be said to lie in the semantic field of 'image, likeness, similarity'. The word *pesel* (פסל) means 'graven image' (of a god) and is immediately related to the verb *pasal* (פסל), which means 'to cut or carve stone'. *Masseka* (מסכה) means 'statue made by casting' and is connected with the verb *nasak* (נסך) 'to pour'. The word *demut* (דמות) is connected with *dama* (דמה) 'to be like', *mar'e* (מראה) with *ra'a* (ראה) 'to see' and *tabnit* (תבנית) with *bana* (בנה) 'to build'. The term *tselem* (צלם), however, has no analogy with verbs like this and is not linked with a verb denoting statue, sculpture, or cutting.

> This is important, because certain of the words in the same semantic field may well have been unacceptable to the Genesis writer precisely because of these associations with verbs. *D'mut*, the one easily transparent word which he did use, was related to the straightforward verb *dama* 'to be like' and created no serious obstacle. But *mar'e* was unsuitable because it clearly suggested that God might be *seen* (Barr 1968: 18-19).

The word *tselem* (צלם) is the most abstract term, which may be used in reference to a physical representation (without a carving, cutting or graving aspect) or to a non-physical representation. It represents something that is not present and may therefore be described by the word 'sign'. A sign is something that refers to something or somebody that is absent. As Clines (1967: 87-88) puts it,

> the function of the image as representative of one who is really or spiritually present, though physically absent. The king puts his statue in a conquered land to signify his real, though not physical, presence there. The god has his statue set up in the temple to signify his real presence there, though he may be in heaven, on the mountain of the gods, or located in some natural phenomenon, and so not physically present in the temple. According to Genesis 1.26ff, man is set on earth in

order to be the representative there of the absent God who is nevertheless present by His image.

On the basis of this linguistic analysis of the word *tselem* (צלם), one
could conclude that, according to Gen. 1.26-27, the human being was
created on earth to be a sign or representative of God, to make God
visible on earth (van Wolde 1996b).

In short, the story of creation is not about human beings dealing
with the universe, it is about the universe itself in which all elements
are interrelated. In this universe, human beings are defined in relation
to the earth (and not to the heaven): the earth is their continuum
against which they are profiled. In their being related to the earth,
they are intended to be an image or sign of God. Their profile on earth
is to represent God, to make God present and visible.

Genesis 11 in the context of Genesis 1–11

In the flood story in Gen. 6.5–9.17, YHWH's concern for the earth is
also the main theme. God decides on a flood because the human
beings are ruining the earth.

> YHWH saw that the wickedness of humankind was great in the earth,
> and that every inclination of the thoughts of their hearts was only evil
> continually. YHWH was sorry that he had made humankind in the
> earth, and it grieved him to his heart. So YHWH said, 'I will blot out
> from the earth the human being I have created' (Gen. 6.5-7a).

The flood comes and goes and at the end of the story YHWH
expresses a changed attitude:

> I will never again curse the ground because of humankind, for the
> inclination of the human heart is evil from youth; nor will I ever again
> destroy every living creature as I have done. As long as the earth
> endures, seedtime and harvest, cold and heat, summer and winter, day
> and night shall not cease (Gen. 8.21).

YHWH removes his curse from the ground and concludes a covenant
with all living beings. He uses the word covenant (ברית) seven times:
five times he mentions the covenant with Noah, and six times the
covenant with all living creatures on earth. It is not just a matter of a
covenant between YHWH and Noah, but of a covenant between
YHWH and everything that lives on earth, including Noah and his
descendants. The final conclusion in Gen. 9.12-16 says:

> This is the sign of the covenant that I make between me and you and
> every living creature that is with you, for all future generations. I have

> set my bow in the clouds, and it shall be a sign of the *covenant between*
> *me and the earth.*

The story of creation, the story of the flood and that of the dispersion show that God does not necessarily share the human perspective;
God also, and perhaps more often, shares the perspective of the earth.
The earth cannot be restricted to an environment human beings have
to live in; it is not only a product of human beings, not only another
word for the human world, but it is a world in its own right. This
implies that one cannot restrict the earth's perspective to the human
one. This can probably be made clear by a comparison with feminism.
Once feminism had made it clear that women are subjects in their
own rights, with their own points of view and perspective, it could no
longer be accepted that women as subjects had to be restricted to the
space or responsibilities given to them by male human beings. This is
the same point I would like to stress here with regard to the earth. The
earth cannot be restricted to 'human environment'. Being in a relationship with the earth does not mean that the human beings determine that what suits them is also best for the earth.

In Genesis 1–11, it is not only stated thematically, but also explicitly,
that the earth has its own face. Human beings are not described as
having a face; only the ground and the whole earth are presented
with a face (פְּנֵי הָאֲדָמָה, Gen. 2.6; 8.13; and עַל־פְּנֵי כָל־הָאָרֶץ, Gen. 1.29;
8.9; 11.4, 8, 9). The human beings are defined and articulated with
respect to the earth: the earth has a face and against this face people
get their profile. Who faces whom? We are used to thinking that it is
the human being that faces the earth, but it is the other way around:
the human being is viewed from the perspective of the earth: in the
eye of beholder earth, the human being is distinguished, or to sum it
up using Latin: *humus* makes human beings *human*.

Finally, at the end of this article it is possible to explain why, in
Gen. 11.1 and 11.9, the earth, and not the human beings, is presented
as the subject with the language in the text. The earth has not only a
face, but a mouth as well. The earth's mouth becomes visible in the
story of Cain and Abel where the earth opens its mouth to take the
blood from the murdered brother and YHWH listens to the blood's
voice crying out from the earth (Gen. 4.11). But here, in the story of
the dispersion, it is the earth's language that is heard by YHWH.
YHWH is the only one listening to it. It is significant therefore that in
Gen. 11.1-9 שָׂפָה, literally 'tongue', but generally translated as 'language', is only connected with the earth: 'the whole earth was of one
tongue' in Gen. 11.1 and 'the tongue of the earth' in Gen. 11.9, whereas the face of the whole earth is to the human beings. In the story of

dispersion God is the only one who acts on behalf of the earth: God listens to the earth's tongue and shares the earth's perspective. This is opposed to the present-day view that the earth is at our disposal. This is the Earth Story as presented by the 'Tower of Babel' narrative.

Chosen People in a Chosen Land:
Theology and Ecology in the Story of Israel's Origins

Gene McAfee

Introduction

The story of Abram/Abraham turns on the two fundamental facts of human interaction with the natural world: biological and social reproduction. Next to God's command to the first human beings to 'be fruitful and multiply' in Gen. 1.28, the call of Abraham in Genesis 12 is the most important passage in the Hebrew Bible concerning the interaction of human beings and the natural environment. Its importance lies in that it both recognizes and profoundly reconceptualizes the fundamental fact of human interaction with the natural world, that is, social population. From the perspective of ecojustice, based on such principles as the intrinsic worth and active subjectivity of the natural environment, the interconnectedness of all beings, and the purpose of all parts of the whole, the story of Abraham is an ominous bellwether of a broad religious tradition, encompassing Judaism, Christianity and Islam, that defines itself in fundamental ways by a utilitarian view of the natural environment (understood as the passive instrument of the divine will), the separation (and self-elevation) of specific social groups from the whole, and the active denigration, vilification and exclusion of many parts of the physical and social world.

The command to Abraham to lay claim to Canaan is the second-order execution of the command in Gen. 1.28, to 'fill the earth and subdue it'. What, exactly, does it mean to 'subdue' the earth? How does one subdue the earth? One does it by settling it, and that requires population.

This subjugation, of course, is second order because it requires subjugation not only of those natural, non-human resources on which humans depend—arable land, water, materials for food, clothing and shelter—but it requires also the subjugation of human competitors: the Canaanites, the indigenous population of the area (e.g. Gen. 12.6; 13.7; 24.3; 24.37; for a discussion and thorough review of the identity of the people and territory commonly designated 'Canaanite' see

Lemche 1991). A fundamentally binary worldview, combined with several strands of theological, social and ecological thought—divine justification for environmental and cultural conquest, competitive and unchecked pro-natalism (that is, attitudes and policies encouraging reproduction), and natural phenomena as expressions of divine disfavor—are interwoven in the story of Abraham to produce a narrative that is frequently at odds with the guiding principles of ecojustice. None of that narrative's central concerns are focused on the natural environment as an active participant in Abraham's story; indeed, there is a noticeable shift in Genesis 12 from the primeval narratives of human creation and cultural formation, in which the non-human environment plays a prominent role (as human-constituting clay, as idyllic habitat, as flood), to the natural environment as source, backdrop and prize for human sociopolitical conflict. From the perspective of ecojustice, the story of Abraham sets into motion an extensive narrative of land use and human competition for that use that many environmentalists have indicted as launching and justifying the Western world's exploitative attitude and behavior toward the environment. It is perhaps only a slight exaggeration to say that, from the point of view of ecojustice, the call of Abraham, with its utilitarian depiction of the natural environment—what the American conservationist Aldo Leopold referred to as 'the Abrahamic concept of land' (1949: viii)—constitutes little less than a second fall of humankind.

It is impossible, in the space allotted for this essay, to treat in detail the entire 14 chapters of the Abraham narrative from the perspective of ecojustice. Three aspects of that narrative, therefore, will serve to illustrate what I perceive to be its preeminent concern with bio-social reproduction and the deleterious effects of such a concern from the perspective of ecojustice: the 'barren matriarchs' ideology of fertility, the expulsion of Hagar and Ishmael, and circumcision as the sign of the Abrahamic covenant. Other topics that bear on these subjects will be discussed in less detail.

Biological and Social Reproduction

Human ecological behavior is intimately linked to human sociological and political behavior. As Lynn White sensibly noted in his influential 1967 article, 'What people do about their ecology depends on what they think about themselves in relation to things around them' (White 1967: 1205). The thinking reflected in such texts as the patriarchal narratives of the Hebrew Bible, composed over a period of centuries to provide a 'historical' foundation for corporate religio-ethnic identity (see Mullen 1997: esp 10-17), is oriented primarily toward human–human and human–divine interaction, and only secondarily toward human–nature interaction. The patriarchal narratives, beginning with the story of the migration of Abraham's family from Mesopotamia and its settlement in Canaan, are concerned fundamentally with providing a 'historical' explanation and theological justification for biblical Israel's territorial claims. The *terminus a quo* ('point of departure') for this explanation and justification is the development of Abraham's family, consisting of an aged, sterile pair with an ancillary relative, Lot, into a numerically powerful ethneme (*goy gadol*, 'a great nation', e.g. Gen. 12.2). The promise to Abraham of fertility recapitulates and redefines the blessing to the primeval pair in Gen. 1.28 of land, descendants and a divine–human relationship (see Clines 1978: 106). This blessing/promise is linked, however, for the first and most important time in the Hebrew Bible, with ethnicity: the fertility of a particular group is to be distinguished from the fertility of other groups. This is social, as distinct from biological, reproduction. While the purpose of this distinction is to establish (or, better, reiterate) a particular divine–human relationship, one of the ecological effects of this distinction is to pit the fertility of the chosen group against the fertility of non-chosen groups. Reproduction becomes an instrument of colonization; as the Israelites are promised by Yahweh, their divine patron, 'Little by little I will drive them [the indigenous populations of Canaan] out from before you, until you have increased and possess the land' (Exod. 23.30). By identifying human reproduction with social reproduction, the biblical concept of 'being chosen' shifts attention from reproduction as an ecological fact requiring balance and moderation to reproduction as the means of cultural survival and dominance. The ecological result of competitive (or simply unregulated) bio-social reproduction is invariably environmental degradation. Concomitantly, social degradation in the form of racism, sexism, militarism and classism undermines the foundations of sustainability and mutual cooperation and support.

Population, Emigration and the Myth of the Frontier

The first point to be noted about the story of Abraham from the perspective of ecojustice is that the migration of Terah's family from the urban center of Ur in southern Mesopotamia, through the urban center Harran in northern Mesopotamia, and, eventually, to the area of Canaan to the west of Mesopotamia reflects ordinary human migratory patterns from (actual or perceived) more densely settled regions to (actual or perceived) less densely settled regions. In other words, the emigration of Terah's family from Mesopotamia to Syria-Palestine was likely the result of perceived population pressure.

That Mesopotamian civilization perceived itself as crowded by the time of the creation of the patriarchal narratives (c. 1000 BCE at the earliest) is evidenced by the Old Babylonian epic of Atrahasis (inscribed shortly before 1600 BCE), lines 352-60 of which read:

> Twelve hundred years had not yet passed
> When the land extended and the people multiplied.
> The land was bellowing like a bull,
> The god got disturbed with their uproar.
> Enlil heard their noise
> And addressed the great gods:
> 'The noise of mankind [*sic*] has become too much for me,
> With their noise I am deprived of sleep.
> Let there be a pestilence (upon mankind [*sic*])'
> (translation of Lambert and Millard 1969: 67, in Kilmer 1972: 166.
> Permission sought).

There follow many lines of Akkadian text devoted to various attempts by the gods to decimate the human population, none of which is successful. Despite massive suffering and appalling human conditions,

> The peoples are not diminished,
> but have become more numerous than before!
> (rev. col. 4, line 39; see also Kilmer 1972: 169; Foster 1996: 160).

Eventually, the gods destroy the human population (except Atrahasis) with a flood, only to realize, too late, that with the end of human life on earth comes also the end of the sweet-smelling sacrifices so beloved of the gods (tablet 3, col. 5, lines 34-35). The compromise reached is that human population will be controlled, on the one hand, by human mortality, and, on the other, by the creation of both she-demons who snatch newborn children away, and an order of priestesses for whom reproduction is taboo (tablet 3, col. 7).

Although the gods recognize the mistake of an all-consuming flood, the problem for which the flood was sent—excessive human population, with its concomitant disruption of the divine order—remained a potential threat that required constant checking through other means, at least one of which became institutionalized (apparently with some high regard) in Mesopotamian society. That the mythographers of ancient Mesopotamia perceived their society to be overpopulated—regardless of actual numbers, it is the perception which matters—is sufficient evidence to accept population pressure (again, a perceived condition, regardless of actual numbers) as a plausible factor in Terah's decision to homestead less densely populated regions.

In marked contrast to the surviving literature from Mesopotamia, the literature of ancient Israel reflects a society that saw itself, physically and spiritually, as a frontier society, and the foundational mythology of ancient Israel, of which the Abraham cycle is the opening chapter, reflects the values of such societies: divine patronage, simple and flexible social and political organization, economic self-sufficiency, the perception of unlimited natural resources, local folktales, social and cultural introversion, suspicion of outsiders, an emphasis on simplicity and domesticity and a marked pro-natalism.

This last feature forms the core of the Abraham narrative and is a central theme throughout all the patriarchal narratives. The problem of the Abraham story is stated bluntly in Gen. 11.30: 'Now Sarai was barren; she had no child.' The Hebrew word for barren ('*aqarah*) is used to describe the matriarchs Sarah, Rebekah (Gen. 25.21) and Rachel (Gen. 29.31), and its use here establishes the drama to come: the dilemma of the childless patriarch divinely commissioned to establish the line of the chosen people, and the intervention of the patriarch's patron deity in order to bring this to pass. It also functions to locate the source of Abraham's childlessness in his wife's barrenness rather than his own sterility. Abraham's childlessness moves from the incidental to the critical in the next episode of his story, the divine summons to emigrate (Gen. 12.1-9, [Yahwist source]). The significance of the notification of Sarai's barrenness in Gen. 11.30 now becomes clear: how is a childless man to found a mighty nation? For that matter, how is he to establish a family that shall become paradigmatic for the other families of the world?

The list of the blessings for Israel's obedience to Yahweh in Deut. 7.14 states that 'You shall be more blessed than all other peoples; there shall be neither sterile male nor barren female among you, or among your livestock' (see Wigedor 1989: 103). Both the masculine and the feminine forms of the adjective for 'infertile' are used in this verse, indicating infertile males as well as infertile females. The separation is vital and telling: the writer understood that males could be infertile apart from females, and that infertility, therefore, could be as much the fault of a male as of a female; this applies to humans as well as to non-human animals. Deuteronomy 7.14 is unmistakable evidence for the ancient awareness of inherent male sterility.[1] This indicates, there-

---

1.   By 'inherent' I mean not caused by external human trauma such as injury or removal of the reproductive organs. The sterility of eunuchs, of course, was a

fore, that the ascription of infertility exclusively to females in the patriarchal and deuteronomistic literature (except for Deut. 7.14)—the theme of the 'barren matriarchs'—is ideological, and does not rest on the ancient writers' ignorance of the physiological role of males in reproduction. Whatever the ancients perceived the male's role to be in conception, the evidence of Deut. 7.14 indicates that there was an awareness that a man could be incapable of bringing conception about in an otherwise fertile female. This suggests that it was possible for stories about sterile patriarchs to circulate in ancient Israel and be preserved in the canon alongside the stories about barren matriarchs. The fact that they did not is evidence of both the creation and effect of patriarchal society.

The inability of the patriarchs to secure sons, therefore, although always ascribed to the barrenness of their wives, is not necessarily a reflection of the ancient Israelite perception of reproduction. It is, rather, an ideological (or, in the terms of Berger and Luckmann, a social) construction of reality. Marital infertility is always a woman's fault in Hebrew narrative. And it is a fault, as the snarling exchange between Rachel and Jacob in Gen. 30.1-2 makes clear:

> When Rachel saw that she bore Jacob no children, she envied her sister; and she said to Jacob, 'Give me children, or I shall die!' Jacob became very angry with Rachel and said, 'Is it I, rather than God, who has withheld from you the fruit of the womb?'

It is impossible, in light of the ideology of fertility that pervades the Hebrew Bible, not to hear moral overtones in this response. Infertility, as the book of Deuteronomy (among others) reiterates, is a sign of divine displeasure, and, closer to Jacob's response to Rachel is the story of Abimelech (Gen. 20), whose harem is rendered infertile because of his unwitting transgression of the divine will (Gen. 20.3-7, 17-18). A barren wife indicates divine displeasure,[2] and Jacob's response is an

commonsense understanding among all ancient peoples, including ancient Israelites (e.g. Isa. 56.1-8; Sir. 30.20; see also McAfee 1993: 205).

2.   The theme of infertility as punishment for moral infidelity was both recognized and criticized in the rabbinic commentary on Hagar's pregnancy and Sarah's barrenness. When Hagar perceived that she was pregnant, she used to belittle Sarah to her mistress's friends when they would come to call. 'My lady Sarah is not inwardly what she appears to be outwardly. She makes the impression of a righteous, pious woman, but she is not, for if she were, how could her childlessness be explained after so many years of marriage, while I become pregnant at once?' (Ginzberg 1909–38: I, 238). Hagar is expressing orthodox deuteronomistic theology, but in her mouth the sentiment is self-critical: Hagar has jumped to an

attempt to exonerate himself from the possibility of culpability. Fertility and morality are part of an overarching system in the Hebrew Bible, namely, cosmology. The failure of the wives of the patriarchs to realize the promise of fertility—see Gen. 1.28 and the study of it by Jeremy Cohen (1989)—is the counterpart in patriarchal narrative to the failure to realize the promise of morality in the primeval narrative: just as the first woman was incapable of maintaining her original design for morality (*be-tselem 'Elohim*) so the women subsequently joined to the patriarchs, Adam's descendants, are incapable of maintaining their original design of fertility. Their infertility is the reflection of their morally blemished condition.

The first explicit reference to ecologically motivated behavior in the Abraham cycle is Abraham's migration from his new homeland to Egypt in response to a shortage of food in Canaan: 'Now there was a famine in the land' (Gen. 12.10). Although famines may result from sociopolitical as well as climatological reasons (e.g. siege warfare, governmental collapse, or non-sustainable farming patterns), the silence of the biblical text regarding any precipitating human factors in the shortage suggests that the famine was the result of environmental rather than sociopolitical factors. Although the riverine societies of Egypt and Mesopotamia were not immune from famine, the rain-based agricultural and pastoral systems of Canaan were more susceptible to periodic fluctuations in rainfall, temperature and pestilence. Moreover, the more loosely organized (and less densely populated) city-states that comprised the political skeleton of Late Bronze Age Canaanite culture did not permit the efficient harvesting and storage of food reserves that were a standard and expected feature of Mesopotamian and Egyptian royal administrations. This contrast is a major feature of the novella concerning the fourth biblical patriarch, Joseph (Gen. 37–50).

The frequent references to famine in the patriarchal narratives (Gen. 12.10; 26.1; 41.54) may be nothing more, taken together, than a literary trope (occurring, as they do, in the lives of all three major patriarchs, Abraham, Isaac and Jacob). On the other hand, it is possible that the frequent references to famine in the patriarchal narratives reflect a historical memory of the last major shift in the climate of the ancient

---

obvious but erroneous conclusion concerning Sarah. The commentary is ameliorating some of the ambiguity surrounding the figure of Sarah in the biblical text, a tendency found also in the rabbinic elaborations on Sarah's generosity and forbearance toward her presumptuous servant (see Ginzberg 1909–38: I, 237-39; but cf. also the elaborations on Sarah's culpability, pp. 239, 264).

Near East, a sustained dry period extending from roughly 2300–2000 BCE. Support for this possibility comes from the existence of a large number of Egyptian texts concerning famine that date from roughly the same period (Shea 1992: 770-71).

In contrast to numerous other biblical texts that attribute drought and famine to divine displeasure (e.g. Lev. 26.18-26; Deut. 11.17; 28.23-24; 32.24; 2 Sam. 21.1; 1 Kgs 8.35-37; 17.1; Isa. 14.30), there is no indication that the famine experienced by Abraham was perceived by the biblical writer as anything other than a naturally occurring misfortune (so also, e.g., Ruth 1.1; Job 5.20; Neh. 5.3). Although biblical writers sometimes understood human beings to be part of a world that included events and phenomena that were either outside divine purview ('chance', e.g., 1 Sam. 6.9), or beyond human (but not divine) reckoning (e.g. Qoheleth), such a view is a distinctly minority opinion. The overwhelmingly dominant perspective of the Hebrew (and Christian) Bible is that both natural and social phenomena are the result of divine will, devolving, for good or ill, on those in divine favor or divine disfavor, determined by their adherence to covenantal obligations. Neither nature nor culture has an autonomous status apart from Yahweh's purposes, and any idea of divine 'immanence' is strictly utilitarian: it is Yahweh who acts through natural and cultural phenomena, not the phenomena acting as part of an independent system. This radically theistic worldview is the fundamental difference between the perspective of the ancient world and the modern perspective.

While in Egypt, Abraham resides 'as an alien' (Gen. 12.10; better, 'resident alien'), a status that reflects his self-conscious awareness of himself as an outsider, without legal or moral claim to insider status. Although Abraham and his line are referred to as 'aliens' in Canaan as well (e.g. Gen. 17.8; 23.4; 28.4), that status is clearly understood to be temporary, until Abraham's descendants have taken possession of the land as its new divinely appointed 'insiders'.

The second explicit reference to ecologically motivated behavior in the Abraham cycle occurs in Gen. 13.5-12, the separation of Abraham and his nephew Lot. Abraham returns to the site of his original encampment in Canaan, the area between Bethel and Ai (less than five miles apart), to resume his life as a pastoralist. The area in which he and Lot—now possessed, like his uncle, of considerable livestock—initially settle is among the more fertile (though rocky) regions in Canaan, receiving a mean annual rainfall exceeding 30 inches (compared to a national average of 26.3 inches). Although the sizes of Abraham's and Lot's herds are not specified (an ideal biblical figure for the livestock of a man of means, according to the book of Job [1.3], is 7000 sheep and goats, and 1000 cattle), the strife that erupts between the herders of Abraham and the herders of Lot is entirely in keeping with the inevitable conflicts over water and grazing rights in the fertile but fragile ecosystem of the confined valleys and slopes of the western hill country of Canaan.

The text's emphasis on the size of the flocks of Abraham and Lot—Abraham's wealth is commented on or alluded to four times in eleven verses—is, on the one hand, meant to enhance the luster of the figure of the patriarch, and, on the other, to prepare the reader for both the clout Abraham will wield in heading a military expedition to rescue Lot in Genesis 14, and the generosity Abraham will display toward Lot in this encounter (Gen. 14.8-12) and toward numerous others throughout the narratives that center on him (e.g. Gen. 14.17-24; 18.1-15; 22.1-24; 23.3-16). This magnanimity will stand in stark contrast to the cowardice and weakness that the patriarch occasionally displays, especially in domestic situations (e.g. Gen. 12.10-20; 16.6; 20.1-18). The issue of exclusive rights to property and, more significantly, lineage, will form the core of the narratives concerning Abraham's children (e.g. Gen. 16.1-16; 21.8-21; 22.1-24; 25.1-6).

Lot's selection for himself of the fertile Jordan valley is partly predicated, according to the text, on an alleged topographical change that had not yet occurred: the decimation of the region surround the Dead Sea. According to Gen. 14.10b, Lot chose the 'plain of the Jordan', probably a reference to the more than 35,000 hectares of cultivable land along the Jordan River between the Yarmuk River in the north and the Dead Sea in the south (Ibrahim 1992: 958). The biblical description of the plain compares it to, on the one hand, the 'garden of Yahweh' (a reference to the Garden of Eden) and, on the other, the 'land of Egypt', perhaps a reference to the Nile-like floodplain that lies at the bottom of the Jordan valley (although see the divergent opinions on the floodings of the Jordan and the Nile in Thompson 1992). At the literary level, the references connect Lot's choice to locations in Hebrew tradition that, while initially hospitable, ultimately proved to be deceptively beneficent.

Yahweh repeats his promise to Abraham of both land and progeny (Gen. 13.14-17), elaborating with a vivid simile the extent of Abraham's descendants: 'like the dust of the earth' (Gen. 13.16). Although cast as a rhetorical hypothetical—'if one can count the dust of the earth'—the implication of the image is innumerability: human fertility beyond reckoning. The same idea will be repeated to Abraham in Gen. 15.5 in astronomical imagery: Abraham's descendants will be as numerous as the innumerable stars. There is, of course, a certain irony, never noted in the history of the Abrahamic religious tradition, in the promise of innumerable descendants to a man who has already encountered conflict over living space with his most important collateral family member.

Reproduction and the Politics of Colonization

The theme of Abraham's childlessness is resumed in Genesis 15, this time in a theological context, the covenant between Yahweh and Abraham. Possession of land in the patriarchal narratives of the Hebrew Bible, no less than in human history in general, consists fundamentally of occupation. If possession, as folk wisdom has it, is nine-tenths of the law, occupation is nine-tenths of possession. The divine promise of the land of Canaan to Abraham is essentially worthless without the promise of descendants—numerous descendants. This fact is articulated in Abraham's plaintive question to Yahweh in Gen. 15.8, following the third divine promise of descendants and land (15.1-7): 'O Yahweh God, how am I to know that I shall possess it?' Yahweh's response is a mysterious appearance to Abraham, in which the promise of possession of Canaan is now qualified for the first time: a delay of 400 years—the Egyptian bondage of the Israelites, explicitly referred to for the first time in biblical narrative (Gen. 15.12-16)—will elapse between Abraham's generation and the generation of his descendants who will ultimately possess Canaan. The reason for this delay is theological: the Amorites (i.e. the Canaanites) have not yet sinned sufficiently to be dispossessed of their land (Gen. 15.16b).

The shift from a concern with biological reproduction to a concern for social reproduction accelerates in the account of Abraham's attempt to secure offspring through the Egyptian slave woman, Hagar (Gen. 16). The key to understanding the very troubling episodes that comprise this domestic drama lies in comparing the roles of Hagar and Abraham, rather than, as is normally done, Hagar and Sarah.

As has been noted by other scholars, the promise of numerous descendants to Hagar in Gen. 16.10 is surprising; it is a typical patriarchal promise delivered to a woman. The only other instance in which a woman is the subject of the term 'seed' is in the blessing of Rebekah. Here the unusual use of the term is a deliberate juxtaposition: the expelled woman Hagar, who becomes the ancestress of a great nation, is placed alongside the ancestor of another great nation, Abraham, who shared responsibility for her expulsion. But the juxtaposition results in more than a comparison; it constitutes a transformation. Unlike the case of Rebekah, whose sons continue the line of Abraham from their father Isaac, here Hagar functions in the capacity of founder of a line; the 'seed' which shall become a great nation is not designated by the name of the inseminating patriarch, but by the bearing matriarch (see Trible 1984: 22).

This fact is not without significance. Hagar's functional parallel in the narrative in which she appears is Abraham. This point becomes clearer when we consider the Yahwist's plotline describing the births and fortunes of their respective children. The childless Abraham, who secures a son through Hagar, loses his son because of Sarah's anger, but nonetheless becomes the founder of a great line through a second son miraculously born. Similarly, the childless Hagar becomes a mother through Abraham, but is expelled and faces the extermination of that line even before its appearance, only to be rescued miraculously and promised that her line, too, will continue and flourish. One might visualize the parallel careers of these founding parents in the following way:

>   childless Abraham: secures line—loses line—line restored
>   childless Hagar: secures line—loses line—line restored

By portraying Hagar as a type of patriarch, a type of Abraham in fact (though a type not entirely acceptable within the Israelite cultural context), the narrator has built into a simple story sufficient flexibility to allow the narrative to take on multivalence. While matriarchs may found nearby cultures that are closely related to Israelite culture,[3] within Israel itself, only patriarchs are recognized as founders. Self-definition here is a product of defining a feature of 'the other'. In this case, unlike the case of the Ammonites and Moabites, the definition of the other is not negative (or it is only mildly so): Hagar was a member of the household of the first family of Israel. Her expulsion was the result of either pride on her part (according to Sarah) or an unwarranted sense of inferiority on the part of her mistress.[4] In either case,

---

3.   So Pedersen's explanation for the Ugaritic Kirta epic (1941); so also Gray (1964: 4, 9, 10), but he appears to err on p. 4 in citing Gordon as the source of this idea.

4.   The qal of the verb *qll*, which is used in Gen. 16.4, means 'to be slight, swift, trifling'; the customary causative, as one would expect, is the hiphil (so 2 Sam. 19.44; Isa. 23.9; Ezek. 22.7), 'to make light, trifling, to treat with contempt'. It is not clear, at first glance, therefore, from either the text or context, that Hagar is the subject of 'her eyes', and that *wa-teqal gevirtah be-'eyneyha* should be rendered 'she looked with contempt on her mistress' (as most translations render). Sarah may be

her expulsion is a breach of the hospitality that became emblematic of Israel's first family, and both her mistress and her master/husband are indicted in that ethical breach (Rosenberg 1986: 93-98).

It is impossible to avoid the conclusion that the final redactors of the Abraham cycle perceived and preserved a striking similarity between the identities of Hagar and Abraham, as evidenced in their respective fortunes with their sons. Yet it is important to note also that Hagar pays a price for this transformation of her identity: the first matriarch in the Hebrew Bible does not become the first matriarch of the people Israel. In the narrative that preserved Hagar's identity as a type of Abraham, Hagar's autonomy is purchased at the price of exclusion from the society that provided the patriarchal foil against which that identity could be shaped in the first place (see D.S. Williams 1993: 5). The common scholarly opinion (see, e.g., Driver 1920: 108, 213; Speiser 1964: 121; contrast von Rad 1972b: 194-95, 234-35) that the story of Hagar and Ishmael is an etiological explanation for the origins of the Ishmaelites and the mutual hostility between them and their Israelite neighbors correctly perceives that one purpose of this narrative is to distinguish 'us' from 'them', and Hagar's unusual actions are those of a woman consistently depicted as one of 'them'. Hagar's ethnic identity has come full circle from her initial identification: she begins as an outsider, an Egyptian slave woman in a Hebrew household, and she ends as an outsider, the Egyptian matriarch of the Ishmaelite clans. Hagar's intervening sojourn among the Hebrew people is the inverse of the Hebrew Abraham's sojourn among her own (Gen. 12.10-20); in this Hagar again appears as a mirror image of Abraham, an image in which Israelite society could see its own reflection and define itself accordingly.

With the expulsion of Hagar and Ishmael, the movement of the Abraham narrative continues toward exclusion—first the Canaanites, then the foreign element within the household of the chosen line—in precisely the direction opposed to that demanded by ecojustice. This movement will reach its peak in the Abraham cycle in Genesis 17, the Priestly recasting of the Yahwistic covenant made with Abraham in Genesis 15 (see, e.g., Driver 1920: 184). At the heart of this chapter is

the subject of 'her eyes' in this verse, and the description is of Sarah's reaction to Hagar's pregnancy: 'and her mistress became diminished in her [own] eyes'. Sarah perceives her status in Abram's household to have been diminished, and nothing is said in this verse about Hagar's feelings about her pregnancy or her mistress. Sarah will eliminate this ambiguity (perhaps unfairly) in her next words, imputing the action to Hagar but the fault to Abram. The ambiguity is almost certainly to be credited to the deliberate narrative skill of the storyteller.

the rite of circumcision, the preeminent sign of the covenantal relationship between God and the people of Israel.

Outward and Visible Sign/Inward and Invisible Grace

Howard Eilberg-Schwartz (1990) has analyzed the Israelite rite of circumcision drawing on literary and anthropological data. Beginning
with Lévi-Strauss's observation that flora and fauna often serve as
foundational metaphors for people who live close to nature, Eilberg-
Schwartz argues that floral and faunal categories served as root
metaphors for ancient Israelite society no less than for any other
largely agrarian society (1990: 119). Employing symbolic exegesis (for
a definition of which see Eilberg-Schwartz 1990: 143), ethnographic
comparisons and metaphoric analysis, Eilberg-Schwartz argues that
in the Priestly community that presented and preserved the rite of circumcision as the foundational symbol of the covenant between God
and Israel, circumcision, despite its symbolic role as covenantal sign
and its observance just after birth, 'nonetheless symbolized the fertility of the initiate as well as his entrance into and ability to perpetuate
a lineage of male descendants' (1990: 143). Eilberg- Schwartz rejects
the prevalent scholarly interpretation of circumcision as an arbitrary
sign of the covenant with no intrinsic relation to the substance of
the covenant itself (see, e.g., von Rad 1972b: 201). Arguing that the
description of circumcision as a 'symbol' (*'oth*) of the covenant means,
on the basis of other uses of the word *'oth* in the Pentateuch (e.g. Gen.
9.12, 17; Exod. 12.13), that the symbol participates in significant ways
in that which it symbolizes; it is not arbitrarily chosen. The intimate
connection Eilberg-Schwartz sees between circumcision as the symbol
of the covenant and that which is the substance of the covenant is
fertility, God's promise of numerous descendants to Abraham (Gen.
17.2, 4-6).

As Eilberg-Schwartz observes, it should come as no surprise that
fertility should be at the heart of P's version of God's covenant with
Abraham, since the Priestly writer was 'pre-eminently concerned with
human reproduction and its implications' (1990: 147). The seven
repetitions of the blessing (or command) of fertility in the P document
(Gen. 1.28;[5] 9.1, 7; 28.3;[6] 35.11; 48.3; Exod. 1.7), as well as P's well-
known concern for genealogical continuity (e.g. Gen. 5.1-28, 30-32;
10.1-7; 11.10-26; 25.12-18; 36.1-14; 46.6-27), make it clear that human

---

5.   Incorrectly cited in Eilberg-Schwartz (1990:147, 167) as Gen. 1.22.
6.   Contrast J's version of the same in Gen. 27.28-29.

fertility is a central concern to the dominant shaping force of post-exilic biblical literature (1990: 147). Eilberg-Schwartz agrees with Isaac (1964: 453) that incising the male reproductive organ as the preeminent mark of God's covenant with Abraham is 'an appropriate symbol for a covenant made with the generations and dealing with descendants' (1990: 148). It is particularly appropriate in the Israelite context, Eilberg-Schwartz continues, 'because in this community the male organ is viewed as the primary vehicle by which reproduction and intergenerational continuity are ensured' (1990: 148).[7]

This understanding of circumcision as a symbol of fertility in God's covenant with Abraham allows Eilberg-Schwartz to attempt to make sense of the most anomalous feature of Genesis 17, Abraham's circumcision of his son Ishmael (Gen. 17.23-25), who is, on the one hand, promised fertility along with Abraham's other descendants (Gen. 17.18-20) yet, on the other hand and in virtually the same breath, is specifically excluded by the Priestly writer from participation in the covenant (Gen. 17.18-22). Most commentators are content to note the difference,[8] and explain the oddity etiologically, that is, by arguing that the text is trying to explain circumcision outside of Israel, as other evidence suggests it was (so, e.g., the Ishmaelites/Arabs).[9] Eilberg-Schwartz argues that God acquiesces to Abraham's wish for intergenerational continuity for his son Ishmael and symbolizes this fact by including Ishmael in the ritual of circumcision:

> The circumcision of Ishmael is entirely in keeping with its symbolism of fertility. But Ishmael's circumcision would make no sense at all if

---

7.   The Hebrew word used for establishing a covenant is most commonly *krt*, to 'cut' a covenant (e.g. Gen. 15.18; Exod. 34.27; Deut. 5.3; 28.69; 31.16; 2 Sam. 3.12, 13, 21), believed to be derived from the practice of cutting a sacrificial victim into pieces to ratify the covenant. The relationship, if any, between this gesture and that of cutting off a portion of the male reproductive organ is unclear. Eilberg-Schwartz's interpretation of the rite, combining ethnographic comparisons with African tribal rituals and the priestly metaphor of 'uncircumcised' body parts and juvenile fruit trees (e.g. Exod. 6.12, 30; Ezek. 44.7, 9; Lev. 19.23-25; 26.41), sees the removal of a male's foreskin as analogous to pruning, preparing (even an immature) male to more effectively impregnate women (eventually) by increasing the maximum yield of seed (Eilberg-Schwartz 1990: 144-45, 149-50, and see the lengthy grammatical comment on Lev. 19.23 by Jo Ann Hackett [1984: 251-52 n. 11]).

8.   E.g. Westermann (1985: 255): while the promise of posterity is given to all of Abraham's children, the promise of divine presence is only with Isaac.

9.   See Driver 1920: 189-91; Speiser 1964: 126-27; Eilberg-Schwartz 1990: 141; Hall 1992. For the older ethnographic literature as it bears on religion, see Gray (1961); for an updated survey see Beidelman (1987).

circumcision was only a sign of the covenant, since the priests exclude
Ishmael from the covenantal promise (Gen. 17.18-22) (1990: 148).

Despite the considerable light cast by Eilberg-Schwartz on the
whole question of the function of circumcision in ancient Israelite
belief, his solution to the problem of Ishmael's circumcision (and it is
a problem) does not finally explain how, on the one hand, circumcision can function as the preeminent sign of the exclusive and obliga-
tory covenant between Israel and its God, and, on the other hand,
how non-Israelite peoples can share that sign.

A warning from structuralist thought is appropriate here. Intelligi-
bility in symbol systems, as in language, arises from the understanding of bundles of relations 'as a system of discontinuous oppositions'
of the order p/not-p, within which 'continuity in any form [i.e. across
the boundary of the opposition] means cognitive disorder' (Jay 1992:
139). Circumcision cannot, on the one hand, function in Priestly theology as an exclusive mark of the covenantal relationship between
Israelite males and their god and, on the other hand, be shared with
many of Israel's neighbors; the circumcised/not-circumcised opposition would be specious and the symbol would lose most of its signifi-
catory power.

So we must look elsewhere for an explanation of the anomalous fact
of Ishmael's circumcision in light of its function as a symbol of a
unique and exclusive covenant. I would suggest that it is precisely
here that we find in the story of Abraham the distinction between
sexual reproduction and social reproduction and the awareness on
the part of the Priestly theologians that cultural continuity depends
on both but more on the latter.

Eilberg-Schwartz is correct in noting that the Priestly circle was
concerned, far more than the other Pentateuchal sources, with human
sexuality and reproduction, and this general concern would be the
logical preoccupation of those anxious to preserve the cultural identity of a decimated people. What this view does not recognize, however, is the 'fuzziness' with which the Priestly circle applies the idea
of sexual reproduction to creation: as is clear from its presence as a
leitmotif throughout the Priestly document, reproduction is not
simply a blessing for Israel, nor for Israel's neighbors, nor even for all
the people of the world; it is a blessing extended even to the non-
human creation. Fertility per se, then, is a blessing Israel shares with
creation. There is nothing distinctively Israelite about it; for purposes
of Israelite identity, therefore, fertility is a necessary but not sufficient
condition.

But what we see in the Priestly covenant with Abraham in Genesis

17 is the simultaneous linking and separation of fertility with and from something else, namely, the covenant with Yahweh, which no one but Israel possesses. Ishmael's exclusion from the covenant is his exclusion from that which constitutes, in Priestly and biblical theology, the very essence of Israelite identity:

> 'And now, if you, on your part, will listen to me and preserve my covenant, you shall be more treasured to me than all other people, since the whole earth is mine. You shall be to me a kingdom of priests and a sanctified nation' (Exod. 19.5-6).

The covenant, understood in Priestly theology as the corpus of cultic prescriptions, constitutes Israel's distinct identity from all other people; holiness is Israel's social identity, both as individual Israelites and as a people (see Gammie 1989). While other peoples may share, like Israel, in the blessing of sexual reproduction (represented symbolically by Ishmael's circumcision), they may not share in Israel's blessing of Israelite social reproduction, which, in Priestly theology, is borne preeminently by Israel's unique possession of the law. The Priestly schema of narrowing covenants, from the blessing of fertility on all creation (Gen. 1.26), to the covenant with Noah (Gen. 9.1-17), to the covenant here with Abraham, will reach its culmination with the disclosure of the full meaning of covenant—the revelation of the commandments—at Sinai (Exod. 19–24). One scholar, writing of the origin traditions of the Israelites, has said that 'it is the social fabric of the Torah which holds them together as a people' (Thompson 1987: 193). Social reproduction and religious reproduction, in Israel's stories of origin, are coterminous.

We see in the biblical account of the failure of the expected solution to Abraham's childlessness (Ishmael) and its actual solver (Isaac) the clearest understanding and presentation of the difference between biological identity and social identity. Ishmael, whose biological identity comes from his father Abraham, does not receive his social identity from him, but from his mother Hagar; it is Isaac who receives, both by his miraculous birth from Sarah and, more importantly, in the covenant from which Ishmael is specifically excluded, his social identity. For the biblical theologian(s), social identity as well as biological identity are both divine gifts, although neither comes without a price.

Conclusion

We return to where we began, with Aldo Leopold's 'Abrahamic concept of land'. That concept, as I have analyzed it, embraces far more

than the simple anthropocentric understanding of land use that
Leopold lamented. The story of Abraham is radical in the etymologi-
cal sense of that word, serving as a root metaphor (see Eilberg-
Schwartz 1990: 119) for Western religious ideas of culture, religious
fidelity, bio-social reproduction, and human worth and relatedness.
The desideratum of a chosen people in a chosen land emphasizes separation, distinctiveness, hierarchical relationships and exclusiveness—
a worldview that is deeply at odds with a sensibility that views interconnectedness as the fundamental fact of ecological existence. From
the perspective of ecojustice, which takes as its point of departure the
connectedness of all things in the system of which the earth and its
inhabitants are parts, the story of Abraham is a radical challenge, so
radical, in fact, that some may find the concept of a chosen people in a
chosen land ultimately incompatible with ecological sensitivity.
Others will find that the story of Abraham presents fundamental and
far-reaching opportunities for those ecologically sensitive adherents
of the Western religious tradition who look to the Bible for guidance
and support.

The Priestly Promise of the Land:
Genesis 17.8 in the Context of P as a Whole

Suzanne Boorer

Introduction

At first glance the promise of the land in the Priestly material (P)[1] would appear (not surprisingly given Gen. 1.28) to be primarily anthropocentric. In Gen. 17.8, within the covenant with Abraham (Gen. 17), the land of Canaan is promised by God to Abraham and his descendants as an 'everlasting possession' (see also Gen. 28.4; 35.12; 48.4b; Exod. 6.4); Abraham buys a portion of this land from Ephron the Hittite to bury Sarah (Gen. 23); the descendants, the nation of Israel, subsequently move across the desert to the land of Canaan with the goal of possessing this land God has promised to give them (Exodus–Numbers). The land of Canaan thus appears to be an object that can be passed from pillar to post: an object to be given away by God, sold by the Hittites, and to be owned and used by Israel as its possession. Like most first impressions there is an element of truth to this, but a closer reading of the promise of the land in P, in its unfolding and as situated within the progression of thought within P as a whole, produces a more complex picture of the land. It will be argued that the portrait that emerges is one in which the land is intrinsically valued, at least by God, with its protection a central theme in the unfolding of P's thought.

The Promise of the Land in Genesis: Genesis 17.8 and Genesis 23

P's promise of the land first occurs in Gen. 17.8 as part of the Abrahamic covenant (Genesis 17). Genesis 17 is a key text within the P ancestral material since the promises of this covenant (of descen-

---

1.   Although there is some debate about the delineation of the Priestly material there is a surprising amount of agreement (see the chart outlining the delineation of Pg by various scholars in Jenson [1992: 220-24]. For our purposes the material that will be designated here under the terminology of P will be Pg as delineated by Noth (1972: 17-19).

dants, land, and to be their God) set the agenda for the rest of the P ancestral material and the unfolding of P's story of the nation of Israel.[2] Although the bulk of the content of the covenant promises in Gen. 17.1-8 comprises the promise of descendants to Abraham (Gen. 17.2, 4-6), the promise of the land to Abraham and his descendants in Gen. 17.8a is at least equally significant. It is framed, and thus focused and highlighted, by the promise to be their God (Gen. 17.7b, 8b). And both these promises are introduced emphatically and solemnly in Gen. 17.7a as the content of the *berit olam*, 'everlasting covenant' (ברית עולם, cf. 'my covenant' in 17.2, 4) that God is establishing with not only Abraham but significantly also with the very descendants promised to him in Gen. 17.2, 4-6.[3] The promise of descendants to Abraham alone is appropriately emphasized in this context since it reflects the focus of the ancestral material in Genesis on the unfolding of this promise. Correspondingly, and of equal weight, the promise of the land (along with the promise to be their God) to Abraham's descendants as well looks forward to the unfolding of these promises not only in the ancestral material but, in particular, beyond this, in the story of the nation, Israel. The importance of the promise of the land in P's schema is also attested in its repetition in the ancestral material in Gen. 28.4; 35.12; 48.4b; and at the beginning of the story of the nation in Exod. 6.4 where it describes the content of the covenant. Accordingly P's account of the Mosaic generation (Exodus–Numbers) is structured around an itinerary that goes from Egypt to the edge of the promised land.

P's particular formulation of this land promise in Gen. 17.8 is significant. The land is portrayed as God's promised gift (*natati*, נתתי) to Abraham and his offspring. The promised land is to be legally handed over by God to Abraham and to Israel.[4] Moreover it will be

2. See Boorer (1977: 14-15) for a discussion of how the promises are unfolded throughout P.

3. See McEvenue (1971: 166-67), who stresses the importance of the land promise as linked to future generations; cf. Westermann (1986: 255, 259-60, 262) who argues that the promise of descendants takes precedence in Gen. 17, while the promise of the land is very much in the background overshadowed not only by the promise of descendants but also the promise of divine presence that encloses it (Gen. 17.7b, 8b). However, the arguments given here that show the importance of the land promise in Gen. 17.8a, and Westermann's own admission (1986: 262) of the centrality of Gen. 17.7, which seems to me to introduce Gen. 17.8, outweighs his concern that the land promise, unlike the repetition of the other promises, is only mentioned once.

4. See Westermann 1986: 229, 263; Van Seters 1975: 283, 289.

granted to them by God as 'an everlasting possession' *(achuzzat olam,*
אחזת עולם). And the land is described distinctively by P[5] as 'the land of
your sojournings' *(ereṣ megurekâ,* ארץ מגריך), and 'all the land of
Canaan'.

'All the land of Canaan' as P's promised land (see also Exod. 6.4;
Num. 13.2, 17) denotes a specific geographical territory west of the
Jordan, defined further in Num. 13.21.[6] 'The land of your sojournings'
is a technical phrase in P referring to the status of the land of Canaan
in relation to the ancestors in Genesis while they are living in it (see
Gen. 28.4; 36.7; 37.1; Exod. 6.4).[7] It is the land in relation to which they
live as resident aliens. They live in it but do not own it, and are
therefore dependent on the hospitality of the citizens for privileges.[8]
That this land, however, is to be granted to them as 'an everlasting
possession', means that they will own this land as property *(achuzzat,*
אחזה) (Clines 1993: 187-88), indefinitely into the future.

Thus the Priestly promise of the land in Gen. 17.8 speaks of the land
as the territory of the land of Canaan where the ancestors lived as resident aliens, which is to be granted by God to Abraham and his
descendants as their property forever. The fate of the land as portrayed here would seem to be as a political entity that draws its identity from Israel and its ancestors as their property. The land thus has
no voice of its own, and the Earth community has no say in this. It is
simply to be the object of divine action in God's handing over of it to
be a possession owned by Israel and its ancestors.

The identity of the land as an object of ownership is reinforced in
Genesis 23 where Abraham purchases a burial plot in the land, the
field containing the cave of Machpelah.[9] Abraham, a resident alien in
the land of Canaan and owning no land *(ger wetoshab,* גר ותושב, Gen.
23.4), after necessarily acquiring the approval of the citizens of the

5.   Cf. the non-P material concerning the land promise in Gen. 12.7; 13.14-15;
15.7, 18; 26.3; 28.13.

6.   See McEvenue (1971: 119-20).

7.   The only other reference to *megur* (מגור) linked with *erets* (ארץ) is in Ezek.
20.38 where it refers to the land where Israel is exiled.

8.   See Kellerman, 'עור (1975: 439-49); Speiser (1964: 170).

9.   There is some debate about whether Gen. 23 was originally part of P or a
later addition. Carr (1996: 111-12) follows Blum, in seeing this chapter as a later
addition, as do Smend and Rendtorff (see Emerton 1988: 388). However, the view
will be taken here that Gen. 23 is part of P, as maintained, for example, by von Rad
(1972a: 246-47); Van Seters (1975: 293); Westermann (1986: 371-72); Noth (1972: 17);
Emerton (1988: 381-400).

land, the Hittites,[10] in order to own some land legally buys the field containing the cave of Machpelah from Ephron the Hittite for a burial site, thus changing his status from resident alien to landowner. Indeed it could be argued that Genesis 23 is even more anthropocentric in relation to the land than Gen. 17.8 for here Ephron sells (*natan*, נתן)[11] the plot of land to Abraham, in contrast to Gen. 17.8 where God (El Shaddai) promises to grant (*natan*, נתן) them the land.

This scenario represents the initial unfolding of the promise of the land in Gen. 17.8 as that promise relates to Abraham and the ancestors.[12] This plot of land is in 'the land of Canaan', mention of which frames the passage (Gen. 23.2, 19); and the repeated description of it in terms of a 'possession' (*achuzzah*, אחזה, Gen. 23.4, 9, 20) suggests a link back to Gen. 17.8 where as we have seen possession (*achuzzah*, אחזה) qualifies the future status of the promised land of Canaan where Abraham is a resident alien.[13] Indeed, this plot of land containing the cave of Machpelah that Abraham buys is repeatedly referred to here and throughout the P ancestral material in Genesis as a 'possession for burial' (*achuzzat qeber*, אחזת קבר, Gen. 23.4, 9, 20; 49.30; 50.13). Thus the granting of the land of Canaan, promised in Gen. 17.8, is initially focused symbolically[14] in this small area of land in which Sarah and

10. 'Hittites' is a late (exilic) term for the pre-Israelite inhabitants of Palestine; see Westermann (1986: 373).

11. See ensuing discussion.

12. This view is held, for example, by von Rad (1972a: 250); McEvenue (1971: 119-20, 142-44); Brueggemann (1982: 196); Fretheim (1994: 504); Wenham (1994: 130). This view is, however, disputed by, for example, Van Seters (1975: 294-95) and Westermann (1986: 376). They argue on the grounds that the non-theological language of Gen. 23 speaks against a theological explanation and therefore a link with Gen. 17. Van Seters favours Gunkel's view that Gen. 23 represents a polemic against the cult of the dead or hero worship (see also Bray [1993: 69-73] for a similar view). Westermann argues that the primary focus is the family rite of burial. In response to this I will argue in what follows that the human (i.e. Ephron's) giving or granting (*natan*, נתן), of the land in Gen. 23 can be seen to mirror the divine granting (*natan*, נתן), of the land, which can itself be interpreted as a theological move, especially in the context of the other linguistic links between Gen. 23 (e.g. *achuzzah*, אחזה) outlined below.

13. See McEvenue 1971: 142 n. 77a.

14. Various commentators nuance this in various ways; for example, McEvenue (1971: 119, 142-43) speaks of Gen. 23 as a 'symbolic fulfilment' of Gen. 17.8, or, taking up Elliger's term, as fulfilling it 'in nuce'; Wenham (1994: 130) speaks of 'partial fulfilment'; Brueggemann (1982: 196) sees the securing of this property for the grave as 'a symbolic but concrete guarantee of possession of the land... This little piece of land signifies the whole land, certainly promised and undoubtedly to be possessed.'

then the other ancestors are buried (Gen. 23.19; 25.9-10; 49.29-32; 50.13). The ancestors may have lived in the promised land of Canaan as resident aliens, but in death they owned as their own property the place where they were buried.[15] The promise of land as an 'everlasting possession' (*achuzzat olam*, אחזת עולם) to Abraham and his immediate offspring in Gen. 17.8 looks to this 'possession for a burial place' (*achuzzat qeber*, אחזת קבר); while the promise of the land as an 'everlasting possession' (*achuzzat olam*, אחזת עולם, Gen. 17.8; 48.4) to the descendants on a long-term scale, the nation of Israel, looks to the more distant goal of Israel's future possession of 'all the land of Canaan'.

Looking more closely, then, at the portrayal of the land in Genesis 23 as it begins to unfold the land promise in Gen. 17.8 for the ancestors, it is clear that its primary identity is as property: it is the object of buying and selling at every turn.

With regard to form Genesis 23 is generally seen to be a report of a sales transaction in which a property, this plot of land, is legally transferred from one owner, Ephron the Hittite, to another owner, Abraham. Its similarity with ancient Near Eastern documents describing commercial transactions, in particular the Neo-Babylonian dialogue documents leads to this conclusion; and comparison with these documents illuminates many of its details.[16] For example, the extended negotiations between Abraham and the Hittites here reflect the ancient Near Eastern custom and style of exaggerated politeness in such transactions. 'Give' (*natan*, נתן), repeatedly used in Genesis 23 in the sales negotiations (Gen. 23.4, 9 [two times], 11 [three times]) is the polite term for selling used in such ancient Near East procedures, as is the verb 'hear' (*shama*, שמע, Gen. 23.16, see also Gen. 23.11, 13, 15) for indicating acceptance of the price of sale, the amount of which, as in Gen. 23.15, is typically stated. The detailed description of the property being bought and sold, as in Gen 23.17, is also a typical feature of these ancient Near Eastern texts (Tucker 1966: 74-84).

The plot of land as the object of this commercial sale is further reinforced by the use in relation to it of *qum* (קום), which denotes the transfer of property from one owner to another,[17] linked with its description as a 'purchase' (*miqnah*, מקנה, Gen. 23.18), and *achuzzat*

15. As von Rad (1972a: 250) states, 'In death they were heirs and no longer "strangers". A very small part of the promised land—the grave—belonged to them'.

16. See esp. Tucker 1966: 77-84; Van Seters 1975: 294; Westermann 1986: 371-72)

17. See, e.g., Ruth 4.7; Lev. 25.30; 27.19.

qeber (קבר אחזת) (Gen. 23.20), which as we have seen denotes a property for a burial place. Moreover, that Abraham 'buys' the land is reinforced in references back to this plot of land containing the cave of Machpelah in the land of Canaan in relation to the burial of the ancestors in Gen. 25.9-10; 49.30-31; 50.13, all of which use the verb *qanah* (קנה).

The account in Genesis 23 thus seems to be irredeemably anthropocentric: the land, or at least this plot, is human property that is bought and sold for the use of humankind. In this instance its use is as a burial place for the ancestors of Israel, and thus its identity is intertwined with Israel's national identity.

However, perhaps this is not quite the whole story, for Genesis 23 represents the initial unfolding of the promise of the land for the ancestors in Gen. 17.8, and in interpreting it in this context the glimmer of a different perspective on the land is opened up. The plot of land that Ephron offers to sell (*natan*, נתן, Gen. 23.11) parallels, indeed unfolds in part, God's promise to give (*natan*, נתן) to Abraham and his descendants the land of Canaan. Ephron the Hittite, then, is the human agent of the divine granting (*natan*, נתן) of this symbolic portion of the land of Canaan. Thus the anthropocentric emphasis of the land transaction of Genesis 23 is reinterpreted somewhat by the theocentric dimension that stands behind it. The anthropocentric orientation of the land promise yet predominates: the land is still an object passed from one owner to another. But at base this grant of land for Abraham and the ancestors to own is the gift (*natan*, נתן) of God.

However, this then raises the question: is the land as grant or gift of God, whether a small plot of land or the whole land of Canaan, to be given to Israel and its ancestors, as its owners, for them to use or abuse as they like? To answer this question, we need to move outside the account of the ancestors in Genesis to the further unfolding of the promise of the land of Canaan in P's account, this time for the Mosaic generation of Israel as portrayed especially in Numbers 13–14.[18]

The Promise of the Land in the P Account of Exodus–Numbers:
Numbers 13–14

P's promise of the land in Gen. 17.8 unfolds for the first generation of the nation of Israel (P material in Exodus–Numbers) in the form of an itinerary moving east from Egypt to the edge of the land of Canaan.

18. Num. 13.1-3a, 17b, 21, 25-26, 32-33; 14.1a, 2-3, 5-10, 26-27a, 28-29, 35-38 (Noth 1972: 18-19). These verses will be referred to as Num. 13–14*.

But it is the scenario set at the edge of the land of Canaan in the P material of Numbers 13–14* that provides further insight into what God's promise of the land in Gen. 17.8 actually means for the land and for Israel to whom it is to be given.

It is clear from the P account in Numbers 13–14 that the land of Canaan that God has promised to give to Israel (Gen. 17.8) will not simply be handed over by God to be used or abused in any way they like. The gift of 'all the land of Canaan' will be granted to Israel by God only when they value the land and trust in God as its giver. In this way God seeks to protect the land and ensures that it will be valued and appreciated by those to whom God gives it.

The P account of Numbers 13–14* begins with the tribal leaders being sent by Moses, at Yahweh's command, to survey (*tur*, תור) the land (Num. 13.1-3, 7*). The terminology used for land in Num. 13.2, 'the land of Canaan' that Yahweh 'is giving' (*natan*, נתן) to the Israelites, parallels that used in Gen. 17.8 and thus leads to the initial expectation that the land promise of Gen. 17.8 is about to be fulfilled for these people who have journeyed on an itinerary that leads from Egypt to the edge of the land of Canaan. The task of the tribal leaders in relation to the land of Canaan is described by the verb *tur* (תור) which has the general connotation of searching out or exploring.[19] In this context, as a step in the unfolding of the land promise in Gen. 17.8, the emphasis would seem to be on the leaders exploring for themselves what the land is like: evaluating the land promised to them by God, and, what is more, evaluating it favourably since it is God's gift to them.[20] Moreover, it is the whole 'land of Canaan' that

19. See, e.g., Job 39.8; Eccl. 1.13; 2.3; 7.25; 9.1; Num. 10.33; Deut. 1.33; and esp. Ezek. 20.6 ,which is the only other place apart from the P references in Num. 13–14 (13.2, 17b, 21, 25, 32; 14.6, 7, 36, 38) where תור is linked with land.

20. See McEvenue 1971: 107, 118, 120-22; Lohfink 1994: 110-11; Dozeman 1994: 122. These authors argue that this exploration (תור) of the land, and indeed the whole P account in Num. 13–14 is non-military (cf. the non-P account). Their delineation of the P text, however, is slightly different from that of Noth that forms the basis of our discussion. They exclude from P (along with some other scholars—see Budd [1984: 151-52] for a summary of these), for example, Num. 14.8-9, which as we will see uses military, indeed holy war, language (such as 'do not fear'). I would argue, however, that military overtones are not excluded from the P account of Num. 13–14, not only because Num. 14.8-9 (and other verses that have military overtones such as Num. 14.3) are included in Noth's P text (as do Olson [1996: 79-80]; Budd [1984: 152]; and Coats [1968: 137-39]), but more importantly because of the context of Num. 13–14* in the P account. Num. 13–14* follows on from Num. 1–4, which not only contains a military census in Num. 1 but presents a picture of a cultic military camp (see esp. Num. 2, and Olson [1996: 75]), thus looking forward

they explore for evaluation, as defined more precisely in Num. 13.21, from its southernmost boundary, the wilderness of Zin, to its extreme northern boundary at Rehob near Lebo-Hamath (or the entrance of Hamoth).[21]

The initial expectation that the land promise in Gen. 17.8 is about to be fulfilled for these Israelites, however, does not come to fruition. This is precisely because the tribal leaders, instead of evaluating the promised land positively and appreciating God's gift, reject the land, and in so doing lead the rest of their generation astray (Num. 14.36). The consequence is that that whole generation dies outside the land— with the tribal leaders, with the exception of Joshua and Caleb, dying immediately of plague (Num. 14.37).

The tribal leaders reject the land of Canaan in no uncertain terms: they bring back a defamatory report of the land (*dibbat ha-arets*, רבת הארץ, Num. 13.32) that describes the land as a land that 'devours' (*akal*, אכל) its inhabitants, and as containing people of great size against whom they paled into insignificance (Num. 13.32-33).

The bad report of the land (*dibbat ha-arets*, דבת הארץ), is a defaming or slandering of the promised land. The noun *dibbah* (דבה) is only ever used negatively, that is in the sense of an evil report or defamation;[22] and this is indeed the case here in Num. 13.32; 14.36 and 14.37, where the adjective 'evil' (*ra'ah*, רעה) reinforces this. The way in which the leaders slander the land is made clear in the content of this defamatory report. Their report personifies the land as a land that eats up (*akal*, אכל) its inhabitants, such that no ordinary people, but only giants, can survive in it (Num. 13.32-33). The verb *akal* (אכל) clearly means 'to destroy' here: the land is personified as a land that destroys those who live in it by eating them.[23] This could mean that the land

to a military campaign, even if the emphasis of this campaign is on *cultic* warfare (see Knierim [1990: 160-61]). Indeed Num. 14.29 (P) refers directly back to the military census in Num. 1. In addition, though *tur*, תור, in most instances does not have military overtones, there is one place where it does—in Judg. 1.23 regarding the reconaissance of Bethel.

21. See, e.g., Davies 1995: 134-35; Dozeman 1994: 122. This stands in contrast to the non-P account in Num. 13.17b, 22 where they spy out the southern area of the Negeb only.

22. See, e.g., Ps. 31.14; Jer. 20.10; Prov. 10.18; 25.11; Gen. 37.2; and esp. Ezek. 36.3, which forms the closest parallel to the defamation of the land in Num. 13.32; 14.36, 37, in that it refers to the mountains of Israel as a *dibbat am* (דבת עם), that is as objects of evil gossip, or the insults, of the nations.

23. Again, one of the closest references here is Ezek. 36.13-14 where what is said of the mountains is that they devour (אכל) people. It is the content of the *dibbat am* (דבת עם), the slander of the people referred to in Ezek. 36.3. See Lohfink's

kills off its inhabitants because it is barren and infertile and therefore
unable to sustain its inhabitants;[24] or, as is more likely, given the
description of the large size of its inhabitants immediately following
(Num. 13.33) and the fear of the people (Num. 14.3), that the land
destroys its inhabitants through war or its desolate consequences[25]—
or both.[26] In any case the metaphor is a powerful one: the land kills
those who live on it, rendering it, as McEvenue points out, almost like
Sheol 'which swallows its inhabitants down its dark throat'.[27] This
personification of the promised land as a killer devalues and negates
not only the land itself, but the land as Yahweh's promised gift and
the promise to the descendants in Gen. 17.1-8.

However, in stark contrast, two of the leaders, Joshua and Caleb,
are portrayed as evaluating the land in the best possible light. Whereas the other leaders say 'the land that we passed through (*avar*, עבר) to
evaluate (*tur*, תור) is a land that devours its inhabitants (*akal yosheveha*,
אכל יושביה)' (Num. 13.32), Joshua and Caleb in deliberate counterpoint
say that 'the land that we passed through (*avar*, עבר) to evaluate (*tur*,
תור) is an exceedingly good land (*tovah ha-arets meod meod*, תובה הארץ
מאד מאד)' (Num. 14.7). This refers back to God's recognition or evaluation of the earth (*erets*, ארץ) in Gen. 1.10, 31, only in a yet more intensified manner (*meod meod*, מאד מאד). God 'sees' (*ra'ah*, ראה) or discovers that the earth is already 'good' (Gen. 1.10, 31);[28] Joshua and
Caleb evaluate (*tur*, תור) or discover that the land of Canaan is 'exceedingly good' (Num. 14.7). Thus, Joshua and Caleb's assessment of 'the
land of Canaan' that God has promised to give them (Gen. 17.8) is in
line with God's evaluation of the cosmic earth of which this is a part.
Over against this, the other leaders 'see' (*ra'ah*, ראה) only the large
inhabitants of the land (Num. 13.32-33). Indeed, the contrast between
Joshua and Caleb's valuing of the promised land and other leaders'
denigration and rejection of it could not be more dramatic. And the
consequences are equally dramatic: the other leaders die of plague
(Num. 14.37), but Joshua and Caleb live (Num. 14.38).

discussion of this (1994: 159-60). The other close reference is Lev. 26.38 where to eat
(אכל) is linked with land (ארץ), this time with the land of Israel's enemies that will
consume, that is, kill them.

24. See Gray 1903: 151.

25. See Noth 1968: 107; Coats 1968: 141; Davies 1995: 140.

26. See Budd 1984: 145.

27. McEvenue 1971: 136. McEvenue hints at this metaphor and the mythical
symbol of Mot swallowing his victims, but states that it cannot be pushed that far,
as *akal* (אכל) is never used explicitly in that context.

28. See Habel, 'Geophany: The Earth Story in Genesis 1', in this volume.

There are, however, yet further ramifications of the leaders' evil report of the land in Num. 13.32-33: their slandering of God's promised land leads to the downfall of the people (Num. 14.36). The people react to the prospect of a land that destroys, and its huge inhabitants, by expressing their fear of being killed there in military terms (Num. 14.3, 'sword', 'booty') and wishing they had died (*mut*, מות, twice, Num. 14.2) outside this devouring land, in Egypt or the wilderness (Num. 14.2-3). Furthermore, in Num. 14.10 they reject Joshua and Caleb's counterassurance in Num. 14.7 that, far from being a devouring killer, the land is exceedingly good, and their further exhortation in holy war language not to fear the people of the land who, far from being giants, ironically can be devoured as easily as bread, for Yahweh the giver of the land is with them (Num. 14.8-9).

In response to the people's rejection of the land they believe is a killer and their lack of trust in Yahweh the giver of this promised land,[29] Yahweh guarantees with an oath (Num. 14.28) that they will get their wish: they will indeed die outside the promised land, in the wilderness (Num. 14.28, cf. Num. 14.2, and Num. 14.35 where *mut* [מות] is repeated twice), where their dead bodies will fall (*napal*, נפל, Num. 14.28; cf. Num. 14.3).

Death in the wilderness is also the fate of the tribal leaders (Num. 14.36-37). It is immediate, by plague and, as emphasized by the repetition of the reason twice, it is precisely because of their defamatory report of the land (Num. 14.36, 37). Only Joshua and Caleb who recognized the promised land as exceedingly good live (Num. 14.38) are to proceed into the land in fulfilment of the promise (Gen. 17.8).

The tribal leaders and the whole Mosaic generation stand in stark contrast to their ancestors with regard to the promised land. The tribal leaders and their generation die outside the promised land; whereas the ancestors are buried in the promised land—in death they own a symbolic portion of it: the plot of land containing the cave of Machpelah. The tribal leaders and their generation lack an appreciation of the promised land to the extent of slandering it and fearing it as a devouring monster that will kill them; whereas Abraham wants the land so much that he not only exercises persistence in order to own a

---

29. See the description in Num. 14.35 of 'this wicked congregation gathered together against me' which stands in stark contrast to Num. 1–4 where Israel is portrayed as gathered around the tabernacle with Yahweh amid them, ready to march forward to receive the promised land to be given to them by Yahweh in 'cultic warfare' (see Knierim 1990: 162).

portion of the land but pays a great deal of money for the plot of land (Gen. 23.16), showing his recognition of its value.

It would seem, then, that although the land as portrayed in the Priestly material of Genesis as property, the object of ownership, granted by God through Ephron the Hittite to Abraham, at least this is more positive than where the land is personified in P as subject (Num. 13–14*), for it is personified in the most negative terms as a killer, as the destroyer of its inhabitants (Num. 13.32). The rejection of the promised land through personifying it in this way is condemned by Yahweh in no uncertain terms: the generation and its leaders who perceive the land in these terms are not, ironically, killed by the land, but through the oath and action of Yahweh (Num. 14.28-29, 35-37).

The conclusion to be drawn from this is that although the land promised to the ancestors and Israel (Gen. 17.8) is a possession granted by God and to be owned by Israel, it is not given to them by God if they do not appreciate, value and respect it properly. The promised land will only be given by God to those—symbolized in the figures of Joshua and Caleb—who recognize and value the land as 'good' (Num. 14.7) as God does (Gen. 1.10) and trust God as its giver (Num. 14.8-9). Human respect and appreciation for the land must match the divine respect and appreciation for the earth. Such appreciation implies that the land can only be possessed by those who treat it with respect. Thus the intrinsic value of the promised land is respected in the P account.

Conclusion

P's promise of the land (Gen. 17.8) as it unfolds in P as a whole offers a significant voice for the land in terms of its intrinsic value.[30] Indeed, given P's anthropocentric and theocentric emphasis in Genesis, the intrinsic value of the promised land as that promise looks towards fulfilment in Numbers, is surprisingly well safeguarded.

True, the land of Canaan, promised by God to Israel and its ancestors, is an object, a possession to be passed from God to the ancestors by a sales transaction between Ephron the Hittite and Abraham as in Genesis 23, or to Israel through God's action in cultic warfare as in Numbers 13–14*. But even while this is the case its value is recognized and protected. Abraham persists in his bid to own the plot of land and recognizes its value in paying a high price for it (Gen. 23.16). Its worth as a burial place for the ancestors is prized highly.

---

30. See principle 1: the principle of intrinsic worth.

And, more than this, even though the land of Canaan is a political entity, the (future) possession of one nation who will live, die and be buried in it,[31] God is seen to safeguard the intrinsic value of the land itself in Numbers 13–14*. The promise of the land cannot be fulfilled, the land of Canaan cannot be possessed by the people, if they do not recognize its intrinsic value. Those who slander the land, seeing it as a killer, unlike their ancestors die outside the land by divine decree. Only those who evaluate the land of Canaan as 'good', recognizing and discovering its intrinsic worth just as God sees or discovers the cosmic earth in Genesis 1 as intrinsically good, can receive it as God's gift in fulfilment of the promise (Gen. 17.8). In this way in P respect for, and appreciation of, the intrinsic value of the promised land is shown by God and ensured by Israel through God's decree and action.

31.   This can perhaps be extrapolated to the whole cosmic earth where its various subdivisions will be the possession of the various nations (Gen. 10*).

'For Out of that Well the Flocks were Watered':
Stories of Wells in Genesis

Laura Hobgood-Oster

Introduction

There are an amazing number of well stories in the Bible. Mates are first encountered at wells, battles wage around or because of them, oaths are sworn and altars built around them, human and non-human alike gather at wells, Jesus even rests at a well during one of his few human moments in the Gospel of John. They provide the 'stage' on which the 'drama' often occurs. An anthropocentric construction of history suggests this theatrical imagery as a metaphor for the Earth as a whole—the stage for the human drama of salvation and action. Wells, along with other sources of water, provide a constant framework for biblical stories.

Usually readers think of these wells and springs as the settings for other important events rather than as significant subjects in and of themselves. But can the wells as central characters provide insight as we seek a new understanding of Scripture from the perspective of the Earth? This article approaches the well stories as evidence of both the ever-present voice of Earth and the too often silenced voice of Earth in the first book of the Bible, Genesis.

Before engaging in this interpretive task, several methodological and theological concerns need to be expressed. The Earth Bible project proposes reflecting from the perspective of Earth. Of course, this raises the controversial question of whether or not one can ever speak adequately for another—particularly if the 'other' is as 'other' as Earth! In liberation and feminist thought, to name only two, this central concern shouts and echoes throughout the canyons of theological construction. Questions of authority face unique voicing as ecologically concerned humans begin to address issues of justice related to others than human beings and, indeed, to Earth. We shoulder a task simultaneously bold and presumptuous as we raise such an interpretive and action-oriented possibility. But in becoming 'fellow members of the Earth community' rather than 'readers within the hierarchy of creation' we move into a role of voice with authority (Habel 2000: 34). No longer can we consider ourselves hierarchically superior to or ontologically greater than our fellow Earth subjects. So we audaciously engage the prospect of articulating our Earth voice.

Still, our voices do not speak alone; rather they should be heard as part of a larger chorus. Earth does have a voice, though most humans do not hear it. We can hear if we are open to listening, as some individuals and cultures have been and still are. We can also hear and become one of the voices of Earth if we begin to recognize ourselves as part of this community, not as rulers over 'it' or spirits essentially transcending 'it'. Through projects such as the Earth Bible project humans recognize both our history of exploitation of Earth and the solidarity requisite for survival of all life that is part of Earth community.

With this as background, I briefly explain the hermeneutic approach that will be employed as Earth's voice is sought through the well stories in Genesis. Then, I outline the passages included along with the general themes that emerge from them.

In a recent work on the book of Revelation, ironically the piece that provides the other 'bookend' to the Christian version of the Bible, Elizabeth Schüssler Fiorenza explains an exegetical approach to Scripture which she designates as 'rhetorical'. Several key elements from her rhetorical methodology are intrinsic to the approach I apply. First, Schüssler Fiorenza reminds us that, regardless of our own lens, the 'rights of the text must be respected, and the chasm between the world of the text and that of the present-day interpreter must be maintained' (1991: 1). Simultaneously, however, one must also avoid running 'the risk of shutting up the message of the text and turning it into an artifact of the past' (1991: 1). In other words, though unpacking the historical world behind the text is necessary, the task of interpretation must include an understanding of the text from the world of the reader or the text becomes obsolete.

She further explains that the process of rhetorical analysis, in many ways a dialogue, claims 'that in the act of interpretation one does not just understand and comprehend texts and symbols (hermeneutics), but one also produces new meanings by interacting with them' (1991: 2). The view of the text depends on one's social location, therefore the text cannot be abstractly removed from the reader's own gaze or lens.

These central concepts in her method of rhetorical interpretation supply an appropriate framework for the task I undertake. In addition, the setting from which the well stories emerge, specifically that of the natural world as human cultures engage it, needs to be explained as fully as possible for our purposes. Simultaneously, the voice of Earth, or lack thereof, must be uncovered from the perspective of a human being living at the turn of the millennium in a world facing ecological catastrophe. At the intersection of these two voices, the dialogue takes place.

Wells and Springs Gushing Forth: Specific Texts in Genesis

Reading through Genesis, one comes upon numerous references to water including, most obviously, the popular and horrifying story of the flood. But another recurrent water character cycles into the text consistently—wells, or more accurately in the context of this study, any source of water that Earth provides for the sustaining of life. After examining these texts, the stories group into several telling themes. Some speak a voice of liberation for Earth and life in the Earth community thus uncovering a hidden possibility for a rereading focused on ecojustice. Others echo themes of exploitation and oppression of Earth by human beings, reinforcing the dualism imposed by humanity on Earth for countless generations.

Dieter Hessel contends that an 'elegant complexity of environmental consciousness and an ambivalent human posture toward nature are both built into the Bible and cultures interacting with it' (1996: 21). This becomes apparent as we dig into the well and water sources stories. Referring directly to several of the ecojustice principles central to the Earth Bible project assists in providing an organizational outline for the texts I will address: Gen. 2.5-6; 16.7; 21.15-19, 25-34; 24.10-21; 26.12-33; and 29.1-12. Some of the water characters central to the Genesis passages are human-dug wells, others are 'springs' that come to the surface of the Earth through their own power. All, though, emerge from the 'womb' of the earth in some form and thus provide potential fonts of life for the creatures who inhabit Earth's surface.

Those passages that speak Earth's voice of liberation and the principles they articulate include several wonderfully diverse stories. The beginning of the second creation account (Gen. 2.5-6) points toward the 'principle of intrinsic worth' as Earth provides all forms of life with the necessary gift of water. Two stories involving Hagar and Ishmael (Gen. 16.7; 21.15-19) exemplify Earth's 'principle of resistance' as those who suffer under the hand of oppressive humans are actively aided in the quest for justice. Well stories that include the provision of water for other than humans as a primary role of wells (Gen. 24.10-21) suggest the 'principle of interconnectedness' in the Earth community.

Other stories, however, continue to articulate anthropocentric and exploitative attitudes. Several concern disputes over rights to use wells (Gen. 21.25-34; 26.12-33). Another tells of the denial of communal access to the source of water (Gen. 29.1-12). As various powerful figures—Abraham, Isaac and Jacob—claim sovereignty and exclusive access to Earth's water sources, conflicts ensue and the water of life freely shared by all becomes the property of the few. Anthropocentric assumptions and lifestyles dominate and wells are filled.

The Genesis 'Water World'

In order to comprehend the well stories included in Genesis, one must become somewhat familiar with what I call the 'water world' of the people whose stories are recorded. Though we are primarily concerned with the perspective of Earth, we must realize that this perspective is being interpreted through the lens of the human beings who collected and eventually wrote the Scripture accounts in concrete form.

Palestine was, and is, a natural world of variety and occasional stark contrast. Evidence gathered from sources other than Genesis indicates that small city-states may have existed, scattered throughout Palestine during the middle of the second millennium, the general time period covered by the mythic and historic account. Various powerful political and military entities, including the Egyptians, dominated parts of Palestine for different periods of time through a feudal-type arrangement. Hints of these power systems emerge constantly throughout Genesis stories. In Genesis 12 Abram and Sarai travel to Egypt during a famine, interacting with the pharaoh there, to the dismay of Sarai, and leave Egypt with additional wealth. These foreign powers developed systems of governance that, most likely, included hereditary local rulers serving as intermediaries responsible to the foreign lords (Alt 1989: 139-49). Such domination of indigenous peoples by imperialistic forces rarely proves healthy for the people or for Earth.

The diverse landscape is figured in the power structures. Archeological research suggests that regions developed based on their unique natural order, as has been the case for human and other life throughout the ages. For example, the plains were broken into more obvious city-state units, whereas the mountainous regions, with their lack of arable land, remained sparsely populated. The coastline, with its access to the Mediterranean, may have been settled first and developed an economic system based on trade, fishing and transportation.

In other words, various cultures existed and the development of these cultures, though somewhat dictated by foreign military rule, was based, at least in part, upon the landscape.

A landscape of varying ecosystems offers diversity for both flora and fauna, for human and non-human. From the foothills of Lebanon to the Mediterranean seacoast to the hills of Judea to the valley of the Jordan, the landscape offers incredible variety.[1] It includes regions of intense summer heat and marginal rainfall alongside areas more readily adapted to grazing or agriculture. Because of the lack of a unifying river system, such as the Tigris-Euphrates or the Nile, the land lends itself to regionalism. In other words, it is a landscape of varying ecosystems.

If one reconstructs the generally accepted historical period covered by the book of Genesis several other factors need to be recalled. The population seems to shift as more semi-nomadic peoples settled or claimed 'land use' rights in Palestine, including the figures around whom the Genesis stories revolve. As a result, we hear stories indicating disputes between various groups of people regarding the land and its 'use'. These conflicts intensified if treaties with imperial powers came into play.

Certainly, non-human inhabitants felt the disruption of increased human population pressure and occasional violent conflict as well.[2] In general, from the standpoint of human history, this place and time witnessed the transition from a semi-nomadic, semi-agricultural society, granted one that was extremely complex, to a more settled, agricultural, semi-urban culture. As revisionist history reinterprets such concepts as 'progress' we realize that such a cultural shift does not necessarily imply that a more 'advanced' human society 'developed' or 'replaced' a less advanced one. Rather, various technologies led to a transition that may or may not have been more conducive to life as a whole than the one it replaced.

However, there does not appear to have been a drastic distinction between 'the desert and the town...with the nomadic shepherds on one side and the sedentary farmers on the other' as many scholars once thought (Hiebert 1996b: 24). Israel, once pictured as a people 'born in the desert', had concrete connections to the land. Rather than

---

1. I use the term 'Palestine' to designate the area which is, at the time of this writing, still disputed. It encompasses parts of late-twentieth-century Israel.

2. An interesting interpretation of the events leading to this shift from hunter-gatherer to agrarian societies (designated as 'leavers' and 'takers') is suggested by Daniel Quinn in his novel *Ishmael* (1992).

a 'progressive' movement from a nomadic lifestyle to an agricultural one, an anthropological theory that influenced much late-nineteenth- and twentieth-century thought, the culture of Israel, along with many others, moved through transitions much less easily delineated. Those stories told in Genesis are of a people who, more than likely, practiced both pastoralism and sedentary agriculture simultaneously (Hiebert 1996b: 26-27). Occasionally situations dictated that they wander or move temporarily to other areas. Evidence for this can be found throughout the narrative, even as indicated by the creation account in Genesis 2 where, as Hiebert emphasizes, one can see 'the founding story of an agricultural society whose identity and survival depended upon its tillable land' (1996a: 41). Sometimes because of their own actions or interactions with others and Earth they relocated, maybe even leaving the garden behind.

In this setting water was not to be taken for granted. A resource requisite for survival for all living things—olive trees, sheep, asses, human beings, doves, locusts—it served as a focal point of community. William Irwin describes the place of water in the area aptly:

> as summer wanes the pulsing life falters, and except for the olive groves and vineyards and a few spots blessed with sources of water, the ground lies bare and sere as the desert, a naked land, trodden by the foot of flock and herd and dotted with scattered black tents of the Bedouin (1952: 15).

Reliable sources of water, available even in times of cyclical drought and in the annual dry seasons, were few and far between in some areas. Thus, the strife between people concerning their use of wells can readily be understood.

'but a stream would rise from the earth': Creation (Genesis 2.5-6)

Most scholars agree that the Yahwist creation account (Gen. 2.4b–3.24) is older than the Priestly one (Gen 1.1–2.4a). According to this powerful myth, 'when no plant of the field was yet in the earth' because the 'Lord God had not caused it to rain', Earth speaks with force. From Earth a stream rises and waters 'the whole face of the ground'. What is happening in this passage?

Before the Lord God acts, forming *adam* (a human/ground being) from the *adamah* (arable ground), Earth acts. Nothing could live—no herbs, no plants, no *adam*—until water emerged. Therefore, from the womb of Earth a stream rises. Does Earth initiate life-giving activity first? Or, at the least, is Earth the first subject of divine creativity, before *adam*? Does this emergence of water lead to subsequent rainfall to allow life? The significance of the line is evident.

When the stream rises from the womb of Earth enough water comes forth for 'the whole face of the ground'. In the beginning Earth's principle is one of no segregation between some who need water and others who need water, no hierarchy of rights to the water. Rather, when the stream arises it covers all. The image is of abundance and access to the essential stuff of life. The voice of Earth ushers in life through watering the entire ground.

On an interesting historical note, it has been suggested that the writer or editor of the Yahwist account takes an 'agricultural perspective' (Habel 1995: 25). The Yahwist speaks with the voice of a farmer as, for example, humans are made from arable land (Hiebert 1996b: 28). Hiebert contends that in this account of creation, nature's 'constituent parts, the earth and soil and its various forms of life—plant, animal, human—are distinct features of the same organic system, sharing a common essence derived from the soil' (1996c: 65). The presence of water gushing forth from the ground as a necessary component of any process of life-giving is easily understood from the perspective of a farmer.

Thus we begin with the first primordial, naturally occurring well— a stream that comes from the womb of Earth providing the necessary components for life to emerge. In the beginning water arose for all of life without regard to a hierarchy of being or to one form of life over another. The intrinsic value of all life is reinforced.

Ecojustice I—Hagar and Ishmael: Genesis 16.7-14 and 21.15-19

Hagar and Ishmael remind readers that the stories of the patriarchs and matriarchs of Israel are laden with problematic human relationships. Hagar, the servant of Sarai, becomes the first mother of a child with Abram. In Genesis 16 Hagar, though 'given' to Abram by Sarai, runs away, or is run away by her mistress. Hagar takes refuge 'by a spring of water in the wilderness' and an angel finds her there, presenting her with the blessing of the Lord. She names the well *Beer-lahai-roi*, or 'well of the Living God who sees me'. Often in the Bible divine ones appear by wells.

In the second account (Gen. 21.15-19) Hagar has been banished again and this time she has her son, Ishmael, with her. In the wilderness without food or water, Hagar averts her eyes, awaiting death for herself and her son. She begins to weep. Then, one of the most powerful acts of justice presented in Genesis occurs when 'God opened her eyes and she saw a well of water' (Gen. 21.19). Ishmael receives the promise that he will become a great nation, which implies that Hagar also receives this blessing though the patriarchal language admittedly understates her pivotal role.

In both of these stories, wells provide life-giving water for the most oppressed, the slaves, the banished ones. Though they could be perceived as a threat to the promise of God to Abram and Sarai, therefore as outsiders less deserving of the love of the divine, Earth again acts with justice. As wells are revealed, ecojustice takes place and water brings life to all, regardless of falsely perceived status or culturally assigned worth.

An additional insight into a strained relationship between Earth and human beings comes from the suggestion that God must open our eyes to the power of nature. The well, Earth's source of water for all who thirst, exists, though sometimes human beings do not see it. This suggests a further question: do the oppressors block the view of the oppressed by reserving the resources for themselves? Only when ecojustice principles challenge the powerful ones who claim Earth's resources will the banished ones have access to the wells.

Ecojustice II—Watering Camels: Genesis 24.10-21

Wells also constituted gathering places as all species came in search of water. At the well outside of Nahor, Abraham's servant rested with ten camels waiting to find a wife for Abraham's son Isaac. Rebekah, along with other women from the city, approaches the well to draw water. When the servant asks her for water she gives it to him and then, with great enthusiasm, offers to water his camels as well. Her genuine concern for the camels and the eagerness with which she serves them water provides another story of connection with the Earth.

Here, the water from the well is for all species who gather in search of replenishment. Rebekah models one who considers it her responsibility to assist all creatures in their quest for life. She offered to water all of the camels 'until they have finished drinking' (Gen. 24.19). This was no small task and it necessarily took many trips down the hill to the well and back up with a full jar of water for the camels. As Karen Armstrong points out, 'all the verbs express bustle and activity. Rebekah was constantly in motion, hurrying, hastening and rushing to the well' (1996: 74). Not only did she water the camels, she did so with urgency and concentration. Earth's water provides for all species.

As the twenty-first century dawns, humanity consumes over 40 per cent of the 'net primary product of terrestrial photosynthesis' (NPP) and, in so doing, uses a high percentage of Earth's water (Martin-Schramm 1996: 133). Entire ecosystems sustained by their water-filled environment linger on the edge of total destruction. Hearing Earth's voice declare justice for all creatures in the provision of water for the camels supplies hope amid this obliteration of non-human species. Additionally, witnessing a human who takes seriously her role in community with other species, as Rebekah works passionately to water the camels, sends a transformative image to an anthropocentric world.

Whose Water Is it Anyway? Genesis 21.25-34 and Genesis 26.12-33

In these passages we witness a drastic shift in the presentation of the earth and the water that gushes forth from the ground. From indiscriminate life-giving water, possessed by no specific human being and provided by Earth for the life of all of Earth's inhabitants, to disputed possession of particular peoples or a particular person, the metamorphosis could not be more apparent or bleak.

As is often the case, parallel accounts emerge in Genesis, possibly offered by two different sources—one in Gen. 21.25-34 and another in Gen. 26.12-33. Both of these stories concern conflicts over water rights. Abraham and Isaac, with their great wealth, dispute with other inhabitants of Canaan over the ownership or rights to the wells. Gestures such as stopping up the wells or digging wells and naming them determine the 'ownership' of the water by one group of people or another.

Genesis 21 relates an encounter between Abraham and Abimelech. Abimelech's servants have 'seized' a well to which Abraham claims rights. Abimelech pleads ignorance and Abraham, always a clever negotiator skillfully using other lives as bargaining chips, approaches him with seven ewe lambs. Issues of human 'dominance' and 'ownership' of Earth and all non-human creatures abound. In giving these ewe lambs to Abimelech, Abraham states, 'These seven ewe lambs you shall accept from my hand, in order that you may be a witness for me that I dug this well' (Gen. 21.30). Abimelech and Abraham swear an oath leading to the departure of Abimelech. Abraham has won the 'right' to the water.

The well is 'named' during the ceremony of the oath, a common cross-cultural symbol of control and ownership that has already been raised in Genesis.[3] As humans name various other living beings, including other humans as witnessed in Adam's naming of Eve, and as humans name places they attain a perceived power over them. On this point, one must consistently question the source of the authority. Does naming actually give humans power over others that live and over places or does the voice of Earth deny the names that we assign? Beersheba, which means either Well of Seven or Well of the Oath, is the designated title of the well over which the two people contested. Earth and the sources of water, rather than being understood as subjects in a community of beings, become objects owned and named by humans.

In an interesting twist at the end of this account, Abraham plants a tamarisk tree and calls on the name of '*El Olam* of Beersheba' (Gen. 21.33). This vestige of worship of local, therefore place-related, deities prior to Israel's exclusive devotion to Yahweh does lend itself to further discussion. In the midst of a story that recounts human strife and injustice, a glimmer of hope appears. The general direction of the account of the well at Beersheba left Earth without a voice and denied the life-giving power of water which was, in Genesis 2, available to all living creatures. It has been claimed for the exclusive use of Abraham and his entourage. Yet, in the midst of this claim, Abraham plants a tree thus creating an altar to the local nature deity and, in essence, praising Earth for her life-giving water. Remnants of the relationship between human beings and Earth in an ethos of reciprocity and kinship emerge.

Another interpretation of this story points to its liminality in the earth–water–human circle. Somewhere between an understanding of the earth's water as gift and the earth's water as owned by particular humans lies Abraham's covenant. He establishes a covenant which does, to a certain extent, provide for communities existing in peace.[4] As populations compete for scarce resources, 'covenants' can seek to establish a just human interaction. The hope of such peaceful relationships between human communities and Earth can provide an alternative model. But the covenant concept is quickly overshadowed by the weight of ownership and its many implications.

The second of the passages presents a more hostile scenario, both in regards to the relationship between peoples as they fight over water

---

3.   See Baker (1990: 11) for other examples of this power of naming in the context of humanity and the natural world in Genesis.

4.   A fascinating interpretation of Abraham's covenant can be found in Norman Habel's recent work (1995).

and between Earth and humanity. Genesis 26.12-14 indicates that Isaac 'became rich; he prospered more and more until he became very wealthy. He had possession of flocks and herds, and a great household'. With this entourage, he returned to an area once claimed by his father, Abraham. The Philistines had 'filled with earth all the wells that his father's servants had dug' (Gen. 12.15). Again, Abimelech enters the scene and tells Isaac to leave. Obviously, Isaac's presence, along with his flocks and herds, will put too much of a strain on the land. The people already occupying the land recognize Isaac's strength and ability to take control of the territory. For all to live with sufficient resources, Earth must remain in balance. Isaac's presence will overpopulate the land.

Isaac proceeds to another area, Gerar, and contends with people occupying the land by digging up Abraham's wells, thus re-establishing his 'claim' to the water and to the land. As Abraham had done, he names the wells, thus assuming his dominance over Earth and his exclusive rights to Earth's natural resources. The names he gives reveal much.

First, we hear that the herders of Gerar 'quarreled with Isaac's herders saying, "The water is ours"' (Gen. 26.20). This happens with each well that Isaac's servants dig. Then, we hear their names—*Esek* or Contention ('because they contended with him') and *Sitnah* or Enmity/Strife ('they quarreled'). Fighting over Earth's resources in an area overpopulated with people and domesticated animals leads to contention and strife. Issues of water rights have been with humanity for thousands of years and, by default, forced upon all other beings.

In the last half of the twentieth century, global water consumption has increased drastically; some estimates indicate that it has tripled in less than 50 years. There are 26 countries considered to be water-scarce nations, indicating that the renewable supply per person is below the level requisite to meet agricultural, ecological, industrial and household needs. Estimates suggest that 460 million people live in these water-scarce countries and that the number will increase to 3 billion within the next 30 years (Motavelli 1998). These figures, which focus on scarcity for human use, compound when applied to available water for other than human species and systems. As species disappear rapidly—90 per cent of the wading birds in the Florida Everglades or chinook salmon in the Snake River—issues of water overuse and abuse draw humans into the Earth community.

Yet, even in the Isaac passage, from a story of injustice and war against Earth and the other, a hint of ecojustice emerges as the voice of Earth continues to speak even with her wells filled. As Abraham worshipped *El Olam*, so Isaac builds an altar at Beersheba and then he digs a well. The connection between the divine and the Earth has not been totally discarded (Alt 1989: 8-9). Does this suggest that wells remain liminal places where the dichotomies of history and nature have not yet been established? Can we find in these well stories an image of the God of the patriarchs/matriarchs closely connected to space as well as time?[5] Such possibilities for articulating an immanent concept of the divine provide promise as we transform human connections with Earth.

The second element of hope comes through yet another well—Rehoboth (Gen. 26.22). Still present are the elements of naming and claiming rights to Earth. However, the meaning of the name Rehoboth, 'broad places', suggests the vision of Earth sufficiently spacious for all to exist in community. A similar promise of abundant life comes from the book of Job when God promises life in the 'broad place where there is no cramping' (Job 36.16). A glimmer of possibility in an Earth with broad places and enough water for all remains within reach.

Claiming the Earth's Commons: Genesis 29.1-12

The well that Jacob approaches on his journey provides water for all of the local shepherds and their flocks. Throughout the passage emphasis is placed on the size of the stone covering the mouth of the well. Some sheep wait at the well already, others gather. None drink, however, until all drink in unison. Though Jacob wants to alter this practice for the sake of Rachel and his agenda, the community states, 'We cannot until all the flocks are gathered together, and the stone is rolled from the mouth of the well; then we water the sheep'.

Jacob always seems to subvert the natural order. He takes his elder brother's birthright, he desires the younger daughter (though, of course, he was unable to tell the difference in the heat of passion), and he moves the stone that guarded the shared water source and protected the rights of the community.

Flocks and humans alike suffer when 'the commons' disappear through the flexing of muscle. Jacob, seeking to impress and claim

5.   An ongoing scholarly discussion regarding Israelite worship of local nature deities proves fascinating, particularly as one studies the Hebrew Bible's conception of nature. It is closely connected to issues of Israelite identity emerging in the desert with Yahweh simultaneously understood as a god with no ties to a particular place or as a god with ties to the mountain. Among many other see Brueggeman (1977); Alt (1989); Harrelson (1970).

authority overriding that of the whole, 'violates community customs' (Fretheim 1994: 552). Though the long-term impact of this violation does not emerge from the story, loss of the commons to human and non-human threatens the well-being of Earth. As 'nature' becomes a 'commodity' that can be bought and sold, denial of the intrinsic value of all life results. Wells, flocks, forests and entire ecosystems function as raw material to provide financial gain in an increasingly capitalistic world market. Those humans with the most 'strength' subvert the natural functioning of the whole to forward an individualistic agenda. By moving the stone, Jacob claimed the well for himself alone and denied the rights of the gathered flocks.

Conclusion

In a recent article on the Hebrew Bible and the environment, Gene Tucker posed the question, 'Where does this review lead us with regard to our question concerning the biblical understanding of the place of humanity in the world?' (1997: 16). Here, I pose the same question regarding wells and the voice of Earth in Genesis and come to the same conclusion, 'it leads to both problems and possibilities' (Tucker 1997: 16).

Sources of water evoke images of Earth's fertility and abundance as all creatures gather around them to drink. Sheep, camels, slaves and patriarchs find sustenance in the wilderness as water springs from the womb of Earth. As places of community, wells link the human and all other life together. As places of worship wells recall the immanence of the divine in Earth's depths.

Elsewhere, wells become settings for strife and enmity, as Isaac so aptly names them. With Earth's abundance reserved for the few and denied to the whole, the value of Earth plummets and only humanity is deemed worthy in our own eyes.

Can the Earth story be retrieved in Isaac's naming of the wells? Through this anthropocentric act of dominance, does the voice of Earth actually speak? When Earth is turned into an object and claimed as a possession, contention results. When human beings decide that our greed and consumption defines all that lives, strife is unavoidable. But when the camels are watered as passionately as the humans and the wells are shared in common, then life for all of the flocks of Earth is affirmed and abundant.

Forgotten Voices of Earth: The Blessing Subjects in Genesis 49

Carole R. Fontaine

Starting from the Ground Up

In keeping with the hermeneutical position of the Earth Bible project, the reading presented here will deviate in a marked way from the perspectives usually presented in 'theological commentaries'. Normally, scholars have felt challenged to trace the text-critical or religio-traditional history of the so-called 'Testament of Jacob' found in Genesis 49 with an eye to establishing an 'original' *Vorlage* for the Masoretic Text (MT), or developing a clearer sense of the stages through which the Bible passes in its journey from Yahwistic monolatry (one god worshiped to the exclusion of others) to full-scale monotheism (Freedman 1987; Sæbø 1993; Westermann 1986: 215-44). Here, however, we will concentrate on finding the voice of Earth, mediated through old Canaanite deities and epithets, buried within the patriarchalizing agenda of Israel's naming of tribal predilections. Reading *with* and *for* the Earth community, as a partner in Earth's travails beneath the hands of our own offending species, calls readers to question the theological principle of the alleged superiority of monotheism with its abstracted, transcendent male god over the more 'primitive' nature deities of fertility that early Israelites shared along with their neighbors. To call this precept into question on behalf of the Earth may require a deliberate restraint, as our theological proclivities try to route us down familiar alleys of thinking. In fact, we must leave the elaborate constructions of human (and divine) ascendancy and venture into other, more blessed fields. This cannot be done by inhabiting the persona of the invincible, all-knowing Western-trained biblical 'expert'—Bible and newspaper in one hand, archaeological shovel in the other. As Earth-based readers, we must be 'born again' to an unfamiliar way of engaging theology: an Earth-creature, the newborn mole, sightless, sniffing, feeling its way toward the nourishing scent of its mother, at home in her burrow of soil and leaves. While this provides a less compelling sense of oneself as the 'adept professional' perhaps, this more humble perception suggests both the newness of our venture, its proper venue, and our own dependency on instinct as we search for new ways to be in textual solidarity with the Earth community.

The text of Gen. 49.25-26 is notoriously difficult: there are philological and grammatical difficulties, as well as a lack of general consensus on the date—some scholars view it as very early; others date Deuteronomy 33 as the more original tradition and suggest our text is very late (Sæbø 1993). In a postmodern climate of hermeneutical suspicion, readers and critics are urged in such situations to feel blessed with interpretive license, rather than trammeled by ambiguity and textual corruption. Fractures in the text, as we find in the disputed verses of Jacob's blessing, signal a possibility of suppressed voices, warring traditions, and theological disputes. Rather than settling for a simple label of 'mistakes', made because of, or in service to, archaizing or monotheizing tendencies of a redactor out of his depth,[1] we may choose to reclaim this text under the rubric of the ecojustice 'principle of resistance'. The witness of text and translators alike is that the divine One towards whom these blessings gesture is best represented through a multiplicity of entities and titles, as are the tribes themselves. Listening for the voice of a suppressed Earth-centered theology, we face the fault lines in the theological decorum for naming the Principle of Creation with the question, '*What* or *who* is *really* being invoked here?'

Canaan and Israel: Two Different Worlds?

Given that we will hear the voice of the nature gods of Canaan beneath our text, one more issue must be dealt with before exploring the identity of the sources of blessing in Genesis 49. In scholarly attempts to understand the relationship of Israelite theology to that of its neighbors, we are hampered by a number of problems. We know Canaanite culture primarily through poetic, ritual and administrative texts, or from archaeology; we do not have an explicit voice in that group theologizing in the same way the Bible does, and recent scholarship has problematized both the territory to be regarded as 'Canaan', along with the ethnic, sociological and historical identities of the Canaanite peoples (Lemche 1991). The Bible's story of tribal Israel 'taking the land of Canaan' is equally ambiguous. In fact, more

---

1.   Editor's footnote: while not all redactors are male, on best evidence, the redactors of the text known as the Bible were probably male.

recent archaeology shows that the two cultures were cradled together, with Canaanite cities expanding and collapsing their populations into the hill regions (supposedly the base of Israelite tribal territories) in response to a variety of environmental, social and political factors (Ahlström 1993; Lemche 1995).

What *is* clear is that the textual polemics against the 'heathens' surrounding tribal Israel, and the rejection of imperial gods imposed by conquerors on the later monarchies, has painted a distorted picture of Israel's relationship to the Other; a concomitant devaluation of the Other's beliefs, rites and environmental practices adds an additional complication. In the light of inscriptional evidence of the past two decades, it is no longer possible to say that early Israel was more different from its neighbors than it was alike; it may be that they were, in fact, the very same people (Lemche 1991: 165-69).

Hence, scholars ought not to assume automatically that Canaanite practices were better or worse than those of tribal Israel. In our eagerness to recover more Earth-attentive forms of biblical theology, we must not fall into the overcompensation of idealizing the religions of rebirth and regeneration: the so-called 'nature' or 'fertility' religions. In theory, it was just as possible for Canaanites to abuse their blessings and gifts from Earth as it was for Israel.[2] Once more, we must shift our focus from too much attention to the Bible's theological construction of the problem—who is the *real* god, YHWH or Ba'al? who are to be the *real* 'elect'?—to a perspective that takes the Earth's concern as its center. King or judge, YHWH or Ba'al, early or late dating—what does it matter if the outcome is desolation of the land, cut trees, poisoned wells, sacrificed babies, burnt crops? It is self-evident that Earth-based readers can no longer view the Bible's sanction of the violent conquest and desecration of land and indigenous peoples—which archaeology now decisively denies ever happened (Ahlström 1993: 284-370)—as theologically or environmentally harmless just because the text portrays God as commanding it,[3] nor should we bow to the

---

2.   In particular, we should note the human component in deforestation that contributed to climactic changes in the periods of EB IV and LBA II–Iron I transitions. I would suggest, perhaps out of some degree of green cynicism, that political practice of both Canaanites and Israelites probably put androcentric concerns far ahead of ecological ones, as moderns would understand them. The depiction of the forces of nature as anthropomorphic deities suggests a fair degree of human-centered appropriation of 'reality'.

3.   A reading of King Mesha's inscription on the 'Moabite Stone' is instructive at this point; if 'holy war' can be commanded by another deity, we should hardly consider it a uniquely Israelite theological datum.

Bible's authority in such ethically critical situations (Kwok 1995; Prior 1997).

We cannot simply 'skip over' the difficult sections of the Hebrew Bible in favor of the New Testament: this text has its own set of issues around the Other (those who reject Jesus). The anti-polytheism of the Hebrew Bible has been conceptually replaced by anti-Judaism in the New Testament, leading to similar disastrous applications of text to real life (Levenson 1985; Klein 1978). Additionally, the dualism of matter/spirit, at home in the New Testament's soteriology, is no friend of this planet—Earth is too easily discarded for a heavenly home that is usually thought of as *outside* of time and space, rather than a part of it. It is all too convenient for Christian theology to blame its ethical troubles on Judaism's Bible, while forgetting that its own amalgam of cultural heritages also merits close and critical scrutiny by honorable believers.

The Tribal Sayings: A Pleasant Land, a Doe Set Free

Critics generally agree that the sayings about the tribes probably orig-inated independently, linking eponymous ancestors to features of the tribe's territory or history; they were later joined together in the com-position of the text (Westermann 1986: 215-44). In other words, though the sayings speak as though some of their content is housed in the prophetic future, in fact, the groups' *previous* experience of the land and their actions within it have given structure to their corporate per-sonality as presented in the text. The *land* forms the tribes in their dis-tinctive particularities, not the other way around. This insight should occasion no surprise, since prior to the modern period of industrial-ization over 90 per cent of the populations of Syro-Palestine were engaged in working the land, and the land was fragmented into highly distinct geographical regions (Lemche 1995: 19-21). Out of this encoun-ter with the micro-environments of Canaan was forged a sharp under-standing of distinctive tribal identities, not all of them agreeable, which our passage then brings together and attempts to link to the patriarch Jacob's sons. The special feature of blessings that obtrude into the sayings about Judah (49.10-12) and Joseph (49.24b-26) prob-ably reflects the later political ascendancy that these groups had already acquired by the time all the sayings were brought together in this collection.

It is essential to note that all the sayings—with or without bless-ing—show a deft attention to the role that each environmental micro-system has played in shaping tribal identity. Tribes, via their eponymous ancestor, are for the most part compared to animals or plants. We find that Judah is a lion, Issachar a donkey, Dan a serpent, Napthali a 'doe set free', and Benjamin a wolf. Reuben is a 'first fruit' of his father's sexual harvest but is compared to water—unstable and holding no shape; Joseph, Rachel's firstborn, is a fruited tree by a spring, whose laden branches—perhaps[4]—spread over a restraining wall (Westermann 1986: 237). Explicit references to the fruits of the land's blessing on humans are everywhere: donkeys tethered to grape-vines, garments washed in wine, teeth whiter than milk, cattle pens, rich food and delicacies, baby fawns, safe harbors that serve as havens for ships humans have built and use to trade the good things of the Earth.

The presence of predators (lions, wolves) among these rich gifts betrays knowledge that even when the land is good, sometimes peo-ple are not. Simeon and Levi are singled out for their cruelty to ani-mals as well as humans, and the serpent Dan is a danger to both horse and rider that pass his way. Authors of these sayings made keen observations of Earth's ways, recognizing the cycles of predator and prey, fruit and harvest, birth and death; they find those same rhythms reflected in human society. The most glowing metaphors involve the fertile extremes of life on the land: the birth of elegant fawns and the extravagance of plenty that allows promised lineages the luxury of squandering wine. The fruit tree image for Joseph delineates the nourishment the land provides as a complex interaction: a spring feeds the tree, the tree bears fruit and feeds the tribe, which then spreads out and test the limits of human-made restraints. This descrip-tion of Joseph recalls the textual 'Egyptian sojourn' during which this man's knowledge of the worlds of land and dream allowed him to feed many, even reaching beyond Egypt during famine to make a place for estranged kin to husband their strength (Zornberg 1996:289). The land, again, makes no distinction between nationalities: all will feel famine; all will know rain.

We hear the great love that the people bear for their land in another telling comparison: the tribe of Issachar is 'a strong donkey, lying down between the sheepfolds; he saw that a resting place was good, and that the land was pleasant; so he bowed his shoulder to the bur-den, and became a slave at forced labor' (NRSV, 49.14-15). Envisioned as surrounded by 'Canaanite' cities, this tribe, like its 'totem' beast of burden, finds the land and its blessings so compelling that Issachar is

---

4.   Other commentators read an animal metaphor here (wild colt; son of a heifer), based on a different reading of Hebrew *tarap* in 49.22; compare Deut. 33.17.

willing to trade his freedom in return for a safe, appealing dwelling. Not only people, but the animal kingdom as well is capable of responding to the goodness of the land—and in divine terms, too, since this gentle, useful donkey's assessment of the territory echoes God's delighted characterizations of creation: 'he saw the land was good'. But we find that wildness also has an allotted niche in this land of promise: predators must eat, too. The hind Napthali does not answer to human voice, nor bear her young for human delectation.

These depictions of the land through the identities formed by living within its boundaries show a keen sensitivity to a broad variety of differences, both geographical and sociopolitical, and their very specificity proclaims the tribes' engagement as *members* of the Earth community. Springs water both 'Canaanite' and 'Israelite' land; wild animals are a danger pacing the borders of human attempts at control. There is an awareness here of interdependence and connectedness with the environment that goes well beyond any redactor's attempt to make us attend by coupling the sayings to ancestors about whom we are supposed to care.

The Blessings of Earth

When we move to the origin of the blessings felt by the tribes in the land, the reader is immediately overwhelmed with an inundation of divine names or references, layered within each other—sometimes difficult to interpret because of their very abundance (Sæbø 1993). The point of the passage in its final form is clear enough, however: we have here a deliberate twining together of vines of blessing and the ones who give them. It is not the national god or Exodus redeemer who is evoked here, but the 'god of the fathers' (Alt 1953), with his many changing epithets and strong Canaanite overtones. Mark Smith's translation of 49.24b-26 follows the suggestions of B. Vawter and others:

> By the Bull of Jacob,
> By the strength of the Shepherd, the Stone of Israel,
> By El, your Father, who helps you,
> By Shadday who blesses you
> With the blessings of Heaven, from above,
> The blessings of the Deep, crouched below,
> The blessings of Breast-and-Womb,
> The blessings of your Father, Hero and Almighty,
> The blessings of the Eternal Mountains,
> The delight of the Everlasting Hills,
> May they be on the head of Joseph,

On the crown of the chosen of his brothers
(Smith 1990: 16-17; Vawter 1955. Permission sought).

What immediately catches the eye is the deeply Earth-related nature of these blessing divinities, perceived by later monotheists to be the 'One God'. The 'Mighty One' of Jacob/Bull normally occurs elsewhere as an epithet of YHWH the national redeemer (Isa. 49.26; 60.16; Ps. 132.2-5), and has been convincingly related to the Canaanite/Ugaritic high-god *'El*. Earlier readings of the term proposed a meaning of 'Bull of Jacob', based on Ugaritic parallelism, expressing the virility of the animal; this is still a popular motif in modern discourse (Köckert 1995). The Hebrew Bible's usage suggests strength and power are the primary associations; in a slightly different form it appears in Isa. 34.7 in a series with 'wild bull and bulls'. As we have it in Genesis 49, it stands in parallelism with 'by the name of the Shepherd, the Rock of Israel'; the grammatical form is peculiar and the term 'Stone' is used instead of the more typical 'Rock' (Olofsson 1990: 94-95; van der Toorn 1995).

However one resolves the text critical and grammatical difficulties, the general meaning is coherent: the patriarchal god of Jacob, identified with the Canaanite *'El*, blesses by means of hands and name, both of which carry power. This divine being is characterized by the strength and fertility of male animals; 'the Bull *'El*' is familiar from Ugaritic texts. Further, this strong, creative being 'shepherds' the tribe. The emphasis in this comparison is on the protection of the flock/tribe, drawing upon the standard ancient Near Eastern characterization of kings and gods as 'shepherds' of the people. This sort of metaphorical language draws an implicit connection between the way Israel's god protects the people, and the way the people protect and draw sustenance from their animals.[5] Humanity, deity and Earth are all related by reciprocal notions of the stewardship of resources and their deployment for greater fertility.

The blessing in the next line references the deity in the kinship terms that are so important in the patriarchal understanding of human-divine relationship: Joseph is blessed by "*El* your Father'. This is entirely in keeping with the Ugaritic portrait of the aged, kindly, compassionate, seated, tent-dwelling father-god. From an Earth-based perspective, we might note that the use of kinship terms for this profound sense of connectedness is in fact a cultural construction of the broader, derived meanings of fertility—and fertility of whatever sort is a biological given, bequeathed to all the entities of Earth *by* Earth.

---

5.   And what does Israel's god get from the flock 'he' protects?

Without the cooperation of the physical body and the environment sustaining it, without the urge for reproduction knit into our cells by the planet that made us, no cultural construct could cause coupling or sexual connection to happen. Here, as everywhere, we are the children of Earth, and kinship terminology—which ultimately attempts to codify a social meaning for genetic relationship—is a way of recognizing this.

The blessings on Joseph suggest an equal respect for the female as well as the male role in fertility by invoking the god *Shadday* (with or without the *'El* supplied by translators) to finish off the parallelism with *"El* your Father'. Usually described as an epithet of the Canaanite *'El*, this designation occurs mainly in poetic (archaic, according to some) and late (texts exilic and postexilic). Typical etymologies relate this term to Akkadian 'mountain' (*shadû*), or less frequently, 'field'— that is, the uncultivated wilderness, whether field or mountain, from the urban point of view (Knauf 1995; Freedman 1987). In fact, the word is a homonym with 'breast' (*shad*), whatever its ultimate derivation philologically, though some have also suggested that the particle *-ay* was an old feminine ending eventually not understood as such by later writers (Lutzky 1998: 17). Further, we can note that this archaizing term for the patriarchal god may be found extensively in texts about fertility (cf. Gen. 17.1-2; 28.3; 35.11; 48.3-4), which makes an association with a possible fertility goddess of Canaan at least worth entertaining (Biale 1982; Bakan 1979: 73-77). We might recall here, as well, that mountains are often thought of as resembling breasts, and often bear names that make that quite clear (the Grand Tetons in the US state of Wyoming, for example).

New evidence from inscriptions at Deir 'Allā in the Transjordan provides another clue as to whom is being invoked in Genesis 49. A text dated to the late eighth century records the vision of a seer named Balaam (cf. Num. 24) where he views a meeting of the Divine Council attended by the gods *'El*, the *"ilhn*-gods', the *'shdyn*-gods', and a goddess *'Sh-'* (only one consonant of three can be identified; Hackett 1984; Smith 1990: 31 n. 42).

The presence of these *Shadday*-gods in conjunction with the unreadable goddess name, *'Sh-'*, has caused some scholars to posit that *Shadday* should be read here. Hence, the 'one of the breast' may be understood as a hypostasis of Asherah, the *dea genetrix* and *nutrix* of Canaan, and consort of *'El* in the Ugaritic texts. This has bearing on our passage; *rahmay*—'the one of the womb'—is one of the epithets of Asherah, which, when joined to the reading of *Shadday* as 'the one of the breast' makes a lush and allusive wordplay (Freedman 1987: 324-

35; Lutzky 1998: 21-25; Smith 1990: 18-20). Though the goddess is not mentioned by name in our text, the context of fertility demands her inclusion, so she is clothed in epithets which could later be viewed as having been transferred to YHWH-'*El*, the father god. Inscriptions from the Judean desert have allowed scholars to recover a dimension of Asherah in legitimate Israelite worship—though whether as a cult object in the form of a sacred tree, or as a full-fledged consort has yet to be resolved; whatever the Asherah of Kuntillet Ajrud turns out to be in the last analysis, YHWH certainly had one (Hadley 1994)!

That the *Shadday* of 49.25a is indeed an example of the repressed divine female principle is clear from the continuation of the verse: *Shadday* gives blessings of 'Heaven above', and 'the Deep' crouching below. In the following verse, she is evoked by her epithets 'Breasts and Womb'. Most scholars have understood these terms to be 'demy-thologized' remnants of the Canaanite gods of heaven and Earth, though we might also envision a connection with the Egyptian gods, Geb (Earth) and Nut (Sky), who are curved together in embrace; in the space between them all creatures live. A rabbinic interpretation of Genesis 1 also recalls the sense of lovers once joined as one, but now separated to create the world we inhabit (Phillips 1984: 178 n. 22).

Another procreative goddess crouches in the depths of our text as well: we have here a clear nod to the dragon goddess Tiamat, the primeval ocean—Hebrew's *tehôm*, 'deep'—found in the Babylonian creation epic of the twelfth century BCE (Alster 1995). In the *Enuma Elish*—a violent creation myth written to explain the ascendancy of Marduk, the city god of Babylon—the female principle of the cosmos is more than repressed. The warrior god defeats her in battle, cuts her in half and forms heaven and Earth out of her corpse, and tears out her eyes which then 'bleed' the rivers of the Tigris and Euphrates. Some speculate that this was an innovation in Babylonian theology— probably influenced by the Ba'al and Yam (the Sea) mythic cycle from the Western Levant.[6] Where once the stuff of which Earth is made was the sacred body of a great mother, the conqueror god has created dead matter, suitable for conquest. Our text retains the notion of Heaven and Deep, both dispensers of life-giving waters[7]—not as an opposition, but as part of a single system; with this image, the insta-

---

6.   The Hebrew Bible knows this myth, too: see Isa. 51.9-10; Pss. 74.15-17; 89.9-12; Job 26.12-13.

7.   'Dew' and 'rain' are the heavenly, sweet waters, upon which agriculture in Canaan is particularly dependent (cf. Deut. 33.13).

bility of water found in the 'blessing' of Reuben earlier in Genesis 49 is reversed.

The blessings of Genesis 49 conclude with another invocation of epithets of Father '*El* in 49.26a (Hero, Almighty). Reading this text in conjunction with the more ancient version in Deut. 33.15-16, we might be tempted to view the parallel pair of the 'Eternal Mountains', 'Everlasting Hills' in 49.26b as referring to the *produce* of the Earth (cf. Deut. 33.15; Hab. 3.6); in much the same way, translators have taken the goddess epithets 'Breast-and-Womb' as referring to the 'natural' product of human fertility. However, this reading overlooks the dramatic confluence of Canaanite imagery: mountains and hills are also the places where the gods live, where deities are worshiped, and only verses before, the Shepherd of Israel was also its 'Stone/Rock'. While grammatical difficulties in the concluding lines of the blessings have led many to translate that the Father's (i.e. Jacob's) blessings are 'greater than' the blessings of the mountains and hills, of breast and womb, a reading aware of the meanings of the Canaanite epithets used here suggests otherwise.

Theological Reflections: Earth the Subject

Reading from Earth's perspectives, the recovery of the Canaanite voices of blessing in Genesis 49 allows us to reintegrate our understanding of blessing as a 'natural' phenomenon bestowed upon all species by Earth, rather than a divine thunderbolt of prosperity originating *outside* of the living cosmos. Moreover, we must take note of the profound meaning of finding the voices of Canaanite nature deities speaking to us in the guise of Israelite theology. One of the most classic ways that scholars establish power relations in biblical texts is by tracing the construction of the subject: the one who sees, the one who speaks, the one who acts—these are the hallmarks of a fully developed persona. In our text, the tribes 'see' how the land has shaped their identity; Earth acts to bless, an activity associated both with pronouncing a blessing and the release of the fertile power that nurses the blessing into fruition. Earth finds a voice here, and it induces action. It is essential to note that Earth need do nothing *special* to constitute blessings; simply being Who-Earth-Is is blessing enough.

In the end, our text suggests that it is neither the 'tribal' father nor human king who bestows the blessings of Earth on his offspring, however much ancient patriarchies may choose to pretend otherwise. It is rather the *interplay* of an interdependent Earth community that creates the blessings to which humanity is all too apt to feel *entitled*.

'El and Asherah, bull, breast and womb, father and mother, sky and deeps, sweet water and salt—all these, intermingling together, fashion and bestow blessing. As we have seen, Earth is a subject in its/her own right/rite/write—and such subjects can also *refuse* blessing to those who ignore, waste or debase either blessing or its giver, an observation apparent in Hosea 9 (Krause 1992). If we accept the legitimacy of the Bible's transfer of Earth's subjecthood to YHWH-*'Elohim*, then hearing the 'Word of God' must also entail listening for the voices of Earth. When the deeps cry out to us in torment, we must not only hearken; we must act.

Bibliography

Adams, C. (ed.)
1993   *Ecofeminism and the Sacred* (New York: Continuum).
Ahlström, G.W.
1993   *The History of Ancient Palestine from the Paleolithic Period to Alexander's Conquest* (JSOTSup, 146; Sheffield: JSOT Press).
Alster, B.
1995   'Tiamat', in van der Toorn, Becking and van der Horst 1995: 1634-39.
Alt, A.
1953   'Der Gott von Väter', in A. Alt, *Kleine Schriften*, I (Munich: C.H. Beck): 1-78.
1989   *Essays on Old Testament History and Religion* (Sheffield: JSOT Press).
Alter, R.
1996   *Genesis: Translation and Commentary* (New York: W.W. Norton).
Anderson, B.W.
1977   'A Stylistic Study of the Priestly Creation Story', in G.W. Coats and B.O. Long (eds.), *Canon and Authority: Essays in Old Testament Religion and Theology* (Philadelphia: Fortress Press): 148-62.
1978   'Unity and Diversity in God's Creation: a Study of the Babel Story', *Currents in Theology and Mission* 5: 69-81.
1994   *From Creation to New Creation: Old Testament Perspectives* (Minneapolis: Fortress Press).
Andreasen, N.-E.A.
1972   *The Old Testament Sabbath: A Tradition-Historical Investigation* (SBLDS, 7; Missoula, MT: Society of Biblical Literature).
Antonelli, J.
1997   *In the Image of God: A Feminist Commentary of the Torah* (Northvale, NJ: Jason Aronson).
Armstrong, K.
1996   *In the Beginning: A New Interpretation of Genesis* (New York: Alfred A. Knopf).
Auld, A.G.
1998   'Joshua Retold: Synoptic Perspectives' (repr. of 'Creation and Land: Sources and Exegesis', in *Proceedings of the 8th World Congress of Jewish Studies, Jerusalem, 1982*; Edinburgh: T. & T. Clark): 7-13.
Bakan, D.
1979   *And They Took for Themselves Wives: The Emergence of Patriarchy in Western Civilization* (San Francisco: Harper & Row).
Baker, J.A.
1990   'Biblical Views of Nature', in C. Birch, W. Eakin, and J.B. McDaniel (eds.), *Liberating Life: Contemporary Approaches to Ecological Theology* (Maryknoll, NY: Orbis Books): 9-26.

Bakhtin, M.
    1981   *The Dialogic Imagination: Four Essays* (trans. C. Emerson and M. Hol-
             quist; Austin: University of Texas Press).
Bal, M.
    1987   *Lethal Love: Feminist Literary Readings of Biblical Love Stories* (Bloom-
             ington: Indiana University Press).
Balabanski, V.
    2000   'An Earth Bible Reading of the Lord's Prayer: Matthew 6.9-13', in
             Habel (ed.) 2000: 151-61.
Barr, J.
    1968   'The Image of God in the Book of Genesis—A Study of Terminol-
             ogy', *BJRL* 51: 11-26.
    1998   'Was Everything that God Made Really Good? A Question in the
             First Verse of the Bible', in T. Linafelt and T. Beal (eds.), *God in the
             Fray* (Minneapolis: Fortress Press): 55-65.
Barth, K.
    1958   *Church Dogmatics. III.1. The Doctrine of Creation* (Edinburgh: T. & T.
             Clark).
Batto, B.
    1992   'Creation Theology in Genesis', in R. Clifford and J. Collins (eds.),
             Creation in Biblical Traditions (Washington: Catholic Biblical Associ-
             ation: 16-38.
Beidelman, T.O.
    1987   'Circumcision', in M. Eliade (ed.), *The Encyclopedia of Religion*, III
             (New York: Macmillan): 511-14.
Bell, D.
    1998   *Ngarrindjeri Wurruwarrin: A World That Is, Was, and Will Be* (North
             Melbourne: Spinifex).
Bergant, D.
    2000   'The Wisdom of Solomon', in Habel (ed.) 2000: 138-50.
Bhabha, H.
    1994   *The Location of Culture* (London: Routledge).
Biale, D.
    1982   'The God with Breasts: El Shaddai in the Bible', *History of Religions*
             21: 249-50.
    1997   *Eros and the Jews: From Biblical Israel to Contemporary America* (Berke-
             ley: University of California Press).
Bird, P.
    1987   'Genesis I–III as a Source for a Contemporary Theology of Sexual-
             ity', *Ex Auditu*: 31-44.
  1993–94   'Bone of My Bone and Flesh of My Flesh', *TTod* 50: 521-34.
    1997   *Missing Persons and Mistaken Identities: Women and Gender in Ancient
             Israel* (Minneapolis: Fortress Press).
Boorer, S.
    1977   'The Kerygmatic Intention of the Priestly Document', *ABR* 25: 12-
             20.
Bray, J.S.
    1993   'Genesis 23—A Priestly Paradigm for Burial', *JSOT* 60: 69-73.
Brenner, A. (ed.)
    1993   *A Feminist Companion to Genesis* (Feminist Companion to the Bible,
             1; Sheffield: Sheffield Academic Press).

1998   *Genesis: A Feminist Companion to the Bible* (Feminist Companion to the Bible, Second Series, 1; Sheffield: Sheffield Academic Press).

Brett, M.G.
1991   'Motives and Intentions in Genesis 1', *JTS* 42: 1-16.
2000   *Genesis: Procreation and the Politics of Identity* (London: Routledge).

Bright, J.
1965   *Jeremiah* (AB, 21; New York: Doubleday).

Brueggemann, W.
1977   *The Land: Place as Gift, Promise and Challenge in Biblical Faith* (Philadelphia: Fortress Press).
1982   *Genesis* (Interpretation: A Bible Commentary for Teaching and Preaching, 1; Atlanta: John Knox Press).
1997   *Theology of the Old Testament: Testimony, Dispute, Advocacy* (Minneapolis: Fortress Press).

Budd, P.J.
1984   *Numbers* (Waco, TX: Word Books).

Byrne, B.
2000   'Creation Groaning: An Earth Bible reading of Romans 8:18-22', in Habel 2000 (ed.): 193-203.

Callicott, J.B.
1991   'Genesis and John Muir', in C.S. Robb and C.J. Casebolt (eds.), *Covenant for a New Creation: Ethics, Religion and Public Policy* (Maryknoll, NY: Orbis Books): 107-40.

Carley, K.
2000   'Psalm 8: An Apology for Domination', in Habel (ed.) 2000: 111-24.

Carr, D.
1996   *Reading the Fractures of Genesis* (Louisville, KY: Westminster/John Knox Press).

Cassuto, U.
1961   *Commentary on the Book of Genesis. I. From Adam to Noah, Genesis 1–6.8* (Jerusalem: Magnes Press [1944]).
1964   *A Commentary on the Book of Genesis. II. From Noah to Abraham, Genesis 6.9–11.32* (trans. I. Abrahams; Jerusalem: Magnes Press [1949]).

Clines, D.J.A.
1967   'The Image of God in Man', *TynBul* 19: 53-103.
1978   *The Theme of the Pentateuch* (JSOTSup, 10; Sheffield: JSOT Press).

Clines, D.J.A. (ed.)
1993   *The Dictionary of Classical Hebrew*, I (4 vols.; Sheffield: Sheffield Academic Press).

Coats, G.W.
1968   *Rebellion in the Wilderness* (Nashville: Abingdon Press).
1983   *Genesis with an Introduction to Narrative Literature* (FOTL, 1; Grand Rapids: Eerdmans).

Cohen, J.
1989   *'Be Fertile and Increase, Fill the Earth and Master It': The Ancient and Medieval Career of a Biblical Text* (Ithaca, NY: Cornell University Press).

Conrad, E.
2000   'Messengers in the Sky', in Habel (ed.) 2000: 86-95.

Coote, R.B.
1990   *Early Israel: A New Horizon* (Minneapolis: Fortress Press).

Coote, R.B., and D.R. Ord
1989   *The Bible's First History* (Philadelphia: Fortress Press).

Coote, R.B., and K.W. Whitelam
1987   *The Emergence of Early Israel in Historical Perspective* (Social World of Biblical Antiquity, 5; Sheffield: Almond Press).

Cornford, F.M.
1952   *Principia Sapientia: The Origins of Greek Philosophical Thought* (Cambridge: Cambridge University Press).

Corowa, J., and N. Habel, for the Rainbow Spirit Elders
2000   *The Rainbow Spirit in Creation: A Reading of Genesis One* (Collegeville, MN: Liturgical Press).

Couffignal, R.
1983   'La tour de Bable. Approches nouvelles de Genèse 11.1-9', *RTL* 83: 59-70.

Craigie, P.C.
1983   *Psalms 1–50* (WBC; Waco, TX: Word Books).

Crüsemann, F.
1980   'Autonomie und Sünde. Gen. 4.7 und die "jahwistische" Urgeschichte', in Schottroff and Stegemann 1980: 60-77.
1981   'Die Eigenstandigkeit der Urgeschichte. Ein Beitrag zur Diskussion um den "Jahwisten"', in J. Jeremias and L. Perlitt, *Die Botschaft und die Boten: Festscrift für Hans Hans Walter Wolff zum 70 Geburtstag* (Neukirchen–Vluyn: Neukirchener Verlag): 11-30.

Davies, E.W.
1995   *Numbers* (Grand Rapids: Eerdmans).

Deane-Drummond, C.
1996   *A Handbook in Theology and Ecology* (London: SCM Press).

Delcor, M.
1964   'Habacuc', in A. Deissler and M. Delcor (eds.), *La Sainte Bible*. VIII. *Les Petits Prophètes* (Paris: Letouzey & Ané): 405-33.

Dillard, A.
1982   *Talking to a Stone: Expeditions and Encounters* (New York: Harper & Row).

Dozeman, T.B.
1994   *The Book of Numbers* (New Interpreters Bible, 2; Nashville: Abingdon Press).

Dressler, H.H.P.
1982   'The Sabbath in the Old Testament', in D.A. Carson (ed.), *From Sabbath to Lord's Day: A Biblical, Historical and Theological Investigation* (Grand Rapids: Zondervan): 21-42.

Drewermann, E.
1976   *Strukturen des Bösen*. I. *Die jahwistische Urgeschichte in exegetischer Sicht* (Theologische Studien, 4; Paderborn: Ferdinand Schönigh).

Driver, S.R.
1907   *The Book of Genesis* (Westminster Commentaries; London: Methuen, 6th edn).
1920   *The Book of Genesis* (Westminster Commentaries; London: Methuen, 11th edn).

Eaton, H.
2000   'Ecofeminist Contributions to an Ecojustice Hermeneutics', in Habel (ed.) 2000: 54-71.

Eaton, J.H.
  1961   *Obadiah, Nahum, Habakkuk and Zephaniah* (Torch Bible Commentaries; London: SCM Press).
Eilberg-Schwartz, H.
  1990   *The Savage in Judaism: An Anthropology of Israelite Religion and Ancient Judaism* (Bloomington: Indiana University Press).
Emerton, J.A.
  1988   'The Priestly Writer in Genesis', *JTS* 39: 381-400.
Fewell, D., and D. Gunn
  1993   *Gender, Power and Promise: The Subject of the Bible's First Story* (Nashville: Abingdon Press).
Firmage, E.
  1990   'The Biblical Dietary Laws and the Concept of Holiness', in J.A. Emerton (ed.), *Studies in the Pentateuch* (VTSup, 41; Leiden: E.J. Brill): 177-208.
  1999   'Genesis 1 and the Priestly Agenda', *JSOT* 82: 97-114.
Fishbane, M.
  1998   *Biblical Text and Texture: A Literary Reading of Selected Texts* (Oxford: Oneworld, 2nd edn).
Fokkelman, J.
  1975   *Narrative Art in Genesis: Specimens of Stylistic and Structural Analysis* (Studia Semitica Neerlandica, 17; Assen: Van Gorcum).
Foster, B.R.
  1996   *Before the Muses: An Anthology of Akkadian Literature* (Bethesda, MD: CDL Press, 2nd edn).
Fox, E.
  1983   *In the Beginning* (New York: Schocken Books).
Frankfort, H.A., J.A. Wilson and T. Jacobsen
  1946   *Before Philosophy: The Intellectual Adventure of Ancient Man* (Baltimore: Penguin Press).
Freedman, D.N.
  1987   ' "Who is Like Thee Among the Gods?": The Religion of Early Israel', in P.D. Miller, P.D. Hanson and S.D. McBride (eds.), *Ancient Israelite Religion: Essays in Honor of Frank Moore Cross* (Philadelphia: Fortress Press): 315-35.
Fretheim, T.E.
  1992   'Creator, Creature and Co-Creation in Genesis 1–2', *WWSup* 1: 11-20.
  1994   *Genesis* (The New Interpreter's Bible, 1; Nashville: Abingdon Press).
  2000   'The Earth Story in Jeremiah 12', in Habel (ed.) 2000: 96-110.
Frymer-Kensky, T.
  1977   'The Atrahasis Epic and its Significance for our Understanding of Genesis 1–9', *BA* 40.4: 147-55.
  1983   'Pollution, Purification and Purgation in Biblical Israel', in Meyers and O'Connor 1983: 399-414.
  1992   *In the Wake of the Goddesses: Women, Culture and the Biblical Transformation of Pagan Myth* (New York: Fawcett Columbine).
Gammie, J.G.
  1989   *Holiness in Israel* (Minneapolis: Fortress Press).
García Marquez, G.
  1978   *One Hundred Years of Solitude* (London: Pan Books).

Gardner, A.
1990   'Gen. 2.4b–3: A Mythological Paradigm of Sexual Equality or of the
             Religious History of Pre-exilic Israel?', *SJT* 43: 1-18.
Gates, H.L.
1988   *The Signifying Monkey: A Theory of African American Literary Criti-
             cism* (New York: Oxford University Press).
Ginzberg, L.
1909–38   *The Legends of the Jews* (7 vols.; Philadelphia: Jewish Publication
             Society of America).
Goldingay, J.
1996   *After Eating the Apricot: Men and Women with God* (Carlisle: Pater-
             noster Press).
Gowan, D.E.
1975   *When Man Becomes God: Humanism and Hybris in the Old Testament*
             (Pittsburgh: Pickwick Press).
1986   *Eschatology in the Old Testament* (Edinburgh: T. & T. Clark).
Gray, G.B.
1903   *A Critical and Exegetical Commentary on Numbers* (Edinburgh: T. &
             T. Clark).
Gray, J.
1964   *The Krt Text in the Literature of Ras Shamra: A Social Myth of Ancient
             Canaan* (Leiden: E.J. Brill, 2nd edn).
Gray, L.H. (ed.)
1961   'Circumcision', in J. Hastings (ed.), *Encyclopaedia of Religion and
             Ethics* (New York: Charles Scribner's Sons [1908–1912]): 659-80.
Griffin, S.
1980   *Woman and Nature: The Roaring Inside Her* (New York: Harper &
             Row).
Gunkel, H.
1969   *Genesis* (Göttingen: Vandenhoeck & Ruprecht, 8th edn).
Haag, H.
1975   '*Chamas*', *TDOT*, V: 479-87.
Habel, N.
1965   *The Form and Meaning of the Fall Narrative: A Detailed Analysis of
             Genesis 3* (St Louis: Concordia).
1971   *Literary Criticism of the Old Testament* (Philadelphia: Fortress Press).
1972   'He Who Stretches Out the Heavens', *CBQ* 34: 417-30.
1995   *The Land Is Mine: Six Biblical Ideologies* (Minneapolis: Fortress Press).
2000   'Introducing the Earth Bible', in Habel (ed.) 2000: 25-37.
Habel, N. (ed.)
2000   *Readings from the Perspective of Earth* (Earth Bible, 1; Sheffield:
             Sheffield Academic Press).
Hackett, J.A.
1984   *The Balaam Text from Deir 'Allā* (HSM, 31; Chico, CA: Scholars
             Press).
Hadley, J.M.
1994   'Yahweh and "His Asherah": Archaeological and Textual Evidence
             for the Cult of the Goddess', in W. Dietrich and M.A. Klopfenstein
             (eds.), *Ein Gott allein? JHWH-Verehrung und biblischer Monotheismus
             im Kontext der israelitischen und altorientalischen Religionsgeschichte*
             (OBO, 139; Fribourg: Editions universitaires; Göttingen: Vanden-
             hoeck & Ruprecht): 235-68.

Hadlington, P., and J. Gerozisis
    1988   *Urban Pest Control*, (Kensington: New South Wales University Press, 2nd rev. edn).
Halifax, J.
    1984   *The Fruitful Darkness: Reconnecting with the Body of the Earth* (San Francisco: HarperCollins).
Halkes, J.M.
    1991   *New Creation: Christian Feminism and the Renewal of the Earth* (London: SPCK).
Hall, R.G.
    1992   'Circumcision', *ABD*, I: 1025-31.
Hamilton, V.P.
    1990   *The Book of Genesis 1–17* (NICOT: Grand Rapids: Eerdmans).
Harland, P.J.
    1993   'A Further Note on Genesis VI 13', *VT* 43.3: 408-11.
    1996   *The Value of Human Life: A Study of the Story of the Flood (Genesis 6–9)* (VTSup, 64; Leiden: E.J. Brill).
Harrelson, W.
    1970   *From Fertility Cult to Worship* (Garden City: Anchor Books/Doubleday).
Hayter, M.
    1987   *The New Eve in Christ: The Use and Abuse of the Bible in the Debate about Women in the Church* (London: SPCK).
Hessel, D.T. (ed.)
    1996   *Theology for Earth Community: A Field Guide* (Maryknoll. NY: Orbis Books).
Hiebert, T.
    1996a   'Re-Imaging Nature: Shifts in Biblical Interpretation', *Int* 50: 36-45.
    1996b   'Rethinking Traditional Approaches to Nature in the Bible', in Hessel 1996: 23-30.
    1996c   *The Yahwist's Landscape: Nature and Religion in Early Israel* (New York: Oxford University Press).
Hyams, E.
    1976   *Soil and Civilization* (London: John Murray).
Ibrahim, M.
    1992   'Jordan Valley', *ABD*, III: New York: 958-60.
Irwin, W.
    1952   *The Old Testament: Keystone of Human Culture* (New York: Schuman).
Isaac, E.
    1964   'Circumcision as a Covenant Rite', *Anthropos* 59.3–4: 444-56.
Jacobsen, T.
    1997   'The Eridu Genesis', in William W. Hallo (ed.), *The Context of Scripture. I. Canonical Compositions from the Biblical World* (Leiden: E.J. Brill): 513-15.
Janzen, J.G.
    1994   'On the Moral Nature of God's Power: Yahweh and the Sea in Job and Deutero-Isaiah', *CBQ* 56: 458-78.
Jay, N.
    1992   *Throughout your Generations Forever: Sacrifice, Religion, and Paternity* (Chicago: University of Chicago Press).

Jenson, P.
    1992   *Graded Holiness: A Key to the Priestly Conception of the World*
                (JSOTSup, 106; Sheffield: JSOT Press).
Jewish Publication Society
    1985   *TANAKH, the Holy Scriptures: The New JPS Translation According to
                the Traditional Hebrew Text* (Philadelphia: Jewish Publication Soci-
                ety).
Jobling, D. and N. Loewen
    2000   'Sketches for Earth Readings of the Book of Amos', in Habel (ed.)
                2000: 72-85.
Johnson, M.
    1995   'From Commonsense to Cartography in Genesis 1–13', *Proceedings,
                East Great Lakes and Midwest Biblical Society* 15: 93-112.
Joines, K.
    1975   'The Serpent in Gen. 3', *ZAW* 87: 1-11.
Kahn, I.
    1990   'Jewish Sabbath', in E.J. Fisher (ed.), *The Jewish Roots of Christian
                Liturgy* (New York: Paulist Press): 121-29.
Kapelrud, A.S.
    1974   'The Mythological Features in Genesis Chapter 1 and the Author's
                Intentions', *VT* 24: 17-86.
Kellerman, D.
    1975   'גור', *TDOT*, II: 439-49.
Kikawada, I.M.
    1974   'The Shape of Genesis 1–11', in J.J. Jackson and M. Kessler (eds.),
                Rhetorical Criticism: Essays in Honor of J. Muilenberg (Pittsburgh:
                Pickwick Press): 18-32.
Kilmer, A.D.
    1972   'The Mesopotamian Concept of Overpopulation and its Solution as
                Reflected in the Mythology', *Or* 41: 160-77.
King, K. (ed.)
    1997   *Women and Goddess Traditions in Antiquity and Today* (Minneapolis:
                Fortress Press).
Klein, C.
    1978   *Anti-Judaism in Christian Theology* (trans. Edward Quinn; Philadel-
                phia: Fortress Press).
Knauf, E.A.
    1995   'Shadday', in van der Toorn, Becking and van der Horst 1995:
                1416-23.
Knierim, R.P.
    1990   'The Book of Numbers', in E. Blum *et al.* (eds.), *Die Hebräische Bibel
                und ihre zweifach Nachgeschichte: Festschrift für Rolf Rendtorff zum 65.
                Geburtstag* (Neukirchen–Vluyn: Neukirchener Verlag): 155-63.
Knight, D.A.
    1985   'The Pentateuch', in D.A. Knight and G.M. Tucker (eds.), *The
                Hebrew Bible and its Modern Interpreters* (Chico, CA: Scholars Press):
                263-90.
Köckert, M.
    1995   'Mighty One of Jacob', in van der Toorn, Becking and van der
                Horst 1995: 1073-76.
Korsak, M.
    1993   'Genesis: A New Look', in Brenner 1993: 39-52.

Krause, D.
1992   'A Blessing Cursed: The Prophet's Prayer for Barren Womb and
          Dry Breasts in Hosea 9', in D. Fewell (ed.), *Reading Between Texts:
          Intertextuality and the Hebrew Bible* (Literary Currents in Biblical
          Interpretation; Louisville, KY: Westminster/John Knox Press): 191-
          202.
Kugel, J.L.
1997   *The Bible as it Was* (Cambridge, MA: Harvard University Press).
Kwok, Pui-lan
1995   *Discovering the Bible in the Non-Biblical World* (Maryknoll, NY: Orbis
          Books).
Lambert, W.G., and A.R. Millard
1969   *Atra-ḫasīs: The Babylonian Story of the Flood* (Oxford: Clarendon
          Press).
Landy, F.
1979   'The Song of Songs and the Garden of Eden', *JBL* 98.4: 513-28.
Lévi-Strauss, C.
1962   *Totemism* (Boston: Beacon Press).
Lemche, N.P.
1991   *The Canaanites and their Land: The Tradition of the Canaanites* (Shef-
          field: Sheffield Academic Press).
1995   *Ancient Israel: A New History of Israelite Society* (BibSem, 5; Sheffield:
          Sheffield Academic Press).
Leopold, A.
1949   *A Sand County Almanac* (New York: Oxford University Press).
Levenson, J.D.
1985   'Is There a Counterpart in the Hebrew Bible to New Testament
          Anti-Semitism?', *JES* 22: 242-60.
1988   *Creation and the Persistence of Evil: The Jewish Drama of Divine Omni-
          potence* (San Francisco: Harper & Row).
Lewis, J.P.
1968   *A Study of the Interpretation of Noah and the Flood in Jewish and
          Christian Literature* (Leiden: E.J. Brill).
Lincoln, A.T.
1982   'From Sabbath to Lord's Day: A Biblical and Theological Perspec-
          tive', in D.A. Carson (ed.), *From Sabbath to Lord's Day: A Biblical,
          Historical and Theological Investigation* (Grand Rapids: Zondervan):
          343-412.
Linzey, A.
1991   'The Theological Basis of Animal Rights', *Christian Century* 108.28:
          906-909.
1993   'Liberation Theology and the Oppression of Animals', *SJT* 46: 507-
          25.
Lohfink, N.
1994   *The Theology of the Pentateuch: Themes of the Priestly Narrative and
          Deuteronomy* (Edinburgh: T. & T. Clark).
Long, A.
1993   *In a Chariot Drawn by Lions: The Search for the Female in the Deity*
          (Freedom, CA: The Crossings Press).
Lutzky, H.
1998   'Shadday as a Goddess Epithet', *VT* 48: 15-36.

MacIntyre, A.
    1981   *After Virtue* (Notre Dame: University of Notre Dame Press).
    2000   *Dependent Rational Animals* (London: Duckworth).
Martin-Schramm, J.
    1996   'The State of the Debate in Christian Ethics', in Hessel 1996: 132-42.
Mays, J. (ed.)
    1988   *Harper's Bible Commentary* (San Francisco: Harper & Row).
McAfee, G.
    1993   'Eunuch', in B.M. Metzger and M.D. Coogan (eds.), *Oxford Companion to the Bible* (New York: Oxford University Press): 205-206.
    1996   'Ecology and Biblical Studies', in Hessel 1996: 31-44.
McEvenue, S.E.
    1971   *The Narrative Style of the Priestly Writer* (Rome: Biblical Institute Press).
McKeown, J.
    1997   'The Theme of Land in Genesis 1–11 and its Significance for the Abraham Narrative', *IBS* 19: 51-64.
Meek, T.J.
    1955   'The Code of Hammurabi', *ANET*: 163-80.
Meier, S.
    1991   'The Sabbath and Purification Cycles', in T. Eskenazi *et al.* (eds.), *The Sabbath in Jewish and Christian Traditions* (New York: Crossroad): 3-11.
Mendenhall, G.
    1974   'The Shady Side of Wisdom: The Date and Purpose of Genesis 3', in H.N. Bream *et al.* (eds.), *A Light unto My Path* (Philadelphia: Temple University Press): 319-35.
Merchant, C.
    1982   *The Death of Nature: Women, Ecology, and the Scientific Revolution* (London: Wildwood House).
Meyers, C.
    1978   'Roots of Restriction: Women in Early Israel', *BA* 41: 91-103.
    1983   'Gender Roles and Genesis 3:16 Revisited', in Meyers and O'Connor 1983: 337-54.
    1988   *Discovering Eve: Ancient Israelite Women in Context* (New York: Oxford University Press).
    1993   'Gender Roles and Genesis 3.16 Revisited', in Brenner 1993: 118-41.
Meyers, C., and M. O'Connor (eds.)
    1983   *The Word of the Lord Shall Go Forth: Essays in Honour of David Noel Freedman in Celebration of his Sixtieth Birthday* (Winona Lake, IN: Eisenbrauns).
Mies, M., and V. Shiva
    1993   *Ecofeminism* (London: Zed Books).
Milgrom, J.
    1985   'You Shall Not Boil a Kid in Its Mother's Milk', *BR* 1.3: 48-55.
Miller, J.M.
    1974   'The Descendants of Cain: Notes on Genesis 4', *ZAW* 86: 164-73.
Moberly, W.
    1992   *The Old Testament of the Old Testament: Patriarchal Narratives and Mosaic Yahwism* (Minneapolis: Fortress Press).

Moltmann, J.
1985   *God in Creation: An Ecological Doctrine of Creation* (London: SCM Press).

Motavelli, J.
1998   'Flushed with Success', *The Environmental Magazine* 9: 44-55.

Mullen, E.T.
1997   *Ethnic Myths and Pentateuchal Foundations: A New Approach to the Formation of the Pentateuch* (Atlanta: Scholars Press).

Mumford, L.
1966   *The City in History: Its Origins, its Transformations and its Prospects* (Harmondsworth: Penguin Books).

Neusner, J.
1991   *Confronting Creation: How Judaism Reads Genesis. An Anthology of Genesis Rabbah* (Columbia: University of South Carolina Press).

Niditch, S.
1998   'Genesis', in C.H. Newsom and S. Ringe (eds.), *Women's Bible Commentary* (Louisville, KY: Westminster/John Knox Press, expanded edn.): 13-29.

Noth, M.
1968   *Numbers* (London: SCM Press).
1972   *A History of Pentateuchal Traditions* (Englewood Cliffs, NJ: Prentice–Hall).

O'Brien, M.
1981   *The Politics of Reproduction* (London: Routledge & Kegan Paul).

Oded, B.
1986   'The Table of Nations (Genesis 10)—a Socio-cultural Approach', *ZAW* 98: 14-31.

Oden, R.A., Jr
1987   'Grace or Status? Yahweh's Clothing of the First Humans', in *idem* (ed.), *The Bible without Theology* (San Francisco: Harper & Row): 92-104.

Oduyoye, M.
1984   *The Sons of the Gods and the Daughters of Men* (New York: Orbis Books).

Olofsson, S.
1990   *God Is my Rock: A Study of Translation Technique and Theological Exegesis in the Septuagint* (ConBOT, 31; Stockholm: Almqvist & Wiksell).

Olsen, C. (ed.)
1983   *The Book of the Goddess Past and Present* (New York: Crossroad).

Olson, D.
1996   *Numbers* (Louisville, KY: John Knox Press).

Owens, J.J.
1990   *Analytical Key to the Old Testament*, I (Grand Rapids: Baker Book House).

Pardes, I.
1992   *Countertraditions in the Bible: A Feminist Approach* (Cambridge, MA: Harvard University Press).

Pardes, I.
1993   'Beyond Genesis 3: The Politics of Maternal Naming', in Brenner 1993: 173-93.

Pedersen, J.
    1941   'Die *Krt* Legende', *Berytus* 6.2: 63-105.
Pedler, K.
    1991   *The Quest for Gaia* (London: Paladin).
Pelikan, J. (ed.)
    1960   *Luther's Works*. II. *Lectures on Genesis Chapters 6–14* (St Louis: Concordia).
Phillips, J.A.
    1984   *Eve: The History of an Idea* (San Francisco: Harper & Row).
Plumwood, V.
    1998–99   'Inequality, Ecojustice and Ecological Rationality' *Ecotheology* 5.6: 185-218.
Primavesi, A.
    1991   *From Apocalypse to Genesis: Ecology, Feminism and Christianity* (Minneapolis: Fortress Press).
Prior, M.
    1997   *The Bible and Colonialism: A Moral Critique* (BibSem, 48; Sheffield: Sheffield Academic Press).
Quinn, D.
    1992   *Ishmael: An Adventure of the Mind and Spirit* (New York: Bantam/Turner).
Rad, G. von
    1961   *Genesis: A Commentary* (Philadelphia: Westminster Press).
    1965   *Old Testament Theology* (London: SCM Press).
    1966   'The Theological Problem of the Old Testament Doctrine of Creation', in *idem*, *The Problem of the Hexateuch and Other Essays* (London: Oliver & Boyd): 131-43.
    1972a   *Genesis* (OTL; London: SCM Press, rev. edn).
    1972b   *Genesis: A Commentary* (trans. J.H. Marks; Philadelphia: Westminster Press, rev. edn).
    1978   *Genesis: A Commentary* (London: SCM Press, 3rd rev. edn).
Rainbow Spirit Elders
    1997   *Rainbow Spirit Theology* (Melbourne: HarperCollins).
Raphael, P.
    1990   *The Hebrew Goddess* (Detroit: Wayne State University Press).
Reid, D.
    2000   'Setting Aside the Ladder to Heaven: Revelation 21.1-22 from the Perspective of Earth', in Habel (ed.) 2000: 232-45
Rendtorff, R.
    1975   'Der "Jahwist" als Theologe? Zum Dilemma der Pentateuchkritik', in A. Alonso-Schökel (ed.), *Congress Volume: Edinburgh 1974* (VTSup 28; Leiden: E.J. Brill): 158-66.
    1976   *Das überlieferungsgeschichtliche Problem des Pentateuch* (BZAW, 147; Berlin: W. de Gruyter).
    1979   '"Subdue the Earth": Man and Nature in the Old Testament', *TD* 27: 213-16.
Rolston, H., III
    1988   *Environmental Ethics: Duties to and Values in the Natural World* (Philadelphia: Temple University Press).
    1996   'The Bible and Ecology', *Int* 50: 16-26.

Rosenberg, J.
    1986   *King and Kin: Political Allegory in the Hebrew Bible* (Indiana Studies in Biblical Literature; Bloomington: Indiana University Press).

Ruether, R.R.
    1985   *Readings Toward a Feminist Theology* (Boston: Beacon Press).

Sacks, R.D.
    1990   *A Commentary on the Book of Genesis* (Ancient Near Eastern Texts and Studies; Lewiston, NY: Edwin Mellen Press).

Sæbø, M.
    1993   'Divine Names and Epithets in Genesis 49:24b-25a: Some Methodological and Traditio-Historical Remarks', in A. Lemaire and B. Otzen (eds.), *History and Traditions of Early Israel: Studies Presented to Eduard Nielsen* (SBT, 50; Leiden: E.J. Brill): 115-32.

Salevao, I.
    2000   ''Burning the Land': An Ecojustice Reading of Hebrews 6.7-8', in Habel (ed.) 2000: 221-31.

Sarna, N.H.
    1989   *Genesis, Torah Commentary* (Philadelphia: Jewish Publication Society).

Sasson, J.M.
    1980   ' "The Tower of Babel" as a Clue to the Redactional Structuring of the Primeval History', in G. Rendsburg *et al.* (eds.), *The Bible World: Essays in Honor of Cyrus H. Gordon* (New York: Ktav): 211-19.

Sawyer, J.F.
    1986   'Cain and Haephestus', *AbrN* 24: 155-66.

Scharbert, J.
    1975   '*brk*', in G.J. Botterwek and H. Ringgren (eds.), *Theological Dictionary of the Old Testament*, II (Grand Rapids: Eerdmans): 279-308.

Schottroff, L.
    1993   'The Creation Narrative: Genesis 1.1–2.5a', in Brenner 1993: 24-38.

Schottroff, W., and W. Stegemann
    1980   *Traditionen der Befreiung: Sozialgeschichtliche Bibelauslegungen.* I. *Methodische Zugänge* (Munich: Chr. Kaiser Verlag).

Schüngel-Straumann, H.
    1993   'On the Creation of Man and Woman in Genesis 1–3: The History and Reception of the Texts Reconsidered', in Brenner 1993: 53-117.

Schüssler Fiorenza, E.
    1991   *Revelation: Vision of a Just World* (Minneapolis: Fortress Press).

Shea, W.H.
    1992   'Famine', *ABD*, II: 769-73.

Shiva, V.
    1991   *The Violence of the Green Revolution: Third World Agriculture, Ecology and Politics* (London: Zed Books).

Simkins, R.A.
    1994   *Creator and Creation: Nature in the World View of Ancient Israel* (Peabody, MA: Hendrickson).

Skinner, J.
    1930   *Genesis* (ICC Commentaries; Edinburgh: T. & T. Clark, 2nd edn).

Smith, M.S.
    1990   *The Early History of God: Yahweh and the Other Deities in Ancient Israel* (San Francisco: Harper & Row).

Speiser, E.A.
  1964   *Genesis* (AB, 1; New York: Doubleday).
  1969   'The Epic of Gilgamesh', *ANET*: 72-99.
Spivak, G.C.
  1988   'Can the Subaltern Speak?', in C. Nelson and L. Grossberg (eds.),
            Marxism and the Interpretation of Culture (Basingstoke: Macmillan):
            271-313.
Steck, O.H.
  1970   *Die Paradieserzählung: Eine Auslegung von Genesis 2.4b–3.24* (Bib-
            lische Studien, 60; Neukirchen–Vluyn: Neukirchener Verlag).
Stone, M.
  1976   *When God Was a Woman* (San Diego: Harcourt, Brace & Company).
Stratton, B.
  1995   *Out of Eden: Reading, Rhetoric and Ideology in Genesis 2–3* (Sheffield:
            Sheffield Academic Press).
Suzuki, D., and A. McConnell
  1997   *The Sacred Balance: Rediscovering our Place in Nature* (St Leonards:
            Allen & Unwin).
Terborg, J.
  1999   *Requiem for Nature* (Washington: Island Press).
Thompson, H.O.
  1992   'Jordan, Jungle of', *ABD*, III: 960-61.
Thompson, T.L.
  1987   *The Origin Tradition of Ancient Israel. I. The Literary Formation of
            Genesis and Exodus 1–23* (Sheffield: JSOT Press).
Tollers, V., and J. Maier (eds.)
  1990   *Mappings of the Biblical Terrain: The Bible as Text* (Lewisburg: Buck-
            nell University Press).
Trainor, M.
  2000   'And on Earth, Peace...' (Like 2.14): Luke's Perspective on the
            Earth', in Habel (ed.) 2000: 125-37.
Trebilco, P.
  2000   'The Goodness and the Holiness of the Earth and the Whole
            Creation (1 Timothy 4.1-5)', in Habel (ed.) 2000: 204-220.
Trible, P.
  1978   'A Love Story Gone Awry', in *idem, God and the Rhetoric of Sexuality*
            (Philadelphia: Fortress Press): 72-143.
  1984   *Texts of Terror* (OBT; Philadelphia: Fortress Press).
Tsumura, D.
  1989   *The Earth and the Waters in Genesis 1 and 2: A Linguistic Investigation*
            (Sheffield: Sheffield Academic Press).
Tucker, G.M.
  1993   'Creation and the Limits of the World: Nature and History in the
            Old Testament', *HBT* 15: 105-18.
  1966   'The Legal Background of Genesis 23', *JBL* 85: 77-84.
  1997   'Rain on a Land Where No One Lives: The Hebrew Bible on the
            Environment', *JBL* 116: 3-17.
Turner, L.A.
  1990   *Announcements of Plot in Genesis* (JSOTSup, 96; Sheffield: JSOT
            Press).
Toorn, K. van der, B. Becking and P.W. van der Horst (eds.)
  1995   *Dictionary of Deities and Demons in the Bible* (Leiden: E.J. Brill).

1995 'Shepherd', in van der Toorn, Becking and van der Horst 1995: 1457-59.

Urbrock, W.
2000 'Angels, Bird Doppings and Fish Liver: The Earth Story in Tobit', in Habel (ed.) 2000: 125-37.

Van Seters, J.
1975 *Abraham in History and Tradition* (New Haven: Yale University Press).

Vawter, B.
1955 'The Canaanite Background of Genesis 49', *CBQ* 17: 1-17.

Vogels, W.
1992 *Nos origines: Genèse 1–11* (Ottawa: Novalis).

Wainwright, E.
2000 'A Transformative Struggle Towards the Divine Dream: An Eco-feminist Reading of Matthew 11', in Habel (ed.) 2000: 162-73.

Wallace, H.
1985 *The Eden Narrative* (Atlanta: Scholars Press).
1988 'Genesis 2.1-3—Creation and Sabbath', *Pacifica* 1: 235-50.

Wallis, G.
1966 'Die Stadt in den Ueberlieferungen der Genesis', *ZAW* 78: 133-48.

Walton, J.H., and V.H. Matthews
1997 *The IVP Bible Background Commentary: Genesis–Deuteronomy* (Downers Grove, IL: InterVarsity Press).

Welker, M.
1991–92 'What is Creation? Rereading Genesis 1 and 2', *TTod* 28: 56-71.

Wenham, G.J.
1987 *Genesis 1–15* (WBC, 1; Waco, TX: Word Books).
1994 *Genesis 16–50* (WBC, 2; Dallas: Word Books).

Westbrook, D.
1990 'Paradise and Paradox', in Tollers and Maier 1990: 121-33.

Westermann, C.
1964 *The Genesis Accounts of Creation* (Philadelphia: Fortress Press).
1984 *Genesis 1–11: A Commentary* (Minneapolis: Augsburg–Fortress).
1985 *Genesis 12–36: A Commentary* (trans. John J. Scullion; Minneapolis: Augsburg–Fortress).
1986 *Genesis 37–50: A Commentary* (trans. John Scullion; Minneapolis: Augsburg–Fortress).

White, L., Jr.
1967 'The Historical Roots of Our Ecological Crisis', *Science* 155: 1203-1207.

Wigedor, G. (ed.)
1989 *The Encyclopedia of Judaism* (New York: Macmillan).

Willers, B. (ed.)
1991 *Learning to Listen to the Land* (Washington: Island Press).

Williams, D.S.
1993 *Sisters in the Wilderness: the Challenge of Womanist God-Talk* (Maryknoll, NY: Orbis Books).

Williams, D.T.
1993 ' "Fill the Earth and Subdue it" (Gen. 1.28): Dominion to Exploit and Pollute?', *Scriptura* 44: 51-65.

Williams, J.
    1982   *Women Recounted: Narrative Thinking and the God of Israel* (Sheffield: Almond Press).

Wilson, R.R.
    1975   'The Old Testament Genealogies in Recent Research', *JBL* 94: 169-89.
    1984   *Sociological Approaches to the Old Testament* (Guides to Biblical Scholarship Series; Philadelphia: Fortress Press).

Wittenberg, G.
    1991   ' "Let Canaan be his slave." (Gen. 9.26) Is Ham also cursed?', *JTSA* 74: 46-56.
    1995   'Wisdom Influences on Genesis 2:11: A Contribution to the Debate about the "Yahwistic" Primeval History', *Old Testament Essays* 8.3: 439-57.

Wolde, E.J. van
    1994   *Words Become Worlds: Semantic Studies of Genesis 1–11* (Biblical Interpretation Series, 6; Leiden: E.J. Brill).
    1996a   *Stories of the Beginning: Genesis 1–11 and Other Creation Stories* (London: SCM Press).
    1996b   'Rhetorical, Linguistic, and Literary Features in Genesis', in L. de Regt, J. Waard and J. Fokkelman (eds.), *Literary Structure and Rhetorical Strategies in the Hebrew Bible* (Assen: Van Gorcum; Winona Lake, IN: Eisenbrauns): 134-51.
    1998   'Facing the Earth: Primaeval History in a New Perspective', in P. Davies and D.J.A. Clines (eds.), *The World of Genesis: Persons, Places, Perspectives* (JSOTSup, 257; Sheffield: Sheffield Academic Press): 22-47.

Wyatt, N.
    1993   'The Darkness in Genesis 1.2', *VT* 43: 543-54.

Young, R.J.C.
    1995   *Colonial Desire: Hybridity in Theory, Culture and Race* (London: Routledge).

Zipor M.
    1991   'A Note on Genesis VI 13', *VT* 41.4: 366-68.

Zornberg, A.
    1996   *The Beginning of Desire: Reflections on Genesis* (New York: Doubleday).

INDEX OF AUTHORS

Lightning Source UK Ltd.
Milton Keynes UK
19 December 2010

164636UK00001B/23/P